1,001 SECRET HOUSEHOLD HINTS & FORMULAS

by Dr. Myles H. Bader

Money–Saving Tips and Problem–Solving

Recipes for the Modern Economical Home

Library of Congress Catalog-in-Publication Data available upon request.

ISBN 1-58663-000-8

Illustrations by: Smacky Bean, San Diego, CA
Desktop Publishing by: Suzanne Merritt, Carlsbad, CA

5 7 9 10 8 6 4

Printed in the United States

Dedication

To My Loving Wife
Paulette Kay Bader

Introduction

The formulas in this book have been tried and tested through the years and only the most common formulas that most people will be able to make have been included. To obtain the best results follow the directions carefully. Use caution when handling the chemicals mentioned in the book. If you plan to make a number of different formulas, you may want to purchase the following items: graduated measuring cups, spoons, glass bottles with caps, and a set of scales.

Many of the formulas, however, do not require any special equipment and can easily be prepared with items found in almost any kitchen. Use enameled ware, hard earthenware, or porcelain containers unless another type of container is specified. The children's formulas and many of the craft formulas can be prepared in a glass bowl or plastic container. Other equipment that may come in handy includes a mortar and pestle for powdering, a good Fahrenheit thermometer, a funnel, mixing utensils, a rotary mixer, brushes, molds, cheesecloth, filter paper, and assorted bottles and cans that seal. A double boiler is required for many formulas and an alcohol lamp and stand may also be required.

When a formula calls for 1 part of a substance or 2 parts of a substance, be sure to use the appropriate liquid or solid measure. For example, use 1 ounce to 2 ounces if the formula calls for 1 part to 2 parts of a liquid, and 1 cup to 2 cups if it calls for a powder. Don't mix liquids with powders unless the formula advises you to do so. When asked to filter or strain a solution, use a piece of fine cloth, muslin, or cheesecloth. Fine filtering can also be done using fine filter paper shaped into a cone and placed into a funnel.

About the Author

Dr. Myles H. Bader (The Wizard of Food) has made more than 4,000 radio show appearances and has been a guest on more than thirty-five major television shows, including the *Oprah Winfrey Show*, *Crook & Chase*, *America's Talking*, The Discovery Channel's *Home Matter*, *Help at Home*, The Home and Garden Channel's *Smart Solutions*, HSN, Trinity Broadcasting, *The Morning Exchange*, and many more. Dr. Bader received his Doctoral Degree in Health Science from Loma Linda University. He is board certified in preventive care and has practiced in major clinics in California for over twenty-two years.

He specializes in nutrition, stress management, cardiac rehabilitation, fitness, weight management, and executive health. He has established programs for thirty-five Fortune 500 companies and many civic organizations and safety departments and has lectured extensively throughout the United States and Canada in all areas of preventive care, weight control, supplementation, and anti-aging.

Some of Dr. Bader's current books include; *10,001 Food Facts, Chef's Secrets & Household Hints*, *5,001 Mysteries of Liquids & Cooking Secrets*, *250 Future Food Facts & Predictions for the Millennium*, *To Supplement or Not to Supplement*, and *The Wellness Desk Reference*. His current books have sold over 500,000 copies. Recently, Dr. Bader has formulated a number of new products, the most exciting of which is his new super anti-oxidant, multi-vitamin, mineral product called "Opti-Max."

Special Note

The formulas in this book are offered as information only. The author or publisher is not responsible for mishaps associated with the handling and use of some of the chemicals needed to produce these formulas. Chemicals can be very dangerous if not handled properly. Even everyday home cleaning products available at the supermarket can cause severe illness and/or injury. Over 1,000 products that can easily be purchased in supermarkets and drugstores are either poisonous or dangerous when misused.

Many of the formulas were revised from formulas that are hundreds of years old. Many of the chemicals in use then are not available today and substitutions have been made to provide you with up-to-date and environmentally safe information.

> Children should always be supervised by an adult
> when mixing any formula.

Please note that any remedies included in this book do not take the place of your physician's advice or of prescribed medications, but are provided as a source of information regarding a number of illnesses and how they were treated before modern medicine came of age.

Read the instructions fully before attempting to produce any of the formulas in this book. When heating chemicals always be sure the area is well ventilated or have an exhaust fan on.

Table of Contents

Chapter 1

General
Home Cleaning

> **CAUTION: never mix chlorine bleach and household ammonia in any formula.**

FLOOR CARE

MARBLE, THE TOUGHEST OF THE TOUGH, BUT BE GENTLE!

Marble, one of the toughest floor surfaces, is a naturally compressed crystallized limestone that can range from somewhat porous to very compact. It can be polished to a high shine and will remain that way with very little care almost forever. The following solutions will clean the marble and keep it shining with a minimum of effort. Strong detergents and abrasives should never be used since they will dull the shine and may cause deterioration of the marble.

GREAT MARBLE CLEANING FORMULA

Mix the following ingredients in a small bucket to make a paste:

> 6% *hydrogen peroxide*
> *White all-purpose flour*

The thick paste mixture must cover the entire surface of the marble—not just the soiled spot—or the marble will not have the same overall clean color. Use enough of the mixture to heavily coat the floor and place plastic sheeting over the mixture, taping down all around the edges. Allow the mixture to sit on the marble for 36 hours, then carefully remove it with a plastic spatula and rinse the marble thoroughly with cool water.

POWDER FOR CLEANING MARBLE

You will need the following ingredients:

> 3 *Cups sodium sulfate*
> 1 *Cup sodium sulfite*

Place the ingredients in a small bucket and mix well. Then place some of the mixture on a damp sponge and rub on the marble to clean it. Wipe off mixture with warm water and a clean cloth that has been rung out very well.

BASIC MARBLE CLEANER

You will need the following ingredients:

4 *Parts soft soap*
4 *Parts whiting*
1 *Part sodium*
       bicarbonate
2 *Parts copper*
       sulfate

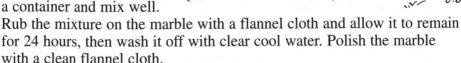

S. DEAN

Place all the ingredients into
a container and mix well.
Rub the mixture on the marble with a flannel cloth and allow it to remain
for 24 hours, then wash it off with clear cool water. Polish the marble
with a clean flannel cloth.

REMOVING OIL STAINS FROM MARBLE

You will need the following ingredients:

$9^3/4$ *Ounces cereal flour*
$13^1/2$ *Ounces hydrochloric acid (use with care)*
4 *Ounces chloride of lime*
2 *Teaspoons turpentine*

Wear gloves and a mask. Place all the ingredients into a glass or porcelain
container and blend into a paste. Smear the paste on the stains and allow
it remain for 6–8 hours. Remove the paste with a brush or piece of soft
leather. Polish the area after the stain has been removed. This formula will
remove grease from marble very easily.

CLEANER FOR PARQUET FLOORS

You will need the following ingredients:

$2^1/4$ *Cups of mineral oil*
$^3/4$ *Cup of oleic acid*
2 *Tablespoons of household ammonia*
$4^1/2$ *Tablespoons of turpentine*

Place the mineral oil and the oleic acid in a bucket and mix well (wear
rubber gloves), then add the ammonia and turpentine while stirring well
to mix completely. This is a concentrated solution. Add $^1/2$ cup of the
solution to $^1/2$ gallon of warm tap water, then mop the floor. Store in a
well-sealed container for future use.

WOOD FLOORS, A TOUCH OF THE OLDEN DAYS

The combination of wooden flooring and carpeting has become more common in the last five years and lends a bit of the olden days to your home. However, caring for and cleaning a wood floor is time-consuming since it must be treated as if it were a fine piece of furniture. Wood floors are more expensive than most carpeting and should be vacuumed regularly or the dirt and grime will scratch the surface and the floor will need re-finishing after a few years. If your floor has been sealed with a varnish or shellac, never clean it with a water based product or even clear water. A turpentine product is recommended. In fact, most wood floors will be damaged if water is used since the water tends to raise the grain and permanently dull the wood. The only exception to the rule is if the floor has been water-sealed. If the wood has been oiled, it is best to clean the floor with a mild solution of dish soap using a damp mop to remove the suds and any scum leftover.

GENERAL CLEANER FOR WOOD FLOORS

You will need the following ingredients:

- 2¼ Cups mineral oil
- ¾ Cups oleic acid (from drug store)
- 2 Tablespoons household ammonia (toxic)
- 5 Tablespoons turpentine (toxic)
- 2 Quarts cool tap water

Place the mineral oil and oleic acid in a container and mix well, then add the ammonia and turpentine and mix well. Place 1 cup of the mixture into the 2 quarts of water, then apply to floor with a sponge mop. Rinsing is not necessary. Keep out of reach of children.

BASIC LIQUID FLOOR WAX

You will need the following ingredients:

- ¼ Pound of beeswax
- 1 Pound of paraffin
- ½ Cup of raw linseed oil
- 3 Cups of turpentine

Place the beeswax and paraffin in a double boiler and heat until melted. Remove from the heat and allow the wax to cool. After it has cooled for 5–10 minutes stir in the linseed oil and turpentine and mix thoroughly. A thin coat of the wax can be applied to the floor and then buffed with a mop buffer or electric polisher.

WAX REMOVER #1

You will need the following ingredients:

> *5+ Cups of washing soda*
> *Warm water as required*

Place the washing soda in a bucket and add just enough water to make a loose paste. Place the paste on the floor and allow it to dry. The wax should bubble up and flake off easily. The floor needs to be thoroughly rinsed until the wax and washing soda residue is removed. The longer the washing soda is left on and moist, the more wax will be removed.

WAX REMOVER #2

You will need the following ingredients:

> 2 *Cups of household ammonia*
> *1/2 Cup of washing soda*
> 4 *Quarts of warm tap water*

Place all the ingredients into a bucket and mix well (wear rubber gloves). Using a sponge mop, place a generous layer of the solution on the floor and allow it to sit for 5-10 minutes. Scrub the floor as you would normally. The old wax should be loosened and easily removed.

BE GENTLE, OR LINOLEUM WILL HAVE A CRACK-UP

Linoleum is manufactured by using a mixture of resins, small particles of cork or wood fibers, and linseed oil that is adhered to a canvas, burlap, or felt backing using high pressure. Never use a strong alkali-based cleaner on linoleum since they tend to ruin the linseed oil binder and may cause the floor to develop cracks, thus shortening the usable life of the flooring. It is best to use a mild detergent solution and dry the floor as soon as it has been cleaned. A linoleum formula should never be used on a wood or cork floor.

PASTE WAX FOR LINOLEUM #1

You will need the following ingredients:

> 2 *Cups of carnauba wax*
> 2 *Cups of ceresin wax*
> *4 1/2 Cups of mineral spirits*

Place the carnauba and ceresin wax in a double boiler and melt. Remove from the heat and allow the wax to cool, then very slowly add the mineral spirits, stirring continually. When the mixture starts to harden around the edges, pour it into a container and allow the mixture to harden.

PASTE WAX FOR LINOLEUM #2
You will need the following ingredients:

2 *Tablespoons of paraffin wax*
4 *Tablespoons of yellow beeswax*
4 *Cups of turpentine*

Place the waxes in a double boiler and heat until melted, then remove from the heat and add the turpentine while continually mixing. Allow the mixture to cool and store in a sealed container.

BASIC LINOLEUM POLISH
You will need the following ingredients:

1 *Part palm oil*
18 *Parts paraffin*
4 *Parts kerosene*

Place the paraffin in a double boiler and melt. Remove from the heat and add the oil and kerosene while mixing very well.

BASIC LINOLEUM CLEANER
You will need the following ingredients:

5 *Parts beeswax*
11 *Parts oil of turpentine*
5 *Parts varnish*

Place the beeswax in a saucepan and melt over low heat. Remove from the heat and very slowly stir in the oil of turpentine, then add the varnish and continue stirring until the mixture is well blended. Apply the cleaner after the floor has been washed with soap and water with a soft cloth mop.

PASTE WAX FOR WOOD FLOORS
You will need the following ingredients:

5 *Tablespoons yellow beeswax*
5 *Tablespoons of ceresin wax*
9 *Tablespoons of carnauba wax*
3 *Tablespoon montan wax*
2 *Cups of mineral spirits*
4 *Tablespoons of turpentine*
3/4 *Tablespoon of pine oil*

Place the waxes in a double boiler and heat until melted, then remove from heat. In another container, add the turpentine, mineral spirits, and pine oil. Mix well and add this mixture to the wax and stir well. When the temperature of the wax mixture is at 135° F., pour into a metal container and allow the wax to cool and set for 8–10 hours at room temperature.

A NON-RESILIENT FLOOR NEEDS TLC

This category of flooring includes ceramic tile, concrete, brick, and all types of stone flooring material. It is best to just clean stone and brick surfaces with a solution of vinegar and water (1 cup of vinegar to 1 gallon of water) whereas concrete needs to be cleaned with an all-purpose detergent or concrete cleaner. If tile is in bad shape and needs to cleaned to remove ground in dirt and residues, the following formula will be needed. Otherwise just use a mild soap solution.

SPANISH TILE CLEANER & CONDITIONER
You will need the following ingredients:

$2^{1}/3$ *Cups of oleic acid*
1   *Tablespoon of triethanolamine (from drug store)*
3   *Cups of cool tap water*

Place the ingredients into a double boiler and heat; do not allow the mixture to boil. Remove from heat and beat with an electric mixer until the mixture becomes milky. Apply the mixture to the tile floor with a sponge and allow it to dry for 8–10 hours before rubbing off with a dry bath towel.

FIRST AID FOR OLD WOOD FLOORS

The following bleach is very poisonous and should be used with extreme caution and not swallowed by children, adults, or pets. However, it is the treatment of choice to remove all the old stains and even the ground in grime from years of abuse and poor cleaning methods. The old wood floor should be cleansed as well as possible first with a good wood floor cleanser.

BLEACH FOR WOOD FLOORS
You will need the following ingredients:

18   *Cups of sodium metasilicate (from drug store)*
2   *Cups sodium perborate (from drug store)*
1   *Gallon very hot tap water*

Place the two sodium ingredients into a bucket and mix well. In another bucket place the gallon of hot water, then add the sodium ingredients into the water, while mixing well. Scrub the floor with a soap and water solution before using the bleach. Place the bleach on the floor with a sponge mop and allow it to remain for about 30 minutes before rinsing the floor with cool, clear water. If you still have spots that are not coming out, just re-do those spots.

FLOOR WAX FOR DANCE FLOORS

You will need the following ingredients:

$^1/_2$ Pound of talc
1   Cup of stearic acid

Place the ingredients into a glass container with a lid and mix well, then sprinkle a small amount around the floor.

NON-SLIP WAX FOR WOOD FLOORS

You will need the following ingredients:

2   Cups of denatured alcohol (flammable)
1   Cup of orange shellac (flammable)
2   Tablespoons of acacia
2   Tablespoon of turpentine (flammable)

Place all the ingredients into a small bucket and blend well, then apply to the floor with a cloth sponge mop and allow the wax to dry for 45 minutes.

DUSTING MAGNET MOP OIL

You will need the following ingredients:

1   Cup of turpentine (flammable)
2   Cups of mineral oil

Place the ingredients into a container and mix well. Place a small amount of the mixture on your dust mop and the dust will jump into the mop.

FLOOR VARNISH

You will need the following ingredients:

3   Parts of Manila copal
     (spirit soluble)
15$^1/_2$ Parts of powdered ruby shellac
3   Parts of Venice turpentine
62$^1/_2$ Parts of alcohol (96%)

Place the alcohol in a large container and dissolve the other ingredients into the alcohol. Filter the solution through a number of thicknesses of wire screening.

COLORLESS FLOOR SHELLAC

You will need the following ingredients:

    1   *Quart of denatured alcohol*
  12 *Ounces of pure flake shellac*

Place all the ingredients into a sealed container and shake repeatedly until the shellac is fully dissolved in the alcohol. Do not use a metal container to store this solution, it will turn the shellac black. Shellac should be used as an undercoat before you varnish a wood floor. This will give you a hard long-lasting beautiful finish for many years.

NO-WAX FLOOR CLEANER

You will need the following ingredients:

    1 *Cup of white vinegar*
  1/4 *Cup of washing soda*
    1 *Tablespoon of Castile soap (liquid)*
    2 *Gallons of very hot tap water*

Place all the ingredients into a bucket and blend well, then mop the floor as usual. This formula will eliminate any greasiness.

BATHROOM CLEANING

REMOVING MILDEW

While many people tend to use a formula containing chlorine bleach, which does work well, I prefer a somewhat milder chemical mixture that will not be as harsh to your lungs.

    Mix the following ingredients together in a medium plastic container:

  1/2 *Cup of Borax*
    1 *Gallon of hot tap water*

Use the solution to remove the mildew. Once the mildew had been removed, coat the area with the same solution and allowed it to remain without rinsing for a lasting effect.

IT'S A DIRTY JOB, BUT SOMEBODY HAS TO DO IT

Toilets are made of either porcelain or ceramic and are acid resistant, which is good since most of the commercial toilet cleaners contain either an acid or ingredients that turn into acid when they come into contact with water. Needless to say, if you swallow most commercial toilet cleaners it will most likely lead to your demise in very short order. If you use one of the following formulas and there is still a ring, try using a pumice bar to remove the ring. Just dampen the bar and gently rub the surface to avoid scratching it. A "00" sandpaper will also do the trick.

TOILET BOWL CLEANER #1

You will need the following ingredients:

- 1   *Cup of hydrogen peroxide*
- 1   *Tablespoon of household ammonia*
- 2   *Quarts of warm tap water*

Place all the ingredients into a bucket and mix well. You will need about 1 quart of the solution for each toilet. Pour the solution in the toilet and allow it to remain for about 30-40 minutes before you scrub and flush. If this is done weekly, residues and discoloration should not occur.

TOILET BOWL CLEANER #2

You will need the following ingredients:

- 3/4   *Cup of alum (powdered)*
- 1/4   *Cup of table salt*
- 1½   *Cups of caustic soda (use with gloves and mask)*

Place the ingredients in a container and mix well with a wooden spoon, then store in a well-sealed container in a cool, dry place. Caustic soda can cause burns if it comes into contact with the skin. When cleaning the toilet, wet the sides with your toilet brush, then sprinkle the mixture on the sides and allow it to remain for 10–15 minutes. Scrub and flush for a sanitary bowl you can show off to your neighbors.

INEXPENSIVE TOILET BOWL CLEANER #1

You will need the following ingredients:

- 1   *Cup of white vinegar*

Place the vinegar into the toilet and allow it to remain for 8–10 hours, then scrub.

INEXPENSIVE TOILET BOWL CLEANER #2

You will need the following ingredients:

- 1   *Cup of Castile soap (liquid)*
- 1/4   *Cup borax*
- 1/2   *Cup baking soda*

Place all the ingredients into a container and mix well. Add a small amount of very warm water if you have a problem blending the ingredients. Pour into toilet and scrub with a brush.

REMOVING SOAP RESIDUE FROM WASHCLOTHS

Mix the following ingredients together in a small bowl:

> 1 Tablespoon of white vinegar
> 2 Cups of warm water

Soap residues tend to build up in washcloths even after they have been washed. If you would like a clean washcloth, just soak the washcloth in the mixture for 10 minutes and ring out before laundering. Lemon juice may be substituted for the white vinegar.

GERM ALERT! CALL OUT THE HEAVY ARTILLERY

The first thing to remember is that germs love moisture. Keeeping surfaces dry will reduce the incidence of bacteria getting a foothold and causing odors and unhealthy conditions. Disinfectants will kill bacteria and almost all molds, but only for a short period of time. Therefore, it is necessary to clean the surfaces that are susceptible to contamination more frequently than other areas of your home.

BATHROOM DISINFECTANT CLEANER

You will need the following ingredients:

> 1 Quart very hot tap water
> 1¹/₃ Cup powdered household laundry detergent
> 1¹/₃ Cup pine oil (Pinesol will do fine)
> 1 Half-gallon plastic container

Place the water and detergent in the ¹/₂ gallon plastic container and mix until the detergent is fully dissolved. Skim off any foam that develops, and then gradually add the Pinesol or pine oil as you continue stirring. To use the solution, add 1 part disinfectant to 1 part warm water. For toilets, use full strength. Store in well-sealed container and, as with all chemicals, store away from children.

ODORLESS DISINFECTANT

You will need the following ingredients:

> 4 Parts of ferric chloride
> 5 Parts of zinc chloride
> 5 Parts of aluminum chloride
> 4 Parts of calcium chloride
> 3 Parts of manganese chloride
> 69 Parts of cool tap water

Place all the ingredients into a container and blend well.

SIMPLE HOUSEHOLD DISINFECTANT FOR BIG JOBS

You will need the following ingredients:

$^1/_2$ Cup of borax
1   Gallon of very hot tap water

Place the ingredients into a large container and mix well.

SIMPLE HOUSEHOLD DISINFECTANT

You will need the following ingredients:

2   Tablespoons of borax
2   Cups of very hot tap water
$^1/_4$ Cup of pure lemon juice

Place all the ingredients into a spray bottle and shake until well blended. This will be as effective as most standard brands.

CERAMIC TILE CLEANER

You will need the following ingredients:

$^1/_4$ Cup of white vinegar
$^1/_3$ Cup of household ammonia
$^1/_2$ Cup baking soda
7   Cups of warm tap water
1   Spray bottle

Place all the ingredients in a medium plastic bucket with a well sealed cover and shake to mix thoroughly. Place the mixture in 2–3 jars. Label the jars and save. Never add chlorine bleach to this mixture. Use with rubber gloves to protect your hands and spray on surface to be cleaned.

SUPER TUB & TILE CLEANSER

You will need the following ingredients:

1   Teaspoon of borax
$^1/_2$ Teaspoon of washing soda
$^1/_2$ Teaspoon of liquid dish soap
$3^1/_4$ Tablespoons of white vinegar
2   Cups of very hot tap water
1   Spray bottle

Place all the ingredients into a spray bottle and mix well. Spray the solution on the area to be cleaned and wipe with a dampened sponge. This is a good powerful solution.

CLEANSER FOR SHOWER NOZZLE RESIDUE

You will need the following ingredients:

> 1   *Cup of white vinegar*
> 1   *Teaspoon of lemon juice*
> 1   *Cup of very hot water*

Place all the ingredients into a small bowl and mix well, then sponge on the showerhead and clean with an old toothbrush.

BATHROOM FIXTURE CLEANER

You will need the following ingredients:

> *1/2*   *Cup of white vinegar*
> 1   *Cup of clear household ammonia*
> *1/4*   *Cup of baking soda (fresh)*
> 1   *Gallon of warm tap water*
> 1   *Spray bottle*

Place all the ingredients in a small bucket and mix well. Pour into a number of smaller jars for storage. Place a small amount into a spray bottle and use on fixtures and soap scum. Wipe clean with a soft cloth.

HERBAL DISINFECTANT

You will need the following ingredients:

> 1   *Teaspoon of essential rosemary oil*
> 1   *Teaspoon of essential lavender oil*
> 1   *Teaspoon of essential lemon oil*
> 1   *Teaspoon of essential eucalyptus oil*
> *1/2*   *Teaspoon of essential peppermint oil*
> *1/2*   *Teaspoon of essential rose oil*
> *1/8*   *Teaspoon of essential love bud oil*
> *2 1/2*   *Ounces of fresh distilled water*

Place all the ingredients in a medium bowl and mix thoroughly. Store the solution in a well-sealed glass jar. Place a small amount in a spray bottle and keep in the bathroom to freshen it up.

GENERAL BATHROOM CLEANING #1

You will need the following ingredients:

> 3   *Tablespoons of baking soda (fresh)*
> *1/4*   *Cup of household ammonia*
> 2   *Cups of warm tap water*

Place all the ingredients in a spray bottle and shake to mix.

GENERAL BATHROOM CLEANER #2

You will need the following ingredients:

    1 Pound of baking soda (fresh)
    4 Tablespoons of liquid hand soap
    1 Cup of warm tap water

Place all the ingredients in a spray bottle and shake to mix. This formula is not as harsh as the one with ammonia. It is also safer around children.

PORCELAIN STAIN REMOVER #1

You will need the following ingredients:

    1 Bar of naphtha soap (grated)
  $1/2$ Cup of mineral spirits (from drug store)
    1 Gallon of very hot water

Place the soap and water into a bucket and mix well, then add the mineral spirits. Scrub the stain with a small medium bristle brush, and then rinse well with cool water. Wear rubber gloves for this job and remember that mineral spirits are flammable, so use caution.

PORCELAIN STAIN REMOVER #2

You will need the following ingredients:

    Oxalic acid or Hydrochloric acid

Wear gloves and a mask. Both of these acids need to be handled with care. Do not mix them together. The safer of the two stain removers is a strong solution of oxalic acid applied with a small brush. If the porcelain has brown stains, use hydrochloric acid and trickle it on the spot until it disappears. Do not allow acid to come into contact with the skin.

SCUM AND MILDEW BUILDUP, ACTIVATE THE SALT

Shower curtains will develop a layer of mildew and scum over time. Most curtains can be washed in the washing machine, which should do the job. However, when you remove them from the washing machine, you should also soak the curtains in the bathtub in a strong solution of salt water before you hang them up. The salt bath should only be needed about once a year. Or, you may want to use the following formula:

SHOWER CURTAIN CLEANER

You will need the following ingredients:

$^1\!/_2$ Cup of soap flakes
$^1\!/_2$ Cup of baking soda (fresh)
 1 Cup of white vinegar
    Mineral oil

Place the shower curtains and 2 large towels in the washing machine. Add the soap flakes and baking soda and run the wash cycle using warm water. Add the vinegar and a few drops of mineral oil to soften the curtains in the rinse water.

GENERAL HOUSEHOLD CLEANING: FIRST REMOVE THE PET CRUMBS, TOYS, AND COINS

As a general rule, all types of upholstered furniture need to be vacuumed regularly to avoid excessive wear (accumulated grit acts like sandpaper in the fabric every time you sit down and squirm around). A foamy type of solution tends to work best on most upholstered furniture since it does not saturate the fabric and will dry quickly. Before cleaning any type of fabric, it is wise to test the cleaner on an inconspicuous area. However, foamy solutions should not be used on any type of velvet or similar fabric.

DRY CLEANER FOR UPHOLSTERED FURNITURE

You will need the following ingredients:

 1 Cup of baking soda (fresh)
 1 Cup of cornstarch

Place the ingredients into a sifter and sift into a small bowl. Mix the powder with enough cool water to form a loose paste. Sponge on the fabric and allow it to stand for 20–30 minutes and dry before brushing off or vacuuming.

BASIC UPHOLSTERY CLEANER

You will need the following ingredients:

> 1 *Ounce of trisodium phosphate (TSP)*
> 1 *Gallon of cool soft water*

Place the ingredients into a container and mix well. Test the solution on an area of the fabric that will not be noticed to make sure that the color will not be damaged (the solution should be safe for most fabrics). Lightly sponge the cleaner on the upholstery.

KEEP CHIMNEY SOOT-FREE

You will need the following ingredients:

> 1 *Cup of table salt*
> 1 *Cup of zinc oxide (from pharmacy)*

Place the ingredients in a medium-sized container and mix well. Sprinkle on logs before igniting to make logs burn cleaner.

INDOOR STONE AND BRICK CLEANER

You will need the following ingredients:

> $1/2$ *Cup of household ammonia*
> 1 *Cup of white vinegar*
> $1/4$ *Cup of baking soda (fresh)*

Place the ingredients into a container and mix thoroughly. Use with a soft bristle brush and rinse with warm water.

CLEANER FOR FIREPLACE GLASS

You will need the following ingredients:

> $1/2$ *Cup of white vinegar*
> 1 *Tablespoon household ammonia*
> 1 *Gallon of cold tap water*
> 1 *Spray bottle*

Place all the ingredients in a small bucket and mix thoroughly. Place some of the solution in a spray bottle and spray on fireplace glass, then rinse with warm water and dry with a soft cloth.

YOU DON'T WANT SANTA TO GET HIS SUIT DIRTY

There are very few cleaners that will work on the creosote buildup that is left over from burning wood. If the buildup is not cleaned out at regular intervals it will build up to such a point that it may cause a fire. Soft woods such as pine deposit more creosote than hard woods such as oak. If you do burn a lot of soft woods, the chimney should be cleaned at least once a year.

FIREPLACE CLEANER

You will need the following ingredients:

$6^1/_2$ Ounces of naphtha soap (grated)
3 Pints of very hot tap water
$3/_4$ Pounds of pumice (powdered)
$3/_4$ Cup of household ammonia

Place the water into a pot and add the naphtha soap. Place the pot on low heat and cook until the soap if fully melted. Remove the mixture from the heat and allow it to cool. Stir in the pumice and household ammonia and mix thoroughly. Wear gloves and use a stiff brush to clean the fireplace, then rinse with clear water.

HI HO SILVER

The most common form of silver tarnish is the result of the silver coming into contact with hydrogen sulfide found in the air. This causes a reaction that forms a brownish coating of silver sulfide on the silver item. A number of common foods such as eggs contain a sulfur compound that will also cause silver to tarnish. Tarnishing will not occur if the silver item is washed thoroughly after each use, dried well, and wrapped as airtightly as possible before being stored. Moisture has the ability to speed up the tarnishing of most silver items.

SILVER CLEANER

You will need the following ingredients:

1 Teaspoons of baking soda
1 Teaspoon of table salt
1 Cup of boiling water

Place a piece of aluminum foil on the bottom of a glass pan and pour in boiling water. Then add the baking soda and the salt and blend all the ingredients well. Place the silverware into the liquid making sure the pieces are touching each other. The tarnish will magically disappear. If the pieces are badly tarnished, additional soakings may be necessary.

SILVER PASTE CLEANER

You will need the following ingredients:

    3 *Tablespoons of cheap vodka*
  $1/2$ *Cup of diatomaceous earth*
  $1/2$ *Teaspoon of liquid dish soap*

Place all the ingredients into a small bowl and mix well, adding just enough water to prepare a thick paste. It is best to store the cleaner in a wide mouth jar. Use with a dampened sponge.

ALL-AROUND HOUSEHOLD CLEANER #1

You will need the following ingredients:

    8 *Cups of warm tap water*
  $1/2$ *Cup of baking soda (fresh)*
  $1/2$ *Cup of household ammonia*

Place the baking soda, ammonia, and one cup of the warm water in a well-sealed $1/2$ gallon plastic jug and mix thoroughly. Add the additional 7 cups of warm water and shake to mix. To use the mixture, pour $1/2$ cup into 1 gallon of hot tap water.

CAUTION: Always test a small hidden area of the surface to be cleaned before using any new chemical to be sure that it is colorfast to that chemical.

ALL-AROUND HOUSEHOLD CLEANER #2

You will need the following ingredients:

    3 *Tablespoons of washing soda*
    1 *Quart of warm tap water*

Place the water in a bucket and add the washing soda. Stir until the washing soda is fully dissolved. This cleaner is also great for heavy dirt areas.

MULTI-ACTION CLEANER

You will need the following ingredients:

  $1/4$ *Cup of baking soda*
    1 *Cup of household ammonia*
  $1/2$ *Cup of white vinegar*
    1 *Gallon of warm tap water*

Place the water in a bucket and add the other ingredients. Mix well. Store in a well-sealed bottle and use as a multi-purpose cleaner.

SPRAY CLEANER FOR MOST JOBS

You will need the following ingredients:

1 Teaspoon of borax
1/2 Teaspoon of washing soda
1/2 Teaspoon of liquid hand soap
2 Tablespoons of white vinegar
2 Cups of very hot tap water
1 Spray bottle

Place the vinegar, soap, borax, and washing soda into the spray bottle and mix well. Add the hot water and mix, then use and wipe with clean sponge.

GREASE CUTTER #1

You will need the following ingredients:

2 Tablespoons of white vinegar
1/2 Tablespoon of washing soda
1/4 Teaspoon of liquid hand soap
2 Cups of very hot tap water
1 Spray bottle

Place all the ingredients into the spray bottle and mix well. To make this mixture even stronger, just add 1/2 teaspoon of borax.

GREASE CUTTER #2

You will need the following ingredients:

1/4 Cup of baking soda (fresh)
2/3 Cup of white vinegar
3/4 Cup of household ammonia
Very hot tap water

Place the baking soda, vinegar, and ammonia into a bucket and mix well. Fill the bucket 3/4 full with the hot water and mix well. Use, then rinse the area well with clean warm water. It is best to use rubber gloves to protect your delicate hands. This is an excellent grease remover.

BASEBOARD CLEANER

You will need the following ingredients:

1 Tablespoon of cornstarch
1/3 Cup of white vinegar
2 Cups of very hot tap water
1 Spray bottle

Place the cornstarch in the spray bottle with the hot tap water and mix. Add the vinegar and mix again.

WINDOWS ARE A PANE

A good tip to remember: never clean windows when the sun is shining on them or they will dry too fast and streak. Newspaper will shine and clean windows when used with a good cleaner. A stronger solution is usually need for the outside glass, especially if the glass is sprayed by hard water from sprinkler systems. Window Cleaning Spray #1 will easily remove hard water spots.

WINDOW CLEANING SPRAY #1

You will need the following ingredients:

$1/4$ Cup of white vinegar
$1/4$ Cup of household ammonia
   1 Tablespoon of cornstarch
$1^1/2$ Cup of warm tap water
   1 Spray bottle

Place all the ingredients in a medium bowl and mix well. Pour the solution into a spray bottle and spray on windows, then wipe with paper towel. Remember: never clean the windows if the sun is shining on them or they will streak.

WINDOW CLEANING SPRAY #2

You will need the following ingredients:

   1 Cup of isopropyl alcohol (flammable, use caution)
   2 Cups of cool tap water
   1 Tablespoon of white vinegar
   2 Drops of blue food coloring

Place the alcohol into the water in a medium bowl and mix well, then add the vinegar and food coloring and mix. This will look and clean just like the blue store-brand cleaner.

S.BEAN

WINDOW CLEANER

You will need the following ingredients:

> 2 *Tablespoons of white vinegar*
> 1 *Quart of cool tap water*

Place the ingredients into a spray bottle and shake to mix.

LEMON GLASS CLEANER

You will need the following ingredients:

> 4 *Tablespoons of reconstituted lemon juice*
> 1 *Gallon of cool tap water*

Place the ingredients into a one-gallon container and mix well. Place a portion into a spray bottle.

HEAVY DUTY CLEANER FOR WINDOWS

You will need the following ingredients:

> $1/4$ *Cup of isopropyl alcohol (70%)*
> $1/4$ *Cup of household ammonia*
> 1 *Teaspoon of liquid detergent*

Place the alcohol and the ammonia into a spray bottle and shake well to mix, then add the detergent and mix gently or it will cause too many suds.

SIMPLE WINDOW CLEANER

You will need the following ingredients:

> $1/2$ *Cup of pure lemon juice*
> 2 *Cups of warm tap water*

Place the ingredients into a spray bottle and shake well to blend.

GREASE-CUTTING WINDOW CLEANER

The following ingredients will not be needed:

> 1 *Tablespoon of deodorized kerosene*
> 1 *Quart of cool tap water*

Place the ingredients into a container (wear gloves) and sponge on glass. Then polish with a piece of newspaper.

NO-STREAK WINDOW CLEANER

You will need the following ingredients:

1   *Tablespoon of cornstarch*
1/4   *Cup of white vinegar*
1   *Quart of warm tap water*

Place all the ingredients into a small bucket and mix well. This mixture may be applied with a rag or sponge or placed into a spray bottle. Shake well before each use.

DEICING WINDOW CLEANER

You will need the following ingredients:

1/2   *Cup of isopropyl alcohol*
1   *Quart of warm tap water*

Place the ingredients into a small container and mix well. Sponge on windows and wipe off with paper towels.

BASIC WALL CLEANER

You will need the following ingredients:

1/4   *Cup of baking soda (fresh)*
1/2   *Cup of white vinegar*
1   *Cup of household ammonia*
    Gallon of warm tap water

Place all the ingredients in a medium bucket and mix well. Sponge on the dirty area, and then rinse well.

I WONDER WHERE THE YELLOW WENT

Furniture made from natural materials must be cared for regularly or it may turn yellow and even crack. Bamboo, rattan, and wicker furniture should be vacuumed frequently and wiped off with a lightly dampened, soft cloth. To prevent yellowing, clean gently with a stiff brush that has been dampened with a strong salt water solution. Most manufacturers of this type of furniture recommend that the furniture be given a light coating of shellac about every 12–18 months.

RATTAN FURNITURE CLEANER

You will need the following ingredients:

2   *Tablespoons of table salt*
2   *Tablespoons of Castile soap (grated fine)*
1   *Cup hot tap water*

In a metal mixing bowl, combine the salt and water and mix until the salt dissolves. Add the soap and stir the mixture until the soap is dissolved, then allow the mixture to cool to room temperature. Place the solution in a spray bottle and spray the wicker/rattan furniture. Wipe off immediately and the furniture should be clean.

BASIC CLEANING POWDER

You will need the following ingredients:

$1/4$ Cup of soap flakes
$1^1/2$ Cups of boiling water
$2^1/4$ Teaspoons of borax
$1/4$ Cup of whiting

Place the water in a bucket and fully dissolve the soap flakes and borax. Allow the mixture to cool to room temperature before adding the whiting, and then mix well. This powder may be stored in a sealed plastic container. It is mildly abrasive but can be used on most fixtures without scratching them. Adding additional whiting will increase the abrasive qualities of the powder.

COMPUTER SCREEN & KEYBOARD CLEANER

You will need the following ingredients:

$1/2$ Cup of rubbing alcohol
 1 Tablespoon of baking soda (fresh)
$1/2$ Cup of cool tap water

Place the ingredients into a small jar and use as needed on a soft cloth. Store in a well-sealed jar in a cool location.

WOOD FURNITURE: THE WONDERFUL WORLD OF NATURAL WOOD

Natural wood furniture provides warmth in your home that cannot be achieved by either metal or glass. Most wood furniture has a finish that utilizes a varnish, shellac, or lacquer that is polished to a high shine and will retain that shine for many years, providing the surface is cleaned with a quality wood cleaner and polished regularly with a soft dry cloth. Most commercial products contain a solvent that will remove previous layers of polish. These should not be used on a natural wood surface that is only protected by a coating of wax. If using oils on wood, use only a small amount to prevent buildup and to keep the surface from becoming gummy.

WOOD POLISH & CLEANER

You will need the following ingredients:

> $1/4$ Cup of lemon juice
> $1/8$ Cup of quality linseed oil (food grade)
> $1/8$ Cup of white vinegar

Place all the ingredients into a small glass jar with a lid and mix well. Apply with a soft, dry cloth; then polish with another clean, dry cloth.

LEMON FURNITURE POLISH

You will need the following ingredients:

> 1   Tablespoon of lemon oil
> 1   Quart of mineral oil
> 1   Spray bottle

Place the ingredients into the spray bottle and mix well before each use. Wipe off the polish with a soft, dry cloth.

FURNITURE POLISH AND CLEANER

You will need the following ingredients:

> $1/3$ Cup of white vinegar
> 1   Cup of Linseed oil
> $2/3$ Cup of turpentine

Place all the ingredients into a large bowl or small bucket and mix well. The solution should be applied with a soft cloth to remove old polish and leave a nice shine. Store in a well-sealed jar.

WAX FURNITURE POLISH #1

You will need the following ingredients:

> 4   Parts of yellow wax
> 1   Part of rosin
> 2   Parts of turpentine

Place the wax and rosin in a pot and heat until they are well blended. Then remove from heat and stir in the turpentine during the cooling period.

WAX FURNITURE POLISH #2

You will need the following ingredients:

> 4   Parts of yellow wax
> 1   Part of linseed oil
> 1   Part of turpentine

Place the wax and linseed oil in a pot and heat until they are well blended, stirring constantly. Remove from the heat and add the turpentine; mix well.

OIL FURNITURE POLISH #1

You will need the following ingredients:

> 1 *Pound of cedar oil*
> 1 *Pint of turpentine*
> 1 *Pint of ammonia water*
> *Small piece of dish soap*

Place the turpentine into a container and dissolve the cedar oil into it completely, stirring well. Add the ammonia water and the dish soap to help prevent the solution from separating and losing its emulsion.

OIL FURNITURE POLISH #2

You will need the following ingredients:

> 1 *Pint of paraffin oil*
> 1 *Pint of kerosene*
> 8 *Ounces of acetic acid (vinegar)*

Place all the ingredients into a container and mix well. Store in a well-sealed container and shake well before each use. This is a fast-drying polish that will not coat the furniture.

FURNITURE POLISH & WOODWORM DETERRENT

You will need the following ingredients:

> 5 *Ounces of linseed oil (food grade)*
> 5 *Ounces of turpentine*
> 2 *Ounces of rubbing alcohol*
> 2 *Ounces of vinegar*

Place all ingredients in a medium jar with a lid and shake well. Apply to wood furniture with a dry soft cloth.

THE MAGIC OF SCRATCH REMOVAL

Most scratches can easily be removed with the right solution and a little know-how. Remember to always go with the grain of the wood when rubbing the area with scratch remover. Use patience if you want the scratch to remain hidden for a long period of time—it is necessary to allow the solution or filler to remain for about 24 hours before attempting to remove any excess. Deep scratches can be filled using special crayons that can be purchased at most hardware stores. Choose a crayon that matches the color of the wood, then melt it into the scratch. There are many different items that can be used to hide scratches, such as eyebrow pencils, permanent markers, crayons, shoe polish, iodine, and nail polish, to name just a few.

HIDING SCRATCHES ON DARK WOOD

You will need the following ingredients:

10 *Drops of white vinegar*
4 *Drops of iodine*

Using a small glass bowl, place the vinegar on the bottom and add the iodine one drop at a time until the color you wish is obtained. Mix and dab on scratch. Wipe off immediately with a soft cloth.

HIDING SCRATCHES ON LIGHTER WOOD

You will need the following ingredients:

2 *Teaspoons of pure lemon juice*
1 *Teaspoon of virgin olive oil (the darker, the better)*
1 *Teaspoon of cool tap water*

Place all the ingredients into a small container and mix well. If this is not dark enough, try adding one drop of iodine. Place a small amount on the scratch and allow it to stand for 5 minutes before buffing it off with a soft cloth and furniture polish.

THE BEST WOOD WAX

You will need the following ingredients:

1 *Tablespoon of carnauba wax*
$1/2$ *Cup of linseed oil (food grade)*
1 *Tablespoon of clean beeswax*
$1/4$ *Cup of white vinegar*
5 *Drops of essential rose oil fragrance (if desired)*

Place all the ingredients in the top of a double boiler, then heat and stir until all the ingredients are melted together. Pour into a heat-resistant container and allow the mixture to cool until the wax becomes solid. The vinegar will go to the bottom and will not be needed. Rub the wax on your furniture with a soft cloth, then dip another cloth into some white vinegar or the residue and rub the waxed area until polished. The vinegar will cut the oil in the wax and make the waxed surface very smooth.

WATER STAIN REMOVER

You will need the following ingredients:

> 1 Ounce of toothpaste (not gel)
> 1/2 Teaspoon of baking powder

Place the ingredients into a small bowl and mix well. The mixture will be a little gritty, which is fine. Gently rub the area and leave the mixture on until it is dry. Then gently buff it off and place a coat of furniture polish on the area.

DID YOUR FRIENDS OR FAMILY GIVE YOU A RING?

When a glass that is damp or has condensation is placed on a waxed, wood surface it may leave a white ring or spots. If the surface is cleaned off within a short period of time, the spot may be easily removed. However, if it is allowed to remain, it will leave a stain that may be more difficult to remove. A mild abrasive made into a paste will usually remove any ring or watermark. The paste can be prepared from any natural oil including olive oil, petroleum jelly, margarine, and even butter, combined with baking soda or salt. Toothpaste, especially the powdered variety, can also be used, often with excellent results. After you remove the stain, be sure to apply a good coating of polish.

RING REMOVER FOR WOOD #1

You will need the following ingredients:

> 10 Drops of lemon oil
> 2 Cup of denatured alcohol

Place the ingredients into a small bottle and mix well before each use. Dab a clean, dry cloth into the mixture and rub the area, then dry with another clean, dry cloth.

RING REMOVER FOR WOOD #2

You will need the following ingredients:

> 1/2 Cup of virgin olive oil
> 1 Tablespoon of pure beeswax

Place the beeswax and olive oil in a small saucepan and heat on low and stir until the wax is melted. Transfer the mixture into a heat-resistant container and allow it to cool before placing the mixture into a jar for future use. Rub the remover on the stained area, then buff with a clean soft cloth that has been lightly dampened with white vinegar.

REMOVING WOOD POLISH BUILDUP

You will need the following ingredients:

> $1/2$ Cup white vinegar
> $1/2$ Cup of cold tap water

Place the ingredients in a small bowl and mix well. Dampen a clean soft cloth and wipe the wood surface. Dry immediately—do not allow the solution to sit on wood after it has been cleaned. Polish as usual.

BASIC WOODWORK CLEANER #1

You will need the following ingredients:

> 1 Quart of vinegar (acetic acid)
> 2 Ounces of butter of antimony
> 2 Ounces of alcohol (any)
> 1 Quart of vegetable oil

Place all the ingredients into a bottle with a lid and shake well before each use. Works well on varnished surfaces.

BASIC WOODWORK CLEANER #2

You will need the following ingredients:

> 1 Part of shellac
> 1 Part of linseed oil
> 25 Parts of alcohol (any)

Place all the ingredients into a container and mix well. This cleaner is best for polished woodwork surfaces. If the wood has any blemished areas, clean those first with boiled linseed oil.

REMOVING WATER STAINS FROM WOOD FURNITURE

You will need the following ingredients:

> White wax
> Olive oil

Water stains can easily be removed from varnished wood surfaces by melting a small amount of white wax in olive oil over low heat, then rubbing the stain with the solution using a soft cloth.

BASIC OAK WOODWORK CLEANER

You will need the following ingredients:

7   *Parts of linseed oil*
2   *Parts of powdered litharge*
2   *Parts of powdered minium*
1   *Part of powdered lead acetate*
16 *Parts of turpentine oil*

This formula may be purchased under the brand name Brunoline, or prepared with these ingredients. Place the linseed oil in a very large pot (lots of foam will be made), then add the litharge, minium, and lead acetate. Place the mixture on the heat and boil while continually stirring until the color is dark brown. Remove it from the heat and add the turpentine oil, then stir very well. Turpentine oil is very flammable so keep it away from any heat source. Oak woodwork should be cleaned with a weak ammonia solution and dried before applying a thin coating of Brunoline.

CLEANER FOR PAINTED WOOD SURFACES

You will need the following ingredients:

2   *Ounces of brown soap*
$1/2$ *Tablespoon of powdered borax*
$17^1/2$ *Ounces of cool tap water*

Cut the soap into small pieces and place in a pot. Then add the borax and dissolve the mixture into the water over low heat. Mix the solution well, then remove from the heat and allow it to cool. A flannel cloth should be used to apply this cleaner and it should be rinsed off immediately afterwards and the area dried with a clean soft cloth.

CARPET CLEANING & DEODORIZING

PROTECTION IS A MUST

Carpet should be vacuumed regularly to protect the fibers from excessive wear due the accumulation of dirt and grime that can damage the fibers. Do not attempt to use the following carpet formulas or any commercial formula on oriental rugs, old carpets, or wool rugs that are more than one color. These carpets should be professionally cleaned. Most carpeting sold is made of synthetic fibers, which may be cleaned with the following formulas. However, always try the formula in an inconspicuous location to be sure that the carpet is colorfast.

GENERAL CLEANING

You will need the following ingredients:

$^1/_2$ *Cup of Castile soap (grated fine)*
2 *Teaspoons of washing soda*
8 *Drops of vanilla essential oil*
5 *Drops of wintergreen essential oil*
4 *Cups of boiling water*

Place the soap flakes into boiling water with the pot removed from the heat. Stir until the soap flakes are fully dissolved, then allow the mixture to cool to room temperature. Add the washing soda and the essential oils and mix well in a large bowl. Check an area of the carpet for color-fastness before cleaning the carpet, just to be safe. Many older carpets are not colorfast.

BASIC CARPET CLEANER

You will need the following ingredients:

4 *Parts of Fuller's earth*
1 *Part of spirits of turpentine*
8 *Parts of pearlash*
  Soft soap

Place all the ingredients into a container, adding enough soft soap to prepare a stiff paste. Make sure to test that the carpet is colorfast before using this solution on the stained area.

CARPET CLEANER WITHOUT SOAP

You will need the following ingredients:

1 *Cup of white vinegar*
1 *Quart of denatured alcohol (cheap vodka would do)*

Place the ingredients into a small bucket and mix, then sponge off the bad spots and rinse lightly with cool water. Allow the carpet to dry and then vacuum.

INEXPENSIVE CARPET DEODORIZER

You will need the following ingredients:

8 *Ounces of baking soda (fresh)*
16 *Drops of essential lemon oil*

Place the ingredients into a container that has holes in the top and mix well, then sprinkle the mixture on your carpet. Allow the deodorizer to remain for 30 minutes, then vacuum it up.

WOOD FLOORS

WOOD FLOOR CLEANER
You will need the following ingredients:

　1　*Cup Fuller's earth clay*
　2　*Cups of Castile soap (grated fine)*
　$1/2$　*Cup of cornstarch (fresh)*
　$1^1/4$　*Cup of washing soda*
　5　*Cups of cold tap water*

Place all the ingredients in a large pot and bring to a slow boil, stirring constantly. Reduce the heat and allow it to simmer for 8-10 minutes, then cool to room temperature before using. When using, a small amount of cleaner should be applied with water, then mopped up immediately with a clean mop.

POLISH FOR WOOD FLOORING
You will need the following ingredients:

　$1/3$　*Cup of linseed oil (food grade)*
　$1/2$　*Cup of beeswax*
　2　*Tablespoons of wheat germ oil (fresh)*
　$3/4$　*Cup of turpentine*

Place the beeswax into a medium pan and heat on low until all the wax is dissolved, then add the oils. Remove from the heat and stir well. Allow the mixture to cool to room temperature, then add the turpentine and mix well. Use a sponge to apply the polish. Allow the polish to set for about 16 hours (it is best to do this at night and allow the polish to dry overnight).

PET ODOR REMOVER
You will need the following ingredients:

　$3/4$　*Cup of white vinegar*
　$3/4$　*Cup of warm tap water*

Place the ingredients into a small bowl and mix well. Place the solution on the area that has been soiled and allow it to remain for about 40 minutes before cleaning off with warm tap water. Care should be taken if the floor has a wax coating, since the vinegar is a mild acid and may remove the wax coating. Re-waxing may be necessary, but at least the odor will be gone.

WAX FLOOR POLISH

You will need the following ingredients:

    12 *Ounces of beeswax*
   2$^1/_2$ *Ounces of powdered resin*
    $^1/_2$ *Pint of turpentine*

Place a large bowl into a container of very hot water, then add all the ingredients into the bowl and mix very thoroughly. This is a flammable mixture and the mixing should not be done on a stove or near any source of high heat or fire. Use a soft cloth to apply the wax, then polish with a brush polisher.

OIL FLOOR POLISH

You will need the following ingredients:

    4 *Ounces of potassium carbonate*
    8 *Ounces of beeswax (shredded or grated)*
  3$^1/_2$ *Pints of cool tap water*

Place 1 pint of the water in a container and dissolve the potassium carbonate in it. Place the beeswax and the remaining water in another container and heat until melted; mix well. Combine the two solutions as soon as the beeswax is melted. Boil the solution until it looks creamy.

CERAMIC TILE & VINYL FLOORS

SUPER CLEANER

You will need the following ingredients:

  $^1/_2$ *Cup of Castile soap (grated fine)*
  $^1/_2$ *Cup of household ammonia (sudsing)*
  $^1/_4$ *Cup of white vinegar*
   7 *Cups of warm tap water*

Place all the ingredients in a medium bucket and mix well. Place some of the solution into a spray bottle and spray on the floor and wipe off with a soft cloth (or mop with a sponge mop).

GROUT CLEANER

KILLING MOLD & ELIMINATING MILDEW

Mold loves to grow and multiply in warm, damp places and the grout around tiles is the perfect environment for it. The hot water keeps the area damp and warm and allows mold to thrive. Cleaners that kill mold can easily be prepared at home making commercial preparations unnecessary. The best tool to use on grout when cleaning is an old toothbrush that is not too stiff. If the brush is too stiff it will remove a small amount of the grout every time you clean and, eventually, you will have to re-grout. Mildew is very easy to remove with the following formula.

INEXPENSIVE GROUT CLEANER
You will need the following ingredients:

2   *Parts of liquid laundry bleach*
$1/2$ *Part of phosphate-based liquid floor cleaner*
3   *Parts of rubbing alcohol*
$4^1/2$ *Parts of cool tap water*

Place all the ingredients into a large container and mix well. Place a small amount into a spray bottle and use as you would any other grout cleaner. Keep out of the reach of children and pets.

WALLPAPER REQUIRES A GENTLE TOUCH

When cleaning wallpaper you shouldn't scrub too hard or you will be replacing the paper. Older wallpapers, while they may have lasted for many years, are somewhat delicate and easily damaged. One of the reasons the paper may have lasted so long is that it was not cleaned too often. Be gentle with old paper and always try an inconspicuous location before cleaning the center of the wall. Newer papers used in bathrooms and kitchens have been coated to protect them making them easier to clean and allowing them to take more abuse from the cleaning methods.

CLEANING DOUGH #1
You will need the following ingredients:

4   *Ounces of powdered pumice*
1   *Quart of all-purpose flour*
   Cool tap water

Place all the ingredients into a large bowl and mix. Reduce the formula if desired. Add enough water to prepare a stiff dough, then form into rolls 2 inches wide and 6 inches long. Place each roll into a cotton cloth and sew closed. Boil the bags for 40 minutes to make them firm, then remove them from the heat and lay them out on a cookie sheet to cool and set for 4–5 hours. Remove the crust that may have formed and use on wallpaper.

CLEANING DOUGH #2

You will need the following ingredients:

2 *Parts of standard bread dough*
1 *Part of plaster of paris*

Place the bread dough and the plaster of paris in a medium bowl and mix well, then bake in the oven, remove and use the next day. The paper should be dry and dust-free before using this cleaner. Rub the cleaner on the wallpaper with single strokes in one direction only. Do not go back and forth or you will damage the wallpaper.

STRONG CLEANER FOR VERY SOILED WALLPAPER

You will need the following ingredients:

1 *Gallon of cool tap water*
5 *Pounds of table salt*
4 *Ounces of aluminum sulfate*
$4^{1}/2$ *Ounces of kerosene*
$9^{3}/4$ *Pounds of all-purpose flour*

Place the water, salt, and aluminum sulfate into a pot and heat to 180° F., while stirring occasionally. Remove from the heat and stir in the kerosene and allow the solution to cool to 170° F. Sift in the flour very slowly and stir continually to prevent lumps from forming. This cleaner is abrasive and should be used with care.

DISINFECTANTS

BASIC DISINFECTANT FORMULA #1
You will need the following ingredients:

6 Ounces of aluminum sulfate
1¹/₂ Ounces of zinc chloride
2 Ounces of sodium chloride
3 Ounces of calcium chloride

Place all the ingredients into a container and add enough water to make 2 pints.

BASIC DISINFECTANT FORMULA #2
You will need the following ingredients:

5 Parts of rosin
2 Parts of caustic soda (380 Baume)
2 Parts of very hot tap water
7¹/₂ Parts of creosote

Place the water in a pot and boil until the caustic soda and rosin are dissolved. Reduce the temperature below boiling and stir in the creosote, then continue to stir until the solution looks uniform.

CESSPOOL DISINFECTANT
You will need the following ingredients:

10 Parts of calcium oxide (quicklime)
2 Parts of chlorinated lime
1¹/₄ Parts of potassium carbonate

Wear gloves. Place all the ingredients into a container and mix well, then sift thoroughly. Store in a tightly sealed glass or metal container. Do not get on your skin.

PINE OIL DISINFECTANT
You will need the following ingredients:

5 Parts of pine oil
2 Parts of rosin
1 Part of caustic soda (25% solution)

Place the pine oil and the rosin in a porcelain container and heat until the rosin has dissolved. Remove from the heat and allow it to cool to 140° F., then slowly stir in the caustic soda solution. Wait 30 minutes until saponification is complete. Mix 1 part of the solution in 40 parts of cool tap water. This solution is strong enough to clean toilets, bathtubs, and even garbage cans. It can also be used as a spray.

TOILET DISINFECTANT & DEODORANT

You will need the following ingredients:

2 *Parts of ferric chloride*
$2^{1}/_{2}$ *Parts of zinc chloride*
$2^{1}/_{2}$ *Parts of aluminum chloride*
2 *Parts of calcium chloride*
36 *Parts of cool tap water*
5 *Grains of thymol*
$^{1}/_{4}$ *Ounce of oil of rosemary*
3 *Quarts of alcohol (any)*

Place the water into a container and dissolve all the chlorides into water. In another container, add the alcohol, thymol, and rosemary, and mix well. To use, mix the alcohol solution with $^{1}/_{2}$ gallon of the chloride solution.

WALL CLEANERS

DON'T BE A PAINT REMOVER

While most stains can easily be cleaned from most wall surfaces, if the stain has been on the wall for a long time, you may have to re-paint. Wall stains should be removed as soon as you notice them or they may become incorporated into the paint. It doesn't take very much rubbing to remove the paint along with the stain.

GREASE SPOT REMOVER

You will need the following ingredients:

2 *Ounce of fresh white talcum powder*
  New powder puff

Place the powder puff into the talcum and gently rub over the grease spot. Continue with additional applications until the spot is completely gone.

REMOVING PASTE FROM WALLS

You will need the following ingredients:

> 3   Ounces of cornstarch
> Cool tap water

Add the water to the cornstarch to produce a paste that can then be applied with a brush to the paste stain. Allow it to remain for about 1 hour, then remove the paste with a brush and repeat if necessary.

WALL CLEANER WITH AMMONIA

You will need the following ingredients:

> $^1/_4$ Cup of washing soda
> $^1/_4$ Cup of white vinegar
> $^1/_2$ Cup of household ammonia
> 1   Gallon of warm tap water

Place the water in a bucket and add the other ingredients, then mix well. Store in a well-sealed container in a cool dry location. This will work well on enameled and surfaces that are painted with a flat, oil, or water-based paint.

Chapter 2

Personal Care
Products

S.BEAN

FACIAL PRODUCTS

Be sure to wash and dry your face thoroughly before applying a facial
mask. The mask ingredients should never be placed close to your eyes.
The ingredients should always be as fresh as possible—don't use the old
leftovers in the cupboard or refrigerator. Masks are capable of removing
dirt, grime, and, especially, dead skin. They increase circulation, reduce
the eruption of pimples, lower the level of oiliness, provide moisture, and
smooth the skin. Commercial preparations are expensive compared to the
following recipes for facial masks. And facial masks made at home are
just as effective when used properly. The more common ingredients used
in facial masks include cooked oatmeal, egg whites, yogurt, brewer's
yeast, honey, vegetable oils, and mashed fruits. Brewer's yeast is excellent for improving circulation and honey balances the acid/base balance
of the skin. A mask should not be used more than three times per week.

SQUEAKY CLEAN CLEANSING MASK FORMULA

Mix the following ingredients together in a small rounded bowl:

> 1   *Tablespoon fresh plain yogurt*
> 1   *Teaspoon fresh sesame oil (no more than 2 weeks old)*

Mix the ingredients together. Allow the mixture to rest for 10 minutes
before applying to your face and neck. The mixture should remain in
place while you remain still for 12 minutes, then massage the mixture
very gently into the skin and immediately wash off with a very warm
washcloth. Rinse thoroughly at least three times and your skin should
be squeaky clean.

A REAL SKIN TIGHTENER

Mix the following ingredients together in a blender until a smooth pasty
mixture is obtained:

> 1   *Tablespoon very ripe avocado, mashed*
> 1¹/₂ *Tablespoons of pure honey (no artificial ingredients)*
> 2   *Egg whites from medium eggs (less than 3 days old)*

Pour off any excess liquid and use the paste only. Gently massage the
paste onto your face and neck and sit still until the mask dries, which
should take about 15 minutes. Then wash your face and neck with a warm
washcloth. This mask will tighten the skin and increase your circulation.

OILY SKIN BEGONE

Mix the following ingredients together in a small bowl:

$2^1/2$ Teaspoons of Fuller's Earth (from health food store)
$1^1/4$ Tablespoon of pure aloe vera juice
$^1/2$ Teaspoon of fresh plain yogurt

Blend the ingredients into a smooth paste. If any small lumps appear, crush them with the back of a teaspoon. Apply the paste to your face and allow it to remain on for 15 minutes. Wash the mixture off with a warm washcloth.

HOW DRY I AM

Mix the following ingredients together in a small bowl:

1 Medium banana (not too ripe)
$^1/4$ Teaspoon pure honey (no artificial ingredients)

Mash the banana and honey together until a paste is formed. Apply the banana/honey paste to your face and neck and leave on for 15–20 minutes. This mixture will stimulate the skin to become more moist and should eliminate dry skin. Remove the mask with a warm washcloth. The neck is important since it does not contain any oil glands. Wrinkling of the neck is very common as you age.

SUPER DRY SKIN CARE CREAM

The following two sets of ingredients are needed:

Step One Ingredients:
$^1/3$ Cup avocado oil
1 Teaspoon of lanolin
$^3/4$ Cup of cocoa butter
$^2/3$ Ounces of finely grated pure beeswax

Place all the ingredients in a small saucepan and heat over low heat until the beeswax melts and blends with the other ingredients. Stir and remove from heat and allow the wax to cool while you prepare the ingredients from step two.

Step Two Ingredients:
$^1/2$ Cup of pure aloe vera gel
$^2/3$ Cup of rosewater
2 Drops of rose oil fragrance
2 Vitamin E capsules (contents only)

Add all the ingredients from step two to solution from step one and, using a small metal whisk, blend all the ingredients together until the mixture looks like, and has the texture of, a light-colored hand cream. Place the cream in a well-sealed jar and use as needed.

FROWN LINE REMOVER

You will need the following ingredients:

1 *Bottle of milk of magnesia*
1/4 *Cup of virgin olive oil*
1 *Bottle of witch hazel (refrigerated)*

Clean your face thoroughly with mild soap and warm water. Dry your face and wait 10 minutes. Spread the milk of magnesia on your face with a piece of cotton and allow it to dry thoroughly. After it has fully dried, spread another layer of milk of magnesia on your face, which will dissolve the first layer. Remove the milk of magnesia with a damp warm washcloth. Place a small amount of olive oil in a small saucepan and heat on low heat until it is just barely warm to the touch (do not overheat). Apply the olive oil to your face with a cotton ball and allow it to remain for 5 minutes. Use the witch hazel to wipe off the olive oil. The process should be used twice a week. You will be amazed at the difference after 2–3 weeks.

TIGHTEN THOSE PORES

You will need the following ingredients:

2 *Teaspoons of Fuller's earth*
2 *Teaspoons of witch hazel*
1 *Large egg (slightly beaten)*
2 *Drops of essential rose oil*

Place the Fuller's earth and the witch hazel in a medium bowl and mix well until they form a paste. Add the egg and the essential oil and blend well. Place the mixture on your face and allow it to sit for 10 minutes, then remove it with cool tap water and pat dry with a soft cloth.

CLAY FACIAL MASK FOR BLACKHEADS & OILY SKIN

You will need the following ingredients:

2 *Tablespoons of aloe vera*
1 *Teaspoon of witch hazel*
1 *Tablespoon of kaolin (from pharmacy)*
1 1/4 *Teaspoon of grapefruit juice*
1/2 *Tablespoon of bentonite*
2 *Drops of essential lemon oil*

Place the aloe vera, grapefruit juice, and witch hazel in a small bowl and mix well. Add the bentonite and kaolin very slowly to the mixture while continually stirring. Strain the mixture through a strainer, then add the essential oil and mix well. Apply the mask and allow it to remain for 12 minutes before washing off with warm tap water.

NEW RADIANCE MASK

You will need the following ingredients:

> 1 *Tablespoon of Fuller's earth*
> 1^1/$_2$ *Tablespoons of papaya (mashed)*
> ^{3}/$_4$ *Tablespoon of pure honey*

Place all the ingredients into a small bowl and mix well until they form a paste. Apply the mask to your face and leave on 15 minutes before washing off with warm tap water.

STRAWBERRY FACIAL

You will need the following ingredients:

> 5 *Medium-sized ripe strawberries*
> ^{1}/$_3$ *Cup of white vinegar*

Place the vinegar in a small bowl, then mash the strawberries into the vinegar and allow the mixture to sit for 3 hours. Strain the solution through a piece of cheesecloth, then dab the solution on your face and neck just before bedtime. Leave the mask on overnight and wash thoroughly with warm water in the morning. This treatment can be done once per week.

MASK THAT PEELS OFF

You will need the following ingredients:

> ^{1}/$_2$ *Cup of apple juice (unsweetened)*
> 1 *Packet of unflavored gelatin (fresh)*
> 1 *Drop of essential rose oil*

Place the ingredients in a double boiler and slowly dissolve the gelatin into the apple juice. Remove from the heat and allow the mixture to cool until almost set, then add the oil. Mix immediately and apply the mixture to your face. When the mask is fully dry, peel it off and rinse your face with warm tap water.

S. BEAN

PROBLEM SKIN MASK

You will need the following ingredients:

  1 *Tablespoon of fresh cucumber*
  1 *Tablespoon of plain yogurt*
  1 *Tablespoon of fresh parsley (chopped)*

Place all the ingredients into a blender and blend until it is somewhat pasty. Wash your face, then apply the mixture and allow it to remain for 10–15 minutes before removing and washing with warm water.

MASK FOR SENSITIVE SKIN

You will need the following ingredients:

  1 *Tablespoon of instant oatmeal*
  ³/₄ *Teaspoon of pure honey*
  1¹/₄ *Teaspoon of avocado (mashed)*
  1 *Tablespoon of rose clay (from health food store or beauty supply)*
  2 *Drops of essential rose oil*
  1 *Drop of essential lavender oil*
  1 *Drop of essential frankincense oil*

Place all the ingredients except the essential oils into a medium bowl and blend well using warm tap water to prepare a paste. Just before the consistency becomes pastelike, add the essential oils and blend well until a paste forms. Place the mask on your face and allow it to remain for 15 minutes before washing off with warm water.

MOISTURIZERS

A HEALING MOISTURIZER

You will need the following ingredients:

  1 *Teaspoon of beeswax (grated)*
  3 *Tablespoons of grapeseed oil*
  1 *Teaspoon of cocoa butter*
  ¹/₂ *Teaspoon of borax*
  1 *Ounce of lavender infusion*
  8 *Drops of lemon essential oil*

Place the wax, butter, and grapeseed oil in a double boiler and slowly melt, mixing well. Very slowly add the borax to the lavender infusion and heat over low heat in a small saucepan. Add the borax/lavender infusion mixture to the wax mixture very slowly, stirring constantly. Remove it from the heat and allow it to cool. Store in an opaque container in the refrigerator.

DELICATE SKIN REJUVENATOR

You will need the following ingredients:

2 *Teaspoons of evening primrose oil*
4 *Teaspoons of grapeseed oil*
4 *Drops of rose absolute*
5 *Drops of patchouli essential oil*
3 *Drops of germanium essential oil*

Place all the ingredients in a small bowl and mix thoroughly. Store in a dark bottle in a cool, dry location—it will last about 5 months. This preparation should be gently massaged onto the face 5 nights a week as a skin toner and moisturizer.

HAIR CARE

NEW BODY FOR THINNING HAIR

Mix the following ingredients together in a small bowl:

1 *Medium raw egg*
1 *Teaspoon of your normal shampoo*

Shampoo your hair with this mixture, allowing it to remain on your hair for 5–7 minutes. The protein in the egg will bind with the protein in your hair and make the hair strands thicker. Rinse your hair well with warm (not hot) water.

PRE-SHAMPOO TREATMENT FOR MEN

You will need the following ingredients:

1 *Teaspoon of dark rum*
1 *Teaspoon of jojoba oil*
1 *Teaspoon of lecithin*
3 *Drops of Bay essential oil*
  Lemon juice

Place all the ingredients into a small dish and blend well. Massage the solution into your scalp. Wrap a towel around your head and allow it to remain for 1 hour. Wash your hair with shampoo and a small amount of lemon juice.

DANDRUFF REMOVER

You will need the following ingredients:

> 1   *Cup of apple cider vinegar*
> 5   *Aspirin tablets (powdered)*
> *1/3*   *Cup witch hazel*

Place all the ingredients in a sealed bottle and shake to mix well. Shampoo using your normal shampoo, then place the dandruff solution on your hair and allow it to remain for about 10 minutes before rinsing it out with warm tap water. The solution should be shaken well before each use.

OILY HAIR SHAMPOO

You will need the following ingredients:

> 1   *Cup of cold tap water*
> 2   *Tablespoons of dry peppermint*
> 2   *Tablespoons of dry spearmint*
> 1   *Tablespoon of dry sage*
> *2/3*   *Cup of baby shampoo*

Place the peppermint, spearmint, sage, and water in a medium saucepan and bring to a boil. Remove from the heat and allow the mixture to steep for 15 minutes. Strain the herbs out and mix the baby shampoo with the water from the herbs. Store in a sealed plastic bottle.

DRY HAIR SHAMPOO

You will need the following ingredients:

> 1   *Cup of cold tap water*
> 1   *Tablespoon of dry rosemary*
> 1   *Tablespoon of dry comfrey root*
> 1   *Tablespoon of dry chamomile*
> *2/3*   *Cup of baby shampoo*
> 1   *Large egg (beaten well)*
> *1/3*   *Cup of whole milk*

Place the rosemary, comfrey root, chamomile, and water in a medium saucepan and bring to a boil. Remove from the heat and allow the mixture to steep for 15 minutes. Strain the herbs out and mix the baby shampoo, egg, and milk into the water from the herbs. Store in a sealed plastic bottle.

HAIR CONDITIONER

You will need the following ingredients:

$^1/_2$ Cup of virgin olive oil
$^1/_2$ Cup of corn oil
$^1/_2$ Cup of pure honey

Place all the ingredients into a small saucepan and heat until just before it begins to boil. Remove it from the heat and allow it to cool. This conditioner should be used while the hair is still very damp. Massage the conditioner through the hair, wrap the hair with a warm towel, and let it sit for one hour. Then shampoo the solution out of your hair. Rinse and dry as usual. Store the mixture in a cool, dry location in a sealed bottle.

SCRUB-A-DUB-DUB

Commercial shampoos will be considerably thicker than most formulas you prepare yourself. In most cases this is done so that you will think that if the product is more substantial, the quality must be high. Almost all of these products contain a sudsing agent to produce the desired suds, along with a non-sudsing agent to break the suds downóotherwise you would never get the soap out of your hair. The following formulas will do the job, remove the dirt, and freshen your hair just as well as most of the commercial products, even though they are for the most part thinner and more watery.

SHAMPOO TO MAKE YOUR HAIR LIVELY & SHINY

You will need the following ingredients:

1 Large egg
1 Teaspoon of lemon juice
3 Tablespoons of an unscented shampoo
    Fragrance (if desired)

Place all the ingredients in a small bowl and blend well. Shampoo the solution into your hair, then rinse with warm water. The protein in the egg acts as a conditioner. The lemon juice gives a attractive sheen to the hair.

HAIR BRUSH CLEANER

You will need the following ingredients:

1 Pint cold tap water
$^1/_4$ Cup household ammonia
$^1/_2$ Teaspoon liquid dish detergent

Place the ingredients in a medium bowl and mix thoroughly. Place the brush or comb in the bowl and let it sit for 10 minutes. Remove and clean off any residue with an old toothbrush. Rinse under warm, running water and allow it to dry overnight before using.

SHAMPOO PASTE

You will need the following ingredients:

2   *Tablespoons of white Castile soap (grated)*
2   *Tablespoons of ammonia water*
1   *Tablespoon of cologne water*
1   *Tablespoon of glycerin*
12 *Tablespoons of cool tap water*

Place the water in a saucepan on low heat and add the grated Castile soap, allowing the soap to dissolve fully. Remove from the heat and allow the mixture to cool before adding the rest of the ingredients. Mix the soap mixture well and use the as a you would a shampoo. Store in a closed container.

SHAMPOO FOR HEAD LICE

You will need the following ingredients:

20 *Drops of essential lavender oil*
20 *Drops of essential germanium oil*
20 *Drops of essential rosemary oil*
20 *Drops of essential tea tree oil*
6   *Tablespoons of coconut oil*
1   *Tablespoon of jojoba oil*

Place all the ingredients into a small bowl and mix well. Massage shampoo into the scalp. Cover the head with a towel and allow the shampoo to sit for 3–4 hours. Massage the shampoo into the hair, then rinse well with warm water. The treatment should be repeated after 2 days and then again in 7 days to be sure all lice are gone.

OLD-FASHIONED EGG SHAMPOO FORMULA

You will need the following ingredients:

2   *Egg whites (large eggs)*
5   *Ounces cool tap water*
3   *Ounces of water of ammonia*
$1/3$ *Ounce of cologne water*
4   *Ounces of ethyl alcohol*

Place the egg whites in a rounded-bottom bowl and beat until they are frothy. Then add the rest of the ingredients in the order they are given in the formula. Mix each ingredient thoroughly into the mixture as you add each one. Store in a sealed bottle in a cool dry location.

SHAMPOO CREAM

You will need the following ingredients:

> 6 *Tablespoons of white soap*
> 9 *Tablespoons of glycerin*
> 5 *Tablespoons of borax*
> 10 *Tablespoons of cool tap water*

Place the water in a small pot on low heat and add the soap, allowing it to dissolve; then add the glycerin and borax. Stir well and, if desired, add any perfume or essential oil.

HAIR BLEACH #1

You will need the following ingredients:

> 1 *Pint of cool tap water*
> *Juice of 4 Lemons (commercial juice OK)*

Place the ingredients in a small bowl and mix well, then rinse the hair with the solution. This will lighten the hair.

HAIR BLEACH #2

You will need the following ingredients:

> 1 *Ounce of 3% hydrogen peroxide*
> 10 *Drops of ammonia water*
> *Powdered white henna*

Place the peroxide and water in a small container and mix well, then add just enough powdered white henna to prepare a paste. Apply the paste to the hair and allow it to remain for 15 minutes or longer, depending on the shade you desire. Excessive bleaching can damage hair.

1940's HAIR TONIC FOR DANDRUFF

You will need the following ingredients:

> 1 *Tablespoon of resorcin*
> 3 *Tablespoons of tincture of capsicum*
> 2 *Tablespoons of castor oil*
> 20 *Tablespoons of ethyl alcohol*

Place all the ingredients into a small bowl and mix thoroughly. Massage into the scalp before bedtime for 6 nights.

1950's WAVE SET LOTION

You will need the following ingredients:

$1/4$ Ounce of quince seed
$9^3/4$ Ounce of distilled water
$1/2$ Teaspoon of borax
$1/2$ Teaspoon of ethyl alcohol
$1/2$ Teaspoon of glycerin
4 Drops of essential rose or lavender oil

Place the borax into the distilled water in a medium bowl and let the borax dissolve. Place the quince seed in the borax solution and allow it to soak for 10–12 hours. This should produce a pasty substance, which should be strained through a piece of cheesecloth. Add the alcohol, glycerin, and essential oil to the resulting liquid and mix well. Go for the waves!

BRILLIANTINE HAIR LUSTER RESTORER

You will need the following ingredients:

4 Ounces of virgin olive oil
4 Ounces of ethyl alcohol
2 Ounces of glycerin
Essential oil (if desired)

Place all the ingredients into a small glass bowl and mix thoroughly. Apply the brilliantine to the hair to obtain a bright, non-sticky luster.

SCALY SCALP FORMULA

You will need the following ingredients:

2 Ounces of hydrous lanolin
2 Teaspoons of virgin olive oil
$1/2$ Teaspoons of salicylic acid
$1/2$ Teaspoon of boric acid
$1/2$ Teaspoon of cholesterin
$1/4$ Teaspoon of bergamot oil

Place the hydrous lanolin in a small saucepan over low heat and melt. Then add the olive oil, salicylic acid, and cholesterin and mix well. Remove from the heat as soon as all ingredients are blended well. Add the bergamot oil as soon as the formula has cooled and mix well.

HAIR ROOT STIMULATOR #1

You will need the following ingredients:

4 *Ounces of bay rum*
4 *Ounces of ethyl alcohol*
2 *Teaspoons of glycerin*
2 *Teaspoons of resorcinol*
Perfume or essential oil (as desired)

Place all the ingredients into a bowl and mix well. Massage vigorously into scalp to stimulate the hair follicles to grow. Store in sealed bottle and shake before each use. Should be used at least 4 times per week.

HAIR ROOT STIMULATOR #2

You will need the following ingredients:

4 *Ounces of distilled water*
2 *Ounces of ethyl alcohol*
3¹/2 *Ounces of bay rum*
1 *Tablespoon of glycerin*
10 *Drops of oil of bay*

The directions are the same as for hair root stimulator #1.

1950's POMADE

You will need the following ingredients:

¹/2 *Ounce of white beeswax*
2 *Ounces of odorless castor oil*
2 *Ounces of purified lard*
1 *Tablespoon of extra virgin olive oil*
2 *Teaspoons of oil of bergamot*

Place the beeswax into a small saucepan and place on low heat until melted. Place the purified lard, olive oil, and castor oil in another saucepan and heat over low heat, mix well and add the melted beeswax. Remove from the heat and allow the pomade to cool. Stir well, then add the oil of bergamot and mix thoroughly. Store in well-sealed container in a cool location.

GRANDMOTHER'S HAIR STRAIGHTENER

You will need the following ingredients:

- 1 *Pound of beef suet*
- 2 *Ounces of yellow wax*
- 2 *Ounces of castor oil*
- 12 *Grains of benzoic acid*
- 30 *Drops of lemon oil*
- 5 *Drops of cinnamon oil*

Place the wax and suet in a double boiler and melt. Add the castor oil and benzoic acid and mix. Remove from heat and allow to cool a little before adding the oils. Blend all ingredients well and use the fingertips to massage a small amount into the hair twice a day. This preparation should make kinky hair straight and allow it to lie flat.

FOR THE BATH

BATH SALTS WITH VINEGAR

You will need the following ingredients:

- 4 *Cups of white vinegar*
- 1 *Cup of baking soda (fresh)*
- 1/2 *Cup of Epsom salts*
- 1/4 *Cup of salt*

Place all the ingredients in a medium bowl and mix well. Store the mixture in a sealed jar and use about 1/2 cup for each bath. Add the solution while the bath water is running for the best results.

FORMULA FOR STANDARD BATH SALTS

Mix the following ingredients together in a medium jar:

- 1 *Ounce vegetable glycerin (health food store)*
- 1/2 *Ounce rose oil*
- 5 *Pounds of a quality sea salt*
- 2 *Drops any food coloring (optional)*

Blend all the ingredients thoroughly and keep near the bathtub. Use about 3/4 cup with each bath for a soothing, relaxing bath.

MAKE COOKIES FOR YOUR BATH

You will need the following ingredients:

$1/2$ Cup of baking soda (fresh)
2   Tablespoons of light corn oil
2   Eggs (large)
2   Cups of powdered sea salt (health food store)
3   Drops of rose oil fragrance

Place all the ingredients in a medium bowl and knead by hand until a workable dough is formed. Form the dough into small tablespoon-sized balls and place them on an ungreased cookie sheet. Bake the cookies in a pre-heated 350° F. oven for 10–12 minutes, keeping an eye on them so that they do not burn. They should be just lightly browned, not black. A soothing bath can be achieved by adding 2 "cookies" to your bath water.

MILK BATH

You will need the following ingredients:

2   Cups of dry non-fat milk powder
1   Cup of cornstarch
$1/8$ Teaspoon of rose oil fragrance

Place all the ingredients into the blender and blend well. Add $1/2$ cup to very warm bath water.

MILK BATH FOR BABIES

You will need the following ingredients:

1   Cup of powdered whole milk
$1/2$ Cup of cornstarch
$1/2$ Cup of pure honey
3   Tablespoons of distilled water
4   Drops of essential rose oil

Place the honey, powdered milk, and cornstarch into a blender and blend on low while adding the water very slowly. The mixture should become a paste. Add 1 cup of the mixture to bath water while the water is running and stir if necessary.

BATH OIL

You will need the following ingredients:

> 1 Cup of pure honey
> 1 Cup of table salt
> 2 Cups of whole milk
> 1/4 Cup of baking soda
> 1/2 Cup of baby oil
> Essential oil fragrance (if desired)

Place the milk, honey, salt, and baking soda in a medium bowl and blend well. Add the entire mixture to a tub of very warm water; then add the baby oil and 3–5 drops of the fragrance, if desired. Add one rubber duck.

BATH FOR LOVERS

You will need the following ingredients:

> 3 Drops of essential ginger oil
> 3 Drops of essential rose oil
> 3 Drops of essential lavender oil
> 3 Drops of essential Ylang Ylang oil
> 2 Drops of essential sandalwood oil

Place the oils into a very warm bath one-drop at a time while the water is running, then get in with your spouse.

BUBBLE BATH

You will need the following ingredients:

> 2 Cups of grated Ivory soap
> 1/2 Cup of glycerin
> 2 Cups of liquid dishwasher detergent
> 1 Gallon cold tap water
> Essential oil fragrance (if desired)

Place the grated soap, water, and 2 tablespoons of glycerin in a large saucepan and cook over low heat while stirring continuously until the soap has dissolved. Place 2 cups of the solution and the remaining glycerin and dishwasher detergent and mix well. Store in a container that is well sealed. Add 1 cup to a very warm tub as it is filling.

FRAGRANT BATH SOAP

The following ingredients will be needed to make soap:

> 1 Pound of glycerin soap
> 1 Cup of boiling water
> 1/2 Cup of standard oatmeal
> 1/4 Ounce of rose oil

Using a double boiler with one cup of boiling water, melt the glycerin soap and add the oatmeal and rose oil. After the ingredients are blended well, allow it to cool but maintain the solution in a pourable state. Pour the mixture into small molds or a box that has been lined with plastic wrap. When the soap hardens, remove and use. The soap will last longer if it is allowed to dry at room temperature for a few days before being used.

FIZZING BATH BEADS

You will need the following ingredients:

3 Tablespoons of powdered vitamin C (ascorbic acid)
$1/4$ Cup of baking soda
1 Tablespoon borax
2 Tablespoons of almond oil
2 Tablespoons of confectioners sugar (10X)
5 Vitamin E capsules (liquid only)
$1/2$ Teaspoon of rose oil fragrance

Place the vitamin C, baking soda, borax, and sugar into a medium bowl and blend thoroughly. Slowly add the almond oil while stirring until the mixture is dampened. Add the vitamin E and the rose oil and continue to stir until well blended. Form the mixture into small balls and place on a piece of waxed paper (in a location that they can be left alone for about 10 days) and allow to dry for 2 hours. Check the balls, reshaping as necessary (they should be as round as you can make them). Place the balls back on the waxed paper and allow them to dry for 10 days. The balls should be stored in an airtight container and stored in a dry place.

A BOMB FOR THE BATH

You will need the following ingredients:

1 Cup of cornstarch
2 Cups of baking soda (fresh)
1 Cup of citric acid powder (vitamin C)
2 Drops of essential rose oil

Place all the ingredients into a medium bowl and mix well into dough. Roll the dough into small balls and place on a cookie sheet to dry. Store in a sealed container away from moisture. Place a bomb into your bath water—it will look like a fizzing bath. Very refreshing.

1920's FLABBY-FLESH BATH TONIC

You will need the following ingredients:

1 Pint if white vinegar
8 Grams of rosemary
8 Grams of rue
8 Grams of camphor
8 Grams of lavender

Place the vinegar in a container and allow the herbs to soak for 2–3 hours, then strain through a piece of cheesecloth. Store in a well-sealed bottle and add to your bath water.

EFFERVESCENT BATH POWDER

You will need the following ingredients:

9 Parts sodium bicarbonate
6 Parts rice flour
10 Parts tartaric acid (from drug store)
1 Essential lavender or rose oil (if desired)

Place the ingredients into a container and mix well. Place two tablespoons in your bath water for an invigorating bath.

POWDERS

The base of most cosmetic powders is mineral talc. Making your own powder is easy and the formulas can easily be altered with the addition of any number of perfumes or essential oils. When talc is called for, always use USP (United States Pharmacopoeia) talc powder, it is the best quality. The majority of chemicals recommended in the powder formulas can be obtained from a chemical supply house, pharmacy, or health food store. If they do not carry the ingredient, they should be able recommend another source.

When preparing a powder, it is best to use an enameled container. If perfume is added to provide a pleasant aroma, it should be sprayed on, rather than added as a liquid, so as not to cause the powder to become lumpy. Though it is not mentioned in the formulas, all powder should be forced through a fine sieve to remove any extraneous, abrasive material in the powder.

CHILDREN'S BODY POWDER

You will need the following ingredients:

5 *Ounces of talc*
2 *Ounces of boric acid*
1 *Ounce of precipitated chalk*
1 *Ounce of magnesium carbonate*
1/2 *Ounce of orris root*
1/2 *Ounce of zinc oxide*
Perfume spray (if desired)

Place all the ingredients into a small bowl and mix well, then place the powder through a fine sieve before storing in a sealed container.

BODY POWDER

You will need the following ingredients:

4 *Tablespoons of kaolin*
10 *Drops calendula tincture*
8 *Drops of essential lemon oil*

Place the kaolin in a fine sifter and sift onto a small plate. Place the tincture and essential oil in a small dish and mix well, then place the mixture into a small, fine spray bottle and spray on the kaolin. Mix together and store in a small shaker and use as a body powder.

DRY SKIN FACE POWDER

You will need the following ingredients:

6 Ounces of talc
2 Ounces of magnesium carbonate
2 Ounces of zinc oxide
1 Ounce precipitated chalk
1 Ounce of magnesium stearate
   Perfume spray (as desired)

Place all the ingredients into a porcelain bowl and mix well, then place through a sieve before using as you would any other face powder. Store in an airtight container.

OILY SKIN FACE POWDER

You will need the following ingredients:

5 Ounces of talc
3 Ounces of magnesium carbonate
$2^1/2$ Zinc oxide
1 Ounce of precipitated chalk
$^1/2$ Ounce of titanium dioxide
   Perfume spray (as desired)

Place all the ingredients into a porcelain bowl and mix well, then place through a sieve before using as you would any other face powder. Store in an airtight container.

BASIC TALCUM POWDER

You will need the following ingredients:

5 Ounces of talc
3 Ounces of precipitated chalk
1 Ounce of boric acid
1 Ounce of magnesium stearate
   Perfume spray (as desired)

Place all the ingredients into a porcelain bowl and mix well, then place through a sieve before using. Store in a sealed container.

ROSE TALCUM POWDER

You will need the following ingredients:

5 Pounds of powdered talc
7 Drops of essential rose oil
4 Ounces of extract of jasmine

Place all the ingredients into a container and blend well.

1940's DOUCHE POWDER

You will need the following ingredients:

12 *Drops of Lysol*
12 *Grains of menthol*
 1 *Ounce of boric acid*
12 *Grains powdered potassium permanganate*
    Sodium bicarbonate as needed

Place all the ingredients into a small bowl and add enough sodium bicarbonate to produce 6 ounces of powder. Place 2 ounces of the powder in 1 quart of very warm tap water (105° F to 115° F.) and use for 15 minutes.

LIQUID FACE POWDER

You will need the following ingredients:

 3 *Ounces of rose water*
 1 *Ounce of pink calamine (powder)*
$1/2$ *Ounce of zinc oxide*
$1/4$ *Ounce of glycerine*
$1/2$ *Ounce of wheat starch*
    Essential oil for aroma (if desired)

Place the calamine, zinc oxide, and wheat starch into a sifter and sift into a bowl, then mix the powder with the rose water and glycerine to dissolve all the powder. The calamine lends a pink color to the powder. If you want to add fragrance, add the essential oil last. Blend the mixture well and then pour the powder into a well-sealed jar. Shake well before each use.

DRY ROUGE POWDER #1

You will need the following ingredients:

 1 *Ounce of talc*
 1 *Ounce of heavy precipitated chalk*
 1 *Ounce of rice powder*
$1/2$ *Ounce of zinc oxide*
$1/2$ *Ounce of powdered tragacanth*
    Perfume spray (if desired)

Place the ingredients into a small bowl and mix well, then dampen the mixture a little and force the rouge into a compact to replace old rouge.

DRY ROUGE POWDER #2

You will need the following ingredients:

> 7^1/$_2$ Ounces of talcum powder
> 1^1/$_2$ Tablespoons of gum arabic
> 3 Teaspoons of powdered carmine

Place all the ingredients into a small bowl and mix well, then add a small amount of cool tap water to form a paste. Force the mixture into an empty compact.

EYE CARE

EYE MAKEUP REMOVER #1

You will need the following ingredients:

> 1 Tablespoon of light corn oil
> 1 Tablespoon of castor oil
> 2 Teaspoons of canola oil

Mix the ingredients together in a small bowl. Apply to remove eye make-up. This will work as well as almost any commercial remover—at a tenth of the cost. Store in a clean, well-sealed jar. It is best to pour out a small amount into a cap and not dip into the main supply.

EYE MAKEUP REMOVER #2

You will need the following ingredients:

> 1 Teaspoon of beeswax (grated)
> 2 Teaspoons of almond oil
> ^{1}/$_2$ Teaspoon of aloe vera juice
> ^{1}/$_4$ Teaspoons of cocoa butter
> ^{1}/$_2$ Teaspoon of shea nut butter (from health food store)
> 10 Drops of chamomile infusion (from health food store)
> 2 Teaspoons of cetyl stearyl alcohol (from pharmacy)

Place the beeswax, cocoa butter, and shea nut butter in a double boiler and heat until melted. Mix the chamomile infusion and the aloe vera juice together in a small saucepan, then add the alcohol and heat on a low flame. Make sure the wax and infusion mixtures are at 158° F. (use thermometer) then mix them together, stirring constantly. Allow the solution to cool, then store in a sealed glass container in the refrigerator.

HARD CONTACT LENS STORAGE FLUID

You will need the following ingredients:

$^1/_4$ Teaspoon of table salt
$^1/_4$ Teaspoon of baking soda (fresh)
1 Cup of sterile water

Place the ingredients into a sterile container and mix until the baking soda and salt are fully dissolved. Pour the mixture through a coffee filter to remove any particles and store in a sterile bottle with a dropper. Used as storage fluid for hard contact lenses only.

PROFESSIONAL LENS CLEANER

You will need the following ingredients:

1 Tablespoon of glycerin
2 Tablespoons of potassium oleate
$^1/_4$ Teaspoon of turpentine (flammable)

Place the glycerin and the potassium oleate in a double boiler and melt, then mix in the turpentine and stir well. Remove the mixture from the heat allow to cool. Apply a very small amount to the lens with a soft cloth that will not scratch the lens. Polish the lens with another clean soft cloth. Many cloth fibers may be somewhat abrasive; so be careful to use a nonabrasive cloth.

BLACK MASCARA #1

You will need the following ingredients:

2 Tablespoons of tincture of benzoin
5 Drops of black dye (oil base)

Place the ingredients in a small glass bottle and shake well to mix. Apply with a small mascara brush. Store in a well-sealed container and shake well before each use. The mascara should last for 2–3 months.

BLACK MASCARA #2

You will need the following ingredients:

$2^1/_2$ Tablespoons of Castile soap (finely powdered)
1 Teaspoon of lampblack
2 Drops of essential rose oil (if desired)

Place the soap and lampblack into a small bowl and blend well, then add the essential oil (if desired).

BLUE WAX MASCARA

You will need the following ingredients:

1^1/$_2$ Tablespoons of white beeswax
   1   Tablespoon of stearic acid
   3   Teaspoons of triethanolamine
   1   Teaspoon of Vaseline
   1   Teaspoon of oleic acid
   1   Teaspoon of cosmetic ultramarine blue

Place the beeswax, stearic acid, triethanolamine, Vaseline, and oleic acid in a medium saucepan and place on low heat. Melt and blend thoroughly, then remove from heat and add the ultramarine blue and blend well. Allow the mascara to cool before placing in a sealed jar.

MAKEUP REMEDY FOR A BLACK EYE

You will need the following ingredients:

   1   Teaspoon of ammonium chloride
   1   Teaspoon of ethyl alcohol
  10   Teaspoons of distilled water

Place all the ingredients into a small bowl and blend well, then dab on with a piece of cotton or a swab.

S. BEAN

SKIN TONERS AND BALANCERS

LEMON SKIN TONER

You will need the following ingredients:

$2/3$ Cup of witch hazel
$1/2$ Cup of lemon juice (from fresh lemon, not reconstituted)
1 Cup of pure distilled water

Place all the ingredients into a small bowl and blend well. Transfer into a jar with a lid and dab on with a fresh cotton ball. Do not contaminate the batch by using it from the jar.

FACIAL TONER & TIGHTENER

You will need the following ingredients:

2 Ounces of 100 proof cheap vodka
2 Ounces of witch hazel
$1/2$ Ounce of essential tea tree oil

Place all the ingredients in a small dish and mix well, then place into a small spray bottle. To apply, spray a small amount on a cotton ball and dab on your face after washing.

AFTER CLEANSING BALANCER

You will need the following ingredients:

$1/3$ Cup of apple cider vinegar
3 Cups of pure distilled water
7 Drops of an essential oil (any fragrance)

Place the water, apple cider vinegar, and oil into a medium bowl and mix thoroughly. Transfer the mixture into a jar, then only pour out what you need into another small container each day. A balancer is used to return your skin's pH balance to normal after you have used a cleanser.

REDUCING PREGNANCY STRETCH MARKS

You will need the following ingredients:

3 Ounces of emu oil (from health food store)
8 Drops of essential lavender oil
5 Drops of essential rose oil
7 Drops of essential bergamot oil

Place the emu oil in a bowl in a pot of very warm tap water and let it sit for 10 minutes. Then add the essential oils and mix well. Store in a well-sealed jar in the refrigerator and apply twice daily to areas that may develop stretch marks. Seal oil may be substituted if emu oil is difficult to locate.

NAIL CARE

When preparing nail preparations at home, it is safer to prepare powders, pastes, and waxes, rather than flammable laquers. The flammable lacquer polishes are not as safe, but are more popular. Carmine or eosine in powdered form may be added to most formulas to produce the desired level of coloring.

NAIL STRENGTHENER
You will need the following ingredients:

1 1/2   Tablespoons of horsetail infusion (from health food store)
  1   Tablespoon of lanolin
10   Drops of myrrh

Place the horsehair infusion in a small bowl and soak your nails in it for 4–5 minutes. Mix the lanolin and the myrrh in another small bowl and rub the mixture into the nails with a soft cloth. Wash off any excess with warm water.

NAIL POLISH REMOVER
You will need the following ingredients:

6   Parts acetone (from pharmacy)
4   Parts ethyl acetate (from pharmacy)

Place the ingredients into a small, glass bowl and mix thoroughly (be careful to avoid the fumes). Store in a well-sealed jar.

1950's PASTE NAIL POLISH
You will need the following ingredients:

4   Teaspoons of tin oxide
2   Grains of powdered carmine
1   Drop of essential rose oil

Place all the ingredients into a small bowl and add just enough water to form a paste. Store in a sealed jar in a cool location.

CONDITIONER FOR CUTICLES
You will need the following ingredients:

1/2   Teaspoons of cocoa butter
1 1/2   Teaspoons of shea butter
9   Drops essential lemon oil

Place the cocoa butter and shea butter in a double boiler and melt; then slowly stir in the essential oil. Remove the mixture from the heat and allow it to cool. Place the mixture into a storage jar and let it sit for about ten hours to allow it to set, then place the lid on the jar. The conditioner will stay fresh for about 3 months.

SOFTENER FOR CUTICLES
You will need the following ingredients:

1   *Teaspoon of virgin olive oil*
5   *Ampoules of 400IU vitamin E (liquid)*
1   *Drop of essential lemon oil*

Place all the ingredients into a small bowl and blend well, then massage the solution into your cuticles.

LACQUER FOR NAILS
You will need the following ingredients:

2   *Drams of celluloid (photographic film)*
$2^1/_2$ *Ounces of amyl acetate*
$7^1/_2$ *Ounces of acetone*
$1^1/_4$ *Grams of phloxine*

Place the amyl acetate and acetone in a small bowl and mix well, then dissolve the celluloid in it and mix well. Apply with a small camel's hair brush after the nails have been well cleaned. Apply two coats, making sure the first coat is completely dry before applying the second coat.

BLEACH FOR NAILS #1
You will need the following ingredients:

$2^1/_4$ *Ounces of rose water*
$^1/_4$ *Ounce of citric acid*
1   *Teaspoon of zinc oxide*

Place the rose water in a small bowl and add the citric acid and zinc oxide to the water and mix thoroughly.

BLEACH FOR NAILS #2
You will need the following ingredients:

$2^1/_2$ *Ounces of hydrogen peroxide*
2   *Ounces of rose water*
$^1/_2$ *Ounce of glycerin*

Place the rose water in a small bowl and add the hydrogen peroxide and glycerin; stir very well. Store in a well-sealed container.

NAIL WHITENER

You will need the following ingredients:

2   Ounces of hydrous lanolin
1   Ounce of talc
1   Ounce of zinc oxide
$1/2$ Ounce of almond oil
$1/2$ Dram of zinc peroxide
$1/4$ Teaspoon of glycerin
2   Drops of essential rose oil

Place the lanolin in a small saucepan and melt, but do not allow it to boil. Then add the other ingredients—except the essential oil—and mix thoroughly. Remove from the heat and allow the mixture to cool before mixing in the essential oil. Use a small, flat-sided nail stick to apply the whitener under the nails.

SOFTENER FOR NAILS

You will need the following ingredients:

2   Ounces of hydrous lanolin
$1/2$ Ounce of Castile soap (grated)
2   Teaspoons of glycerin
1   Teaspoon of virgin olive oil
2   Drops of essential lavender oil

Place the lanolin in a small saucepan on low heat and melt, then mix in the soap, glycerin, and olive oil. Remove from the heat and stir constantly until the mixture cools. Add the essential oil and mix well, then store in a sealed glass container in a cool location.

SOFTENER FOR CUTICLES

You will need the following ingredients:

$2^1/2$ Ounces of cocoa butter
1   Ounce of hydrous lanolin
1   Ounce of almond oil
$1/2$ Ounce of glycerin
1   Dram of trisodium phosphate (TSP)

Place the cocoa butter and the lanolin in a double boiler and melt while stirring. Then add the other ingredients and blend well. Remove from the heat and allow the mixture to cool while stirring constantly. Store in a sealed container in a cool location.

BALMS

CONDITIONING BALM

You will need the following ingredients:

2   Teaspoons of cocoa butter
10 Drops of essential grapefruit oil

Place the butter in a double boiler and allow it to melt before adding the essential oil. Remove from the heat and allow the mixture to cool and set for about 10 hours. This balm is an excellent natural moisturizer and antiseptic for dry lips.

FOOT BALM

You will need the following ingredients:

2   Teaspoons of beeswax (grated)
3   Tablespoons of almond oil
1   Tablespoon of wheat germ oil
1   Teaspoon of mallow tincture
7   Drops of essential tea tree oil

Place the beeswax and the almond oil in a double boiler and melt, then add the wheat germ oil and the tinctures while stirring continually. Remove from the heat and allow the mixture to cool slightly. Add the essential oil and mix thoroughly, then place the balm into a glass jar and allow it to set before placing the lid on.

ITCH-REDUCING BALM FOR PREGNANT WOMEN

You will need the following ingredients:

1   Tablespoon of wheat germ oil
1   Tablespoon of beeswax (grated)
1/4 Cup of cocoa butter
3   Tablespoons of almond oil

Place all the ingredients into a double boiler and blend well until the wax melts. Remove from the heat and allow the balm to cool. Add a few drops of essential oil after it cools if desired.

HAND AND FACE CREAMS

Creams are used to lubricate the skin and should be applied with a gentle massaging motion. They cannot restore skin or remove wrinkles, but can keep the skin moist and slow the skin aging process. There are a variety of creams, some of which will soften the skin and prevent roughness, and some that will serve as a foundation for powders. One of the more common ingredients in skin creams is mineral oil, which does not have the ability to penetrate the skin, but is used mainly as a cleansing agent. Lanolin and certain vegetable oils are more effective and replace the mineral oil in some of the formulas. Cream formulas will have a better consistency and the ingredients will be more thoroughly blended if mixed with an eggbeater or electric mixer. Be aware that metal spoons and utensils can discolor many cream formulas: wooden spatulas are recommended. When preparing creams, small batches are usually best and should be used up within 3–5 months. To save money, you may purchase a higher strength of rose water or witch hazel than the formula calls for and then dilute it with distilled water.

ROSE HAND CREAM

You will need the following ingredients:

- $1^1/2$ Teaspoons of cocoa butter
- 1 Teaspoon of beeswax (grated)
- 2 Tablespoons of almond oil
- 3 Tablespoons of rosewater
- $^1/2$ Teaspoon of borax
- 8 Drops of essential rose oil

Place the beeswax, cocoa butter, and almond oil in a double boiler and melt while mixing well. In a small saucepan, heat the rosewater and borax over low heat for a few minutes, then slowly stir the rosewater into the wax mixture. Remove from the heat and continue stirring until it cools and forms a creamy texture. Add the essential oil and mix well, then store in a small bottle in the refrigerator. The cream should last for at least 2 months.

BASIC COLD CREAM

You will need the following ingredients:

- $^1/2$ Cup of virgin olive oil
- $^1/4$ Cup of distilled water
- 2 Tablespoons of beeswax (grated)
- $^1/8$ Teaspoon of borax (powder)
- 5 Drops of essential rose oil

Place the beeswax and oil in a double boiler and heat until melted. Blend well. After the wax has melted, dissolve the borax in the distilled water in a small saucepan and mix well, then bring to a very light boil and slowly pour the water mixture into the oil while stirring constantly. This process can also be done in a blender if you prefer. When the mixture cools, add the essential oil, blend well, and store in a glass jar with a well-sealed lid. The cream will thicken as it cools.

LIQUID COLD CREAM

You will need the following ingredients:

    1 *Tablespoon of essential oil of sweet almond*
1^1/$_2$ *Ounces of beeswax*
1^1/$_2$ *Ounce of Castile soap (powdered or liquid)*
    1 *Ounce of borax*
  ^{1}/$_2$ *Ounce of quince jelly*
    1 *Tablespoon of ethyl alcohol*
    2 *Ounces of very hot tap water*

Mix the hot water, soap, and borax in a container until the soap and borax dissolve. Place the beeswax into a double boiler and melt, then add the soap mixture to the beeswax and mix thoroughly. Remove from the heat and add the other ingredients. Allow the mixture to cool somewhat, mix well, then strain the cold cream through a piece of cheesecloth.

GREASLESS COLD CREAM

You will need the following ingredients:

5^1/$_4$ *Ounces of glycosterin*
    2 *Ounces of petrolatum*
1^1/$_2$ *Ounces of paraffin wax*
3^1/$_2$ *Ounces of mineral oil*
    1 *Pint of cool tap water*

Place the wax, glycosterin, and petrolatum in a double boiler and heat to 170° F. In another pan, heat the water to 170° F., then stir the water into the wax mixture. Allow the mixture to heat until all the air bubbles have disappeared. Remove from the heat and add any essential oil to create a pleasant aroma. Allow the cream to cool to about 120° F. before pouring into a jar. This cream has the ability to cool the skin and evaporates very fast.

MINERAL OIL COLD CREAM

You will need the following ingredients:

$1/2$ Pint of mineral oil
   1 Ounce of paraffin
   3 Ounces of white wax
$1^1/2$ Teaspoons of borax (powder)
$1/2$ Pint of warm tap water
   2 Drops of essential rose oil

Place the paraffin, mineral oil, and white wax in a double boiler and melt. In another container, add the borax to the warm water and allow it to dissolve, then combine all the ingredients, remove from the heat, and allow the cold cream to cool for a few minutes. Add the essential rose oil and blend well until it is a creamy consistency.

QUALITY HAND & BODY CREAM

You will need the following ingredients:

$2/3$ Cup of baby oil
$2^1/2$ Ounces of beeswax (grated)
   1 Teaspoon of borax (cosmetic or chemical grade 1 sodium borate)
   4 Ounces of anhydrous lanolin
$3/4$ Cup of cool tap water
   4 Drops of essential rose oil

Place the beeswax, lanolin, and oil in a double boiler and melt them to 160° F. In another saucepan, heat the water and borax to 160° F., then, making sure that the borax has melted, remove from the heat. Add the water mixture to the oil mixture and stir rapidly until the mixture looks like smooth cream. Continue stirring until the mixture cools to 100° F., pour into small jars, and store in a cool, dry location.

MASSAGE CREAM

You will need the following ingredients:

   1 Ounce of white wax (from hobby shop)
   2 Ounces of coconut oil
$2^1/2$ Ounces of lanolin
   4 Ounces of oil of sweet almonds
   2 Ounces of orange flower oil
   5 Drops of tincture of benzoin

Place the wax, coconut oil, lanolin, and oil of sweet almonds in a porcelain pot and heat until the ingredients are melted and mixed. Add the flower water and tincture of benzoin and beat or place in a blender to mix until it is the consistency of a thick cream.

VANISHING CREAM

You will need the following ingredients:

3   *Ounces of stearic acid*
1   *Teaspoon of triethanolamine*
2   *Ounces of glycerin*
1   *Pint of cool tap water*
$^1/_2$ *Teaspoon of perfume oil (health food store)*

Place the triethanolamine, glycerin, and water into a double boiler and heat to 170° F. In another double boiler heat the stearic acid to the same temperature, then add it to the glycerin mixture and stir rapidly for 3–4 minutes. Remove from the heat and add the perfume oil as soon as the temperature lowers to 135° F. Continue to stir slowly until the vanishing cream is cold. Store in a well-sealed container in a cool, dry location.

S. BEAN

YOU DON'T HAVE TO GET STRETCH MARKS

Stretch marks may be the result of a number of factors including heredity, naturally dry skin that has less elasticity, weight gain and loss, and, of course, pregnancy. The marks occur when the skin is abnormally stretched for a long period of time and then returned to its original position. Using a good quality cream 2–4 times per day on areas that may be affected can prevent most stretch marks, even during pregnancy. A common cause of stretch marks in children is rapid growth or weight gain.

MASSAGE CREAM FOR STRETCH MARKS

You will need the following ingredients:

2 *Teaspoons of beeswax (grated)*
1/3 Cup of cocoa butter
1 *Teaspoon of light sesame oil*
11/4 Teaspoon of apricot kernel oil
4 *Capsules of 400IU vitamin E (liquid only)*
1 *Tablespoon of wheat germ oil*

Place all the ingredients into a double boiler and heat until the wax and cocoa butter have melted and the oil is well blended. Remove the mixture from the heat and allow it to cool, then store in a well-sealed jar. Massage the cream into the stretch mark area twice each day.

TISSUE LUBRICATING & TONING CREAM

You will need the following ingredients:

5 *Ounces of almond oil*
2 *Ounces of anhydrous lanolin*
1 *Ounce of rose water*
11/4 Ounces of white beeswax
1/2 Ounce of witch hazel
Small dash of borax
Essential oil as desired for pleasant aroma

Place the beeswax in a double boiler and melt. Heat the almond oil in a saucepan for a minute or so before stirring in the melted beeswax. In another container heat the rose water, lanolin, and witch hazel for a short time, then add the borax, making sure it dissolves completely. When the borax is fully dissolved, add this mixture to the other mixture, remove from the heat and beat well for 3–5 minutes before adding the perfume or essential oils. Mix well and store in a well-sealed jar. Tissue lubricating cream is designed to tone the texture of dry skin and prevent roughness. The lanolin is very effective in penetrating the skin and is used as a carrier, however, lanolin does not have a very pleasant aroma and needs to be made more pleasant-smelling with the addition of a perfume oil or essential oil.

FOOT CARE

DUSTING FOOT POWDER
You will need the following ingredients:

2   Ounces of boric acid
1   Ounce of zinc oxide
3   Ounces of talcum

Place all the ingredients in a container and blend well.

DEODORANT POWDER FOR YOUR FEET
You will need the following ingredients:

3/4   Cup of baking soda (fresh)
3/4   Cup of cornstarch
3   Drops of essential rose oil
3   Drops of essential rosemary oil
3   Drops of essential lemon oil

Place all the ingredients into a medium bowl and mix thoroughly, then store in a well-sealed glass jar. Sprinkle a thin layer of the powder in the shoes and shake to be sure it reaches all areas.

ATHLETE'S FOOT POWDER
You will need the following ingredients:

1   Cup of boric acid
2/3   Cup of talc
1/3   Cup of sodium thiosulfate (powder)

Place all the ingredients into a container and mix thoroughly, then place a small amount of the powder between the toes twice each day.

SHOE FOOT POWDER
You will need the following ingredients:

1   Tablespoon of dried sage
2   Tablespoons of black current leaves
1   Tablespoon of kaolin
3   Drops of essential lemon oil
1   Drops of essential lavender oil

Crush the sage and black current leaves into a fine powder using a mortar and pestle, then add the kaolin and mix well. Blend in the essential oils and mix well. Works well when placed in a cheese shaker with small openings.

SOOTHING FOOT BATH #1

You will need the following ingredients:

> 1 *Gallon of very warm water*
> 3 *Tablespoons of sodium bicarbonate*
> 1 *Tablespoon of citric acid*
> 2 *Drops of essential rose oil*

Place all the ingredients in a large foot bowl and mix well, then place your feet in and soak. Make sure the water is very warm or even hot.

SOOTHING FOOT BATH #2

You will need the following ingredients:

> 1/8 *Teaspoon of menthol crystals*
> 9 *Tablespoons of Epsom salts*
> 4 *Tablespoons of alum (powder)*
> 8 *Tablespoons of boric acid*

Place all the ingredients into a container and blend well, then place one teaspoon of the mixture into 1 gallon of hot tap water and mix well.

DEODORANT FOR SMELLY FEET

You will need the following ingredients:

> 2 1/4 *Tablespoon of witch hazel*
> 4 *Drops of essential lavender oil*
> 4 *Drops of lemon essential oil*
> 2 *Drops of orange essential oil*

Place all the ingredients into a small spray bottle with a fine mist setting and spray feet. Be sure to shake the mixture before each use.

FOOT SCRUB

You will need the following ingredients:

> 3 *Tablespoons of clean filtered beach sand (sandbox sand)*
> 3 *Tablespoons of virgin olive oil*
> 3 *Drops of essential rose oil*

Place the ingredients into a small bowl and mix into a paste.
Massage gently on feet, then wash off with warm water.

MOUTH CARE PRODUCTS

Most homemade toothpaste consists of a base of glycerin or honey mixed with water. The mixture is then heated to the boiling point and other ingredients are added and blended thoroughly before the flavorings are added. Flavorings are easily destroyed and, therefore, are always added last. Your favorite flavoring can always be substituted for the flavoring in any formula. All homemade toothpaste needs to be tightly covered or the flavoring will be lost in a short period of time.

HOMEMADE TOOTHPASTE #1

You will need the following ingredients:

> 1   *Teaspoon of sodium bicarbonate*
> 1   *Teaspoon of glycerin (vegetable source)*
> 2   *Drops of peppermint oil*

Place the bicarbonate and the glycerin in a small dish and mix well, then add the peppermint oil.

HOMEMADE TOOTHPASTE #2

You will need the following ingredients:

> 1   *Tablespoons of bicarbonate of soda*
> 1   *Tablespoon of table salt*
> 1/4   *Cup of cold tap water*
> 3   *Teaspoons of glycerin (vegetable source from pharmacy)*

Place the bicarbonate of soda, salt, water, and glycerin in a small bowl and mix until it forms a thick paste. Add additional water if need. A few drops of peppermint oil can be added to improve the flavor. Store in a sealed container.

HOMEMADE TOOTHPASTE #3

You will need the following ingredients:

> 5   *Ounces of honey*
> 4   *Ounces of cool tap water*
> 4   *Ounces of precipitated chalk*
> 3 1/2   *Ounces of milk of magnesia*
> 2   *Ounces of magnesium carbonate*
> 2   *Teaspoons of virgin olive oil*
> 1   *Powdered tragacanth*
>   *Pinch of soluble saccharine or Equal*

Place the honey and water in a medium saucepan and heat to boiling, then remove from the heat and add all the other ingredients and blend well.

Continue stirring for 1 hour to be sure it is well blended. After the mixture cools completely, place the toothpaste into a sealed container.

HOMEMADE TOOTHPASTE #4

You will need the following ingredients:

5 Ounces of glycerin
2 Ounces of cool tap water
6 Ounces of precipitated chalk
3 Ounces of magnesium carbonate
1 Ounce of confectioners sugar (10X)
2/3 Ounce of Castile soap (powdered)
2/3 Ounce of borax
2 Teaspoons of starch
1 Teaspoon of virgin olive oil
2 Drops of peppermint oil

Place the water and glycerin in a medium saucepan and heat to the boiling point, then add all the other ingredients except the essential oil. Mix the solution well, remove from heat, and allow it to cool before adding the peppermint oil. The mixture should be stirred for 45 minutes to be sure it is well blended. Store in a well-sealed jar or bottle in a cool dry location.

HOMEMADE TOOTHPASTE #5

You will need the following ingredients:

1/4 Cup of glycerin (vegetable source from pharmacy)
1/2 Cup of powdered pumice
2 Drops of cinnamon oil

Place all the ingredients into a small wide-mouth container with a lid and mix well. To brush your teeth, just place the dry bristles of your toothbrush into the mixture and brush away.

TOOTH POWDER #1

You will need the following ingredients:

4 Ounces of precipitated chalk
3 1/2 Ounces of magnesium carbonate
1 Ounce of confectioners sugar (10X)
1/2 Ounce of sodium bicarbonate
1/2 Ounce of borax
1/2 Ounce of powdered white toilet soap
2 Drops of peppermint oil

Place all the ingredients into a medium bowl and blend very thoroughly. Store the tooth powder in a well-sealed bottle and shake before each use.

TOOTH POWDER #2

You will need the following ingredients:

    5   Ounces of precipitated chalk
    3   Ounces of magnesium carbonate
    1   Ounce of powdered white toilet soap
    1   Ounce of boric acid
    2   Ounces of salol
   1/2 Teaspoon of thymol
    2   Drops of peppermint oil

Place all the ingredients into a medium bowl and blend thoroughly. Store the powder in a well-sealed container and shake well before each use.

TOOTH POWDER #3

You will need the following ingredients:

    1   Part of menthol
    8   Parts salol
   10   Parts pumice
   20   Parts of Castile soap (finely grated)
   20   Parts of calcium carbonate
   60   Parts of magnesia carbonate
    2   Parts essential mint oil

Place all the ingredients in a bowl and mix well. All ingredients should be finely powdered. The pumice is added to remove tartar.

TOOTH POWDER FOR CHILDREN

You will need the following ingredients:

   10   Parts of magnesia carbonate
   10   Parts of Castile soap (finely grated)
   80   Parts of sepia powder
    3   Drops of essential peppermint oil

Place all the ingredients into a bowl and mix into a fine powder.

SUPER MOUTHWASH

You will need the following ingredients:

    3   Cups of cold tap water
    3   Teaspoons of fresh parsley
    2   Teaspoons of whole cloves
    2   Teaspoons of peppermint extract

Place the water in a small saucepan and bring to a boil, then remove from the heat. Add the dry ingredients and allow them to steep for 15 minutes.

Add the peppermint extract, mix thoroughly, and store in a sealed bottle. Any flavoring can be used in place of the peppermint.

LEMON MOUTHWASH

You will need the following ingredients:

- 10 *Teaspoons of glycerin (vegetable source)*
- 3 *Teaspoons of lavender tincture*
- 3 *Teaspoons of calendula tincture*
- 4 *Drops of lemon oil*
- 3 *Drops of peppermint oil*

Place all the ingredients into a small bottle and shake well to blend. To use, dilute 1 teaspoon in 2 ounces of water, shake the solution and use.

OLD-FASHIONED MOUTHWASH

You will need the following ingredients:

- 1 *Teaspoon of table salt*
- 1 *Teaspoon of baking soda (fresh)*
- 1 *Quart of cool tap water*

Place all the ingredients into a bottle and mix well. Always shake well before using.

FOAMING WINTERGREEN MOUTHWASH

You will need the following ingredients:

- 7 *Ounces of ethyl alcohol*
- 2$^1/_2$ *Ounces of rose water*
- $^1/_4$ *Ounce of peppermint oil*
- $^1/_4$ *Ounce of glycerin*
- $^1/_4$ *Teaspoon of saponin*
- 5 *Drops of cinnamon oil*
- 3 *Drops of wintergreen oil*
    Pinch of thymol

Place all the ingredients into a medium bowl and blend thoroughly. To use, place 3 ounces of solution in 8 ounces of cool tap water and use as any other mouthwash. This is a foaming action mouthwash. Store in a cool location in a sealed bottle.

EASY BUB, IT'S JUST MOUTHWASH!

S. BEAN

PRE-SHAVE & AFTERSHAVE

PRE-SHAVE FOR ELECTRIC SHAVERS

You will need the following ingredients:

    1 *Tablespoon of glycerin*
    1/2 *Teaspoon of spirit of camphor (from pharmacy)*
    4 *Ounces of cheap 80-proof vodka*
    15 *Drops of essential lime oil*

Place the vodka and camphor in a small bowl and mix well, then add the glycerin and the essential oil and blend thoroughly.

HOMEMADE AFTERSHAVE

You will need the following ingredients:

    2 *Cups of rubbing alcohol*
    1 *Tablespoon glycerin*
    1 *Dried lavender flower (health food store)*
    1 *Teaspoon of dried rosemary*
    1 *Teaspoon of ground cloves*

Place all the ingredients into a medium bowl and blend well, then place the mixture into a sealed jar in the refrigerator for 4 days. Shake the mixture twice each day, then strain through a piece of cheesecloth and retain the liquid in a sealed jar. This aftershave should keep under refrigeration for 2 months.

WAKE UP FAST AFTERSHAVE

You will need the following ingredients:

    2 *Teaspoons of witch hazel*
    2 *Teaspoons of 100-proof cheap vodka*
    1 *Tablespoons of cool tap water*
    1/2 *Cup of aloe vera gel*
    5 *Drops of essential bay oil (optional)*

Place all the ingredients into a small bowl and mix well. Do not drink the aftershave. This aftershave can be used on legs as well as the face.

TANNING OIL AND SUNTAN LOTION

TANNING FORMULA
You will need the following ingredients:

5 Lipton tea bags
1 Cup of wheat germ oil
2/3 Cup of cold tap water
1/4 Cup of sesame oil
1/4 Cup of apple cider vinegar
2 Tablespoons of aloe vera gel
1 Teaspoon of iodine
1/2 Teaspoon of almond extract

Place the teabags in 2/3 cup of water, bring to a boil, and steep for 5 minutes. Squeeze the teabags into the water and throw the bags away. Place the oil and vinegar into a small bowl and mix well. Then gently beat in the aloe vera gel. Add the almond extract and iodine, mix well, and store in a well-sealed jar until needed. **NOTE:** Not to be used by children or people who have sensitive or fair skin.

SUNTAN LOTION #1
You will need the following ingredients:

4 Ounces of witch hazel
4 1/2 Ounces of pink calamine powder
4 Ounces of rose water
2 1/2 Ounces of zinc oxide
1 Ounce of glycerin
2 Teaspoons of boric acid

Place all the ingredients in a medium bowl and blend well, then pour into well-sealed bottles. Shake well before each use.

SUNTAN LOTION #2
You will need the following ingredients:

7 1/2 Ounces of peanut oil
4 1/4 Ounces of virgin olive oil
1 Teaspoon of bergamot oil
3 Teaspoons of laurel-berry oil
1 Teaspoon of chlorophyll

Place the olive oil and the peanut oil into a medium bowl and blend well, then add the other ingredients and blend well. Store in a bottle and shake well before each use.

SUNTAN LOTION #3

You will need the following ingredients:

2   *Ounces of salt-free mayonnaise*
2   *Ounces of black tea*
2   *Tablespoons of lemon juice*
5   *400IU vitamin E capsules (liquid only)*

Place the mayonnaise, lemon juice, and tea in a blender and blend on low for a few seconds. Place the blended mixture into a container and add the contents of the 5 vitamin E capsules and stir well. This formula needs to be refrigerated or it will turn rancid.

BODY SOAPS

> **CAUTION:** Always wear protective gear when working with lye—just to be safe. This includes plastic goggles, rubber gloves, and a facemask. It is best to make the soap out-of doors, and never breathe the fumes. Also, please read information in the glossary regarding lye.

GET OUT THE OLD SOAP KETTLE

The main ingredients in most soap formulas are lye, water, and fat. The lye is used as an emulsifying agent (to keep the ingredients in suspension) and has the ability to remove dirt from clothing or skin. The fat retains the lye in a state that produces lather, and holds the dirt in a state that allows it to be washed away by water. The water has the ability to dissolve the lye, eliminating any residue. Beef tallow is preferred over pork lard since it will produce a longer-lasting, harder soap.

JOJOBA CLAY SOAP

You will need the following ingredients:

$1^1/2$ *Tablespoons of clay*
$1^1/4$ *Pounds of glycerin soap (vegetable base)*
2   *Tablespoons of jojoba oil*
$2/3$ *Cup of pure distilled water*
3   *Drops of essential rose oil*
    Soap molds

Place the soap into a double boiler and slowly melt. Remove about 1/2 pound of the melted soap and place it in a small dish. Add the clay to the soap and mix well. Add the jojoba/soap mixture back into the double boiler and mix well for a few seconds. Remove the mixture and allow it to cool somewhat, then pour into the soap molds to set.

GRANDMA'S OLD-FASHIONED SOAP

You will need the following ingredients:

2	*Quarts of distilled water*
1	*Can of lye*
3$1/2$	*Pounds of grease*
1/3	*Cup of borax*

Place the grease in a small bucket and add the lye while stirring continually. Use precautions mentioned above when working with lye. Mix in the borax, then slowly add the water to the soap solution while stirring continually. Place into molds or cardboard tubes to set. This recipe will produce about 8$1/2$ pounds of soap.

BASIC HAND SOAP

You will need the following ingredients:

5	*Parts of oleic acid*
2	*Parts of caustic soda solution (40° Baume)*
1	*Part of sal soda*
4	*Parts cool tap water*

Place the oleic acid, caustic soda, and water in a pot. Heat on low just enough to form a clear paste. Then boil the mixture and remove it from the heat. Add the sal soda and continue to stir until the soap becomes lukewarm. Pour into molds and allow the soap to cool.

CLEAR HAND SOAP

You will need the following ingredients:

7	*Parts of cochin coconut oil*
4	*Parts of compressed tallow*
3	*Parts of castor oil*
8	*Parts of caustic soda lye (38° Baume)*
5$1/2$	*Parts of granulated sugar*
6	*Parts of cool tap water*
4	*Parts of ethyl alcohol*

Place the coconut oil, tallow, and castor oil in a double boiler and heat to 111° F., then stir in the lye and cover the pot for 1 hour. Dissolve the sugar in the water in another container; then add the sugar water and the alcohol to the lye mixture. Mix thoroughly until very well blended. Pour into molds to cool.

HOMEMADE LIQUID PUMP HAND SOAP
You will need the following ingredients:

2 Cups of Castile soap (grated)
10 Ounces of very hot tap water
2 Tablespoons of baby oil
2 Drops of essential rose oil

Place the water in a bowl, add the soap, and stir well. Slowly add the oil, stirring constantly to keep the soap from separating out of suspension. Add the essential oil and store in a well-sealed container until needed. Shake well each time you fill a bottle.

SOAP POWDER FOR HARD WATER #1
You will need the following ingredients:

4 parts of powdered soap
3 Parts of sal soda
2 Parts of silicate soda

Place all the ingredients into a container and mix well. Make sure that all the ingredients are very dry before mixing.

SOAP POWDER FOR HARD WATER #2
You will need the following ingredients:

10 Parts of powdered soap
1 Part of borax
1 Part of sodium carbonate (soda ash)
1/2 Part of powdered pumice stone

Place all the ingredients into a container and mix well. Any ingredient that is not finely powdered will have to be placed in a mortar and pestle and powdered before blending.

COMBINATION BODY & SHAMPOO BAR

You will need the following ingredients:

12 *Ounces of coconut oil*
5.6 *Ounces of lye*
6 *Ounces of palm oil*
10 *Ounces of castor oil*
3 *Ounces of jojoba oil*
1 *Ounce of aloe vera oil*
8 *Ounces of virgin olive oil*
1 *Ounce rose essential oil*
1/2 Ounce lavender essential oil
15 *Ounces of lukewarm tap water*
1 *Cooking thermometer*
Set of plastic goggles, face mask, and rubber gloves
Soap molds (if desired)

Place the water into a large pot and slowly pour in the lye. A chemical reaction will take place and the solution will become very hot. Place the pot in a cold water bath and let it sit until the temperature is reduced to 100° F. (use your thermometer). This should take approximately 2–3 minutes. The solution will look cloudy. In another pot, place the solid oils on the stove to be melted over medium heat As soon as they have melted, add the other oils. Cool the oils to 100° F. in a cold water bath. The lye solution will take longer to cool. Both solutions must be the same temperature before mixing together. The lye solution can be placed into a warm water bath to if it has become too cool. Very slowly add the lye mixture into the oil mixture, stirring continually until the mixture starts to thicken (about 15 minutes). Rest for a few minutes, then resume stirring for another 8–10 minutes until it gets thicker. Continue stirring and resting until the soap thickens (this may take 1–2 hours). When the soap is thick but still workable, add the essential oils and mix well. Pour the soap into the molds and cover with a piece of cardboard to keep it from cooling too fast. Once set, remove the soap from the molds (wear gloves)and allow it to air dry. This curing reduces the alkalinity and lowers the pH (thus making it more acidic), and makes the soap safe to use.

GENERAL SKIN CARE

DEAD SKIN REMOVER

You will need the following ingredients:

4 *Tablespoons of raw barley (fresh)*
2 *Tablespoons of pure oats*
3 *Capsules of liquid lecithin*
2 *Cups of warm tap water*

Pour one cup of the warm tap water into a medium saucepan, then mix in the barley and oats. Heat the mixture at a slow simmer for 8 minutes then allow it to cool to lukewarm. Thoroughly mix in the contents of 3 capsules of liquid lecithin and add the remaining cup of hot tap water to the mixture. Place the mixture into a blender and blend for a few seconds. Strain through a piece of gauze to remove any particles that did not blend into suspension. To use, place the mixture into a bathtub with very warm (not hot) water and bathe for 10–15 minutes.

NATURAL OILY SKIN CLEANSER

You will need the following ingredients:

6 *Ounces of plain oatmeal*
1 *Ounce of lavender buds*
6 *Ounces of cornmeal*
1½ *Ounces of rose petals*
1 *Ounce of Irish moss powder*
½ *Ounce of kelp granules (very fine)*
½ *Ounce of comfrey root powder*
    (**CAUTION:** Pregnant women should omit the comfrey
    root powder.)

Place the oatmeal and rose petals in the blender and make a powder. Place the remaining ingredients into a medium bowl and add the oatmeal and petals; mix well. To use, rinse your face with warm water, then place a small amount of the mixture onto the palm of your hand with a small amount of water, just enough to make a paste, and gently rub onto your skin. Rinse with warm water then splash your face with cold water to close the pores.

SKIN MASSAGE & STIMULATOR

You will need the following ingredients:

> 1 Cup of table salt
> 1 Cup of light corn oil
> 1 Cup of liquid hand soap

Place the ingredients into a medium bowl and mix well. Gently massage into the skin before you shower.

CLEANSER FOR DRY SKIN

You will need the following ingredients:

> 6 Ounces of plain oatmeal
> 6 Ounces of cornmeal
> 1 Ounce of chamomile flowers
> 1/2 Ounce of Elder flowers
> 1 Ounce of Irish moss powder
> 1 Ounce of slippery elm powder

Place the oatmeal, elder, and chamomile flowers in a blender and blend until powdered. Place the rest of the ingredients in a paper bag and mix well. Add the blended powder and mix thoroughly. To use, rinse your face with warm water, then prepare a small amount of paste using the powdered herbs mixed with a bit of water and apply to your face in a gentle, circular motion. Rinse your face with warm water, then use a cold water splash to close the pores.

FACIAL RINSE

You will need the following ingredients:

> 4 Cups of bottled water
> 1 Tablespoons of dried rosemary
> 2 Tablespoons of dried chamomile
> 3 Cups of dried rose petals (fresh is OK)

Place all ingredients is a small glass or enameled pot and boil over medium heat for 10 minutes. Remove from heat and allow the mixture to cool to room temperature before straining out the herbs. Store in a sealed bottle in the refrigerator and dab on your face to remove all traces of soap.

WHAT IS AN ASTRINGENT?

Very simply, an astringent is a substance that has the ability to tighten, draw together, or contract tissue. It is also used to control bleeding by the use of a styptic.

ASTRINGENT #1
You will need the following ingredients:

   3   Teaspoons of pure lemon extract
   2   Teaspoons of lime juice
   1/2 Cup of rubbing alcohol

Place all the ingredients into a capped jar and shake well. Store in the refrigerator.

ASTRINGENT #2
You will need the following ingredients:

   3/4 Cup of ethanol (from pharmacy)
   1/2 Lemon (thinly sliced)
   1/2 Orange (thinly sliced)

Place all the ingredients in a blender and blend until the fruit is completely pulverized. Remove the liquid by straining through a doubled piece of cheesecloth and store it in a sealed jar. This is an excellent solution to tighten skin and remove oil.

SKIN OIL TO PREVENT PARASITES
You will need the following ingredients:

   1/3 Cup of almond oil
   8   Drops of essential lavender oil
   10   Drops of essential palmarosa oil
   10   Drops of essential wild thyme oil
   10   Drops of essential rosemary oil
   10   Drops of essential lemon oil

Place the almond oil into a small bowl. Slowly add each essential oil while stirring continually. Store the oil in a well-sealed glass bottle in a dry, dark location. The oil should remain good for about 10 months.

BASIC SKIN SCRUB

You will need the following ingredients:

1   *Cup of instant oatmeal (for face, use extra fine cornmeal)*
1   *Cup of virgin olive oil*
1   *Cup of mild liquid hand soap*
3   *Drops of essential rose oil*

Place all the ingredients in a medium bowl and mix well. Gently rub the mixture into your skin just before you start the shower then shower or bathe as usual.

NO-SOAP FACIAL CLEANSER

You will need the following ingredients:

1¹/₂   *Cups of instant oatmeal*
1¹/₂   *Cups of powdered whole milk*
¹/₂   *Cup of raw sugar (turbinado OK)*

Place all the ingredients into a small covered container and mix well. When ready to use, place about 2 tablespoons in your hand and add a small amount of water to prepare a paste. Dab on your face and allow it to remain for about 8–10 minutes before washing it off with warm water and then a cold rinse.

OATMEAL SCRUB

You will need the following ingredients:

2   *Tablespoons of instant oatmeal*
2   *Tablespoons of pure powdered honey*
2   *Tablespoons of powdered milk (whole)*
2   *Vitamin E capsules (liquid only)*

Place the oatmeal and the vitamin E into a blender and pulse for a few seconds until well blended. Add the milk powder and powdered honey and blend for a few more seconds to allow all the ingredients to mix well. Place 2 tablespoons of the mixture into a small bowl and add just enough water to prepare a paste. A few drops of your favorite essential oil may be added.

FLORAL WATER

You will need the following ingredients:

1   *Cup of pure distilled water*
¹/₈   *Cup of cheap vodka*
4   *Drops of essential rose oil*

Place all ingredients into a well-sealed bottle and mix thoroughly. Allow the mixture to stand undisturbed for 1 week in a cool, dark location.

LOTIONS

BACK TO BASICS

Most lotions are prepared using more water than oil and are used to remove excess oil from the skin. Grandpa used to make lotion from glycerin and rose water (from rose petals). Lotions do not have a long shelf life and should be used up in a short period of time or they may grow bacteria, though most of the over-the-counter brands contain some preservatives that prolong their shelf life.

CREAMY BABY LOTION

You will need the following ingredients:

- 1   Cup of pure distilled water
- 2   Tablespoons of beeswax (grated)
- $1/2$ Cup of virgin olive oil
- 20   Drops of essential lavender oil
- 4   Drops of essential rose oil

Place the water in the top of a double boiler and add the wax. Heat until all the wax has melted, then transfer the mixture to a blender. Slowly add the olive oil while blending on low. As soon as all the olive oil has been blended, add the essential oils and blend for a few seconds. Allow the mixture to cool in a heat-safe dish until it is creamy. Store in a well-sealed container and use just like any other lotion.

S. BEAN

HONEY AND ALMOND HAND CREAM

You will need the following ingredients:

1½   Ounces of sweet almonds
5½   Ounces of almond oil
 2   Tablespoons of honey
 2   Tablespoons of virgin olive oil
 2   Tablespoons of ethyl alcohol
½   Teaspoon of oil of bergamot
½   Teaspoon of essential clove oil
½   Teaspoon of essential rose oil

Scald the sweet almonds in boiling water for 6 minutes, then skin them and place them into a medium bowl. Add the almond oil, olive oil, and honey, and mix. Pound the almonds with a mallet until they are very soft. Place all the ingredients into a saucepan and heat until a lotion consistency is obtained. Remove from heat and allow the mixture to cool, then strain the mixture through a piece of cheesecloth or muslin. Place the mixture in a bowl and add the oil of bergamot and the essential oils. Blend and pour into a sealed glass bottle. Shake before each use.

LUXURIOUS LOTION BAR

You will need the following ingredients:

 6   Ounces of beeswax
 2   Ounces of almond oil
 2   Ounces of Virgin olive oil
 3   Drops of essential lavender oil

Place all ingredients except the essential oil into a double boiler and heat until the wax is melted and well mixed with the oils. Add the essential oil and stir well, then pour into a mold to set. Refrigerate the bar, then allow it to return to room temperature before using in place of body or hand lotion. Rub it on for the best results.

ALOE LOTION

You will need the following ingredients:

1¼   Cup of aloe vera
 1   Teaspoon of lanolin
⅓   Cup of virgin olive oil
 3   Capsules of vitamin C (liquid)
¾   Cup of beeswax
 2   Drops of essential rose oil

Place the aloe vera, vitamin E, and lanolin in a small bowl and mix well. Place the beeswax in a double boiler and melt slowly, then add the aloe mixture and remove from heat. Allow to cool, but while it is still warm, place the mixture into a blender and blend on slow, while adding the oil in a slow stream. Blend for an additional 2–4 seconds after depleting the oil. When finished you should have a smooth cream.

MOISTURIZING LOTION
You will need the following ingredients:

2 Teaspoons of castor oil
1 Teaspoon of lanolin
2 400IU capsules of vitamin E (liquid)
1½ Teaspoons of cocoa butter
4 Drops of essential rose oil
3 Drops of essential tea tree oil

Place the castor oil, cocoa butter, and lanolin into a double boiler and melt together. Remove from heat and whisk the liquid from the vitamin E capsules into the mixture. Allow to cool, then add the essential oils and mix well. Store the lotion in a well-sealed glass bottle in a cool dry location.

SUNTAN LOTION
You will need the following ingredients:

3 Tea bags (standard, not instant)
¼ Cup of lanolin
¼ Cup of sesame oil
¾ Cup of cool tap water

Place the water in a small saucepan and bring to a boil, then add the teabags and brew for 15 minutes, pushing them against the wall of the pan with the back of a spoon to release the maximum amount of tea. Remove from heat and allow the tea to cool a little before placing 25% of the tea into a blender with the lanolin and oil. Blend on low for a few seconds, then add the balance of the tea in a slow stream. If you wish to add 3–4 drops of your favorite essential oil, add it just before you finish blending. The cream will repel water and will screen out about 50% of the suns harmful rays. People that burn easily should not use this cream.

GLYCERIN HAND LOTION
You will need the following ingredients:

4 Tablespoons of glycerin
2 Tablespoons of bay rum
2 Tablespoons of ammonia water
2 Tablespoons of rose water

Place the glycerin and the bay rum in a medium bowl and mix well, then add the ammonia and rose water. Blend well and store in a sealed glass container.

GLITTER GELS

SPARKLER GEL

You will need the following ingredients:

- 1 Teaspoon of glycerin
- 1/4 Cup of aloe vera gel
- 1/4 Cup of fine polyester glitter
- 4 Drops of essential rose oil
- 1 Drop of food coloring

Place the aloe vera and the glycerin in a small bowl and mix well, then add the glitter, color, and essential oil and blend.

LIP GLOSS AND LIPSTICK

KEEPING YOUR LIPS KISSABLE

Lipstick was originally formulated to protect your lips. Today it still provides a degree of protection. Lip gloss, however, seems to do a better job. Lip gloss will protect the lips from the heat of the sun and excessive dry conditions that reduce the moisture of the lips. Skiers are especially at risk since their lips are exposed to cold and wind.

BASIC LIP GLOSS

You will need the following ingredients:

- 1/4 Cup of sesame oil
- 2 Teaspoons of beeswax
- 1/2 Ounce of Camphor
- 1/2 Ounce of menthol

Place the beeswax in a double boiler and melt, then add the oil and menthol and mix well. Remove from the heat and beat until the mixture is cool. Transfer into a clean container and continue beating until it is cool and set.

SHINY LIP GLOSS

You will need the following ingredients:

1   *Teaspoon of pure honey*
$2^1/_2$ *Teaspoons of beeswax (grated)*
7   *Teaspoons of jojoba oil*
4   *Drops of essential rose oil*

Place the beeswax and oil in a double boiler. Remove from the heat and add the honey. Blend all the ingredients well and allow to cool before adding the essential oil. Mix well and place into a small glass jar with a good lid. If stored in a cool, dry location the lip-gloss should last about 3–4 months.

NATURAL LIPSTICK FORMULA #1

You will need the following ingredients:

$2^1/_2$ *Ounces of almond oil*
2   *Ounces of white beeswax*
    Essential oil as desired for aroma

NATURAL LIPSTICK FORMULA #2

You will need the following ingredients:

4   *Ounces of coconut butter*
$1^1/_2$ *Tablespoons of almond oil*
$^1/_2$ *Ounce white beeswax*
    Powdered carmine
    Essential oil for aroma (if desired)

To prepare either of these lipstick formulas: place the first three ingredients in a double boiler and heat, stirring gently, until they are thoroughly blended together. Remove from the heat and allow the mixture to cool almost completely before adding any essential oil. The reddish coloring for lipstick is dependent on the amount of powdered carmine that is added. This coloring agent should be added at the same time as the essential oil. After the lipstick has cooled completely it can be poured into molds or any container you wish. Other coloring pigments are available through a chemical supply house for different colors.

LIP SALVES

LIP POMADE
You will need the following ingredients:

80 *Parts of paraffin*
80 *Parts of Vaseline*
$^1\!/_2$ *Part of anchusine*
1 *Part of bergamot oil*
1 *Part of lemon peel*

Place all the ingredients in a container and blend well.

LEG WAX

LEG WAX
You will need the following ingredients:

2 *Cups of granulated sugar*
$^1\!/_4$ *Cup of cold tap water*
$^1\!/_4$ *Cup of lemon juice*
2 *Drops of essential lavender oil*

Place the sugar, water, and lemon in a small saucepan. Mix and bring to a boil. Cook until the mixture is at the softball stage or about 250° F. Remove from heat and allow it to cool, then pour into a jar and store in a cool, dry location.

S. BEAN

BODY WRAPS

OLDEN TIMES SPA WRAP

You will need the following ingredients:

$1/2$ Cup of chamomile
$1/2$ Cup of dried rosemary
$1/4$ Cup of peppermint leaves
  5   Drops of essential lavender oil
  6   Cups of very hot tap water

Place the water in a medium-sized pot and bring to a boil, then remove from the heat. Place the herbs in a piece of cheesecloth and tie the cheesecloth to retain the herbs. Crush the herbs just slightly and place the cheesecloth into the water, place a lid on the pot, and allow it to stand for 20 minutes. This will create an herbal infusion. Remove the cover and stir. Add strips of linen fabric, saturate them well, and wring them out. Place them around your lower arms and feet. Make sure the wrap is not too hot or it will burn. This process is normally done twice with plastic wrap placed on top of the wrap the second time. Do not allow wrap to remain on more than 15 minutes. Let your body cool for 20 minutes before taking a bath or shower. Do not use if you have any type of cardiovascular problem without consulting your physician.

MASSAGE OILS

TOUCH OF MAGIC OIL

You will need the following ingredients:

- *1/4 Cup of sweet almond oil*
- *4 Drops of essential jasmine oil*
- *2 Drops of essential lavender oil*
- *2 Drops of essential bergamot oil*

Place all ingredients in a small bowl and mix thoroughly. Store in a well-sealed jar in the refrigerator—allow it to return to room temperature before using.

NO-SOAP HAND WASH

SOAPLESS HAND FRESHENER

You will need the following ingredients:

- *1 Teaspoon of rubbing alcohol*
- *2 Teaspoons of glycerin (vegetable source)*
- *1 Cup of aloe vera gel*
- *7 Drops of essential tea tree oil*

Place all the ingredients into a small bowl and mix well, then store in a well-sealed glass jar. This is not recommended to remove heavy soil from hands, but as a freshener and germ killer.

DEODORANTS

LE PEW

Deodorants are formulated to do two different things: keep perspiration from forming and reduce or eliminate the odor that it causes. There are many herbal preparations that can be used to mask unpleasant odor but do not have the ability to stop wetness. Many commercially prepared products contain chemicals that may be harmful and the more natural products are recommended in all cases. Diet has a lot to do with body odors, and the healthier the diet, the less body odor a person will have, even if they perspire.

POWDER DEODORANT #1

You will need the following ingredients:

2   *Ounces of bicarbonate of soda*
2   *Ounces of boric acid*
$1/2$ *Ounce of zinc peroxide*
2   *Drops of essential rose oil*

Place all the ingredients into a small bowl and blend well. Store in a sealed jar or bottle in a cool dry location. Shake well before each use.

POWDER DEODORANT #2

You will need the following ingredients:

5   *Ounces of boric acid*
1   *Ounce of zinc oxide*
1   *Ounce of talc*
2   *Drops of essential rose oil*

Follow the directions for powder deodorant #1.

PASTE DEODORANT

You will need the following ingredients:

1   *Ounce of zinc oxide*
1   *Ounce of prepared chalk*
4   *Ounces of cold cream*
2   *Drops of essential lavender oil*

Place the zinc oxide and the chalk in a small bowl and mix well, then add the cold cream and essential oil. Blend well and store in a sealed glass jar.

AFTERSHAVE

BASIC AFTERSHAVE

You will need the following ingredients:

1   *Tablespoon witch hazel*
1   *Tablespoon rosewater*

Place the ingredients into a small container and blend well. Store in a well-sealed bottle.

APPLE CIDER AFTERSHAVE

You will need the following ingredients:

    1   *Tablespoon of apple cider vinegar*
    1   *Tablespoon of vegetable glycerin*

Place the ingredients into a small container and blend well. Store in a well-sealed bottle.

GRANDPA'S AFTERSHAVE LOTION

You will need the following ingredients:

    5   *Ounces of rose water*
  2¹/₂   *Ounces of witch hazel*
   ¹/₂   *Ounce boric acid*
    1   *Ounce of ethyl alcohol*
    1   *Ounce of glycerin*
    1   *Teaspoon of tincture of benzoin*

Place all the ingredients into a medium bowl and mix well. Pour into a sealed, glass container and use as needed. Shake well before each use. This will really wake you up and make you bright-eyed.

FRECKLES

CAN I COUNT YOUR FRECKLES?

I'm sure anyone who has freckles has heard that one before. Freckles are the result of exposure to the sun's rays on the face, back of the hands, and upper torso. They are small, brownish pigmenta-

tion spots and are more noticeable in the spring and summer when you start getting out in the sun and exposing your skin. Fair-skinned individuals are more likely to have freck-les. Freckles can be faded somewhat, but are impossible to remove. Many preparations have been tried, from lemon juice, to all kinds of herbal remedies.

OLD-FASHIONED FRECKLE REMEDY

You will need the following ingredients:

      1   Part of poppy oil
      2   Parts of lead acetate
      1   Part of tincture of benzoin
      5   Parts of tincture of quillaia
      1   Part of spirit nitrous ether
     95   Parts of rose water

Place the oil and the lead acetate into a double boiler and saponify (turn into soap), then add the rose water and mix well. Add the rest of the ingredients and blend well.

COMPLEXION CLAY

SPECIAL MUD CREAM

You will need the following ingredients:

      4   Ounces of modeling clay (powdered and sifted)
      1   Ounce of calamine powder
    $1/2$ Ounce of oxide of zinc
    $1/4$ Ounce of infusorial earth
      7   Grains of benzoate of soda (finely powdered)
      2   Ounces of witch hazel
      1   Ounce of glycerin

Finely powder all the dry ingredients using a mortar and pestle. Place the powder in a container and form a paste by adding the witch hazel and glycerin. Water may be added to produce the consistency you desire. Store in a well-sealed container. The less contact the cream has with the air, the better.

BABY PRODUCTS

BABY TEETHING GEL

You will need the following ingredients:

      1   Ounce of pure vegetable glycerin
      2   Drops of essential oil of cloves

Place the glycerin into a small glass container and add 1 or 2 drops of oil of cloves (depending on the strength desired). Virgin olive oil may be substituted for the glycerin. Rub on the gums as needed to bring relief.

BABY WIPES

You will need the following ingredients:

5 *Large plastic containers with high sides*
1 *Roll of Bounty paper towels*
2 *Cups of cold tap water*
6 *Tablespoons of baby oil*
2 *Tablespoons of baby bath liquid*

Slice the roll of paper towels in half and remove the center cardboard. Place the ingredients into a medium bowl and mix—do not mix too much or the solution will foam and you will have to start over. Place the paper towels in the container and pour the solution over the top. It will take about 1 hour for all the liquid to be absorbed into the paper towels. Place the baby wipes in a well-sealed plastic container and use as needed.

ANTI-FUNGAL BABY WIPES

You will need the following ingredients:

$1/2$ *Cup of distilled water*
$1/4$ *Cup of white vinegar*
$1/4$ *Cup of aloe vera gel*
1 *Tablespoon of calendula oil*
1 *Drop essential rose oil*
1 *Drop essential tea tree oil*

Place all the ingredients in a container and mix well. Store in the refrigerator in a well-sealed glass jar and use a paper towel as needed for an anti-fungal wipe.

BATH AND BABY POWDER

You will need the following ingredients:

$1/4$ *Cup of cornstarch*
2 *Tablespoons of powdered dried chamomile*
1 *Tablespoon of orrisroot (powdered)*
$1/2$ *Teaspoon of alum*

Place all the ingredients in a small bowl and mix well, then sift the powder through a fine sieve and place in a powder-type shaker.

MILD BABY MASSAGE OIL

You will need the following ingredients:

4 *Ounces of virgin olive oil*
4 *Drops of essential rose oil*

Place the ingredients into a well-sealed bottle and shake to blend.

MUSTACHE FIXER

GRANDPA'S FIXING FLUID FOR MUSTACHES

You will need the following ingredients:

1 *Part of balsam of tolu*
3 *Parts of rectified spirits*
1 *Part of Jockey Club (cologne)*

Place the liquids in a container and dissolve the balsam into them. Apply just a few drops to your mustache with a brush then twist into the desired shape. The mustache will keep its shape for a long period of time.

PERFUME, COLOGNE, AND TOILET WATER

SMELL PRETTY AND SAVE MONEY

Next time you visit the health food store, smell the essential oils and choose your favorite ones to mix with either pure ethyl alcohol or distilled water. It's as easy as that to prepare a cologne or toilet water that will smell just as good as the high-priced brands. Commercial brands are expensive because of the packaging, not the ingredients. They are marketed as eye-appealing containers that you will keep after you use up the fragrance.

OLD-FASHIONED BAY RUM PERFUME

You will need the following ingredients:

50 *Drops of essential bay rum oil*
10 *Drops of essential bitter orange oil*
 5 *Drops of essential clove oil*
 1 *Ounce of cheap rum*

Place all the ingredients into a glass bottle that has a cap and shake to blend. Shake well before each use.

LILAC TOILET WATER

You will need the following ingredients:

- 1 Teaspoon of terpineol
- 4 Grains of heliotropin
- 1/2 Teaspoon of bergamot oil
- 6 Drops of neroli oil
- 6 Ounces of ethyl alcohol
- 2 Ounces of cool tap water

Place all the ingredients into a container and blend well, then strain through a piece of fine cheesecloth.

LAVENDER COLOGNE

You will need the following ingredients:

- 1 1/2 Teaspoons of essential oil of lavender
- 1/2 Teaspoons of essential oil of bergamot
- 1/2 Teaspoon of tincture of benzoin
- 6 Ounces of ethyl alcohol

Place all the ingredients into a container and blend well, then allow the cologne to stand for 30 days. Strain the mixture through a funnel with gray filter paper before using.

AUTUMN LEAVES PERFUME

You will need the following ingredients:

- 2 Drops of essential lavender oil
- 2 Drops of essential rose oil
- 2 Drops of essential grapefruit oil
- 4 Drops of essential germanium oil
- 2 Drops of essential sandalwood oil
- 2 Drops of nutmeg oil
- 2 Drops of essential vanilla oil
- 3 Drops of essential rosewood oil
- 1/8 Ounce of jojoba oil

Place all the oils into a glass bottle with a good lid and shake to mix. Shake before each use.

MAKING SOLID PERFUME

You will need the following ingredients:

^{1}/$_2$ *Ounce of beeswax*
1^1/$_2$ *Ounce of infused myrrh oil*
^{1}/$_2$ *Ounce of infused clary sage oil*
25 *Drops of essential clary sage oil*
9 *Drops of essential patchouli oil*
7 *Drops of essential rose oil*
5 *Drops of essential chamomile oil*

Place the beeswax into a double boiler and melt, then remove from the heat and allow the wax to cool to lukewarm. Place the wax into a glass jar that has been held under very warm running water for a few seconds, then add all the oils and blend well. Pour into small metal tins or molds to harden.

Chapter 3

Grandpa's Old-Fashioned Know How

FORMULA TO TEST DRINKING WATER

You will need the following ingredients:

> 1 *Teaspoon of granulated sugar*
> 1 *Cup of cold tap water*

This test will determine if any bacteria are present in your drinking water. Place the sugar in a cup of water and place the cup in a sunny location. Sugar is a food supply for bacteria and they will become very active and feed on the sugar and multiply. If the water becomes milky after about 2–3 days the bacteria are very active.

WRITING ON THE INSIDE OF AN EGG

You will need the following ingredients:

> $1/2$ *Ounce of alum (from pharmacy)*
> $1/2$ *Pint of white vinegar*
> 1 *Large egg*

This formula allows you to write a message on the outside of the egg and have it disappear and reappear on the inside of the shell wall. Place the alum and vinegar in a small bowl and mix thoroughly. Dip a fine-tipped brush into the solution and write something on the eggshell. Allow it to fully dry, then boil the egg for 15 minutes. Let the egg cool and carefully remove the shell. Your words will have disappeared from the outside of the shell but will be visible on the inside. **NOTE:** you should never eat eggs treated with this formula.

HERBS TO THE RESCUE

There are a number of pharmaceutical preparations that will eliminate the craving for alcohol and even make you sick if you take a drink. The most common is "Antibuse." However, there are a number of herbal preparations that are almost as effective, especially when taken in combination. The following herbs will do a great job when prepared as a tea.

ELIMINATE THE CRAVING FOR LIQUOR

You will need the following ingredients:

> 1 *Part of goldthread*
> 1 *Part of goldenseal*

Place an amount equal to $1/2$ a small teabag of the goldenthread and goldenseal into a tea infuser and steep as you would a cup of tea. This will cause a serious distaste for alcohol after one sip. If you really want o kill the desire, add a very small amount of epicae to the tea.

SMOKE NO MORE

You will need the following ingredients:

$^1/_2$ *Teaspoon of rochelle salts (from pharmacy)*
$^1/_2$ *Teaspoon of cream of tartar*
   Ginseng root (from health food store)

Place the rochelle salts and the cream of tartar in a small bowl and mix thoroughly. Add to your morning juice and you will not have the desire for a cigarette all day long. Even better is the ginseng root alone. Just chew a small piece of the root and swallow the juice. This will eliminate the craving as well and tastes better.

DRY ICE CAN BE FUN, BUT USE WITH CAUTION

Dry ice is actually frozen carbon dioxide gas that has been turned into a solid by reducing the temperature to –110° F. If you place the dry ice on your skin it will burn you. Dry ice is very highly compressed—when released, one pound of dry ice produces 8.3 cubic feet of carbon dioxide gas. Dry ice usually costs about $1.00 per pound and may be purchased at ice cream stores, welding supply houses, or chemical supply houses. The "smoke" you see is actually carbon dioxide gas being slowly released. Dry ice stored in a porous container won't last long. A well-sealed plastic container works best. Even in a plastic container, the dry ice will not last very long and you will notice a white "frost" on the outside of the container. Eventually the dry ice will totally dissipate into the air.

MAKING SMOKE WITH DRY ICE

You will need the following ingredients:

1 *Part dry ice*
2 *Parts water*

Place the dry ice in a shop vacuum that will accommodate water and cover with water. Turn on the vacuum and aim the hose. If you use warm water the smoke will dissipate fairly fast.

BACON PRESERVATIVE FOR HUNTING TRIPS

You will need the following ingredients:

> 6 *Tablespoons of white vinegar*
> 1 *Cup of cool tap water*

Place the ingredients into a small bowl and mix well. Saturate a piece of cloth and wrap it around the bacon. Since the bacon will be kept in your cooler chest, you won't need the preservative until the original package is opened. Just keep a bottle of vinegar with you. This preservative will keep the bacon from becoming rancid at least 5 days longer than it normally would last.

SAVING GRANDMA'S PANTYHOSE

You will need the following ingredients:

> 2 *Cups of table salt*
> 1 *Gallon of cold water*

Place the salt and water in a medium bucket or pot and mix well. Add the pantyhose (brand new ones only) and allow them to soak for about 3 hours, then drip dry. This will make the pantyhose stronger and they will last longer.

GRANDPA'S SALT-FREE SEASONING

You will need the following ingredients:

> 1 *Cup of toasted sesame seeds*
> 2 *Tablespoons of garlic powder*
> 1 *Tablespoon of dried marjoram*
> 1 *Tablespoon of dried rosemary*
> 1 *Tablespoon of dried thyme*
> 1 *Tablespoon of dried lime zest*
> 1/4 *Teaspoon on onion powder*

Place all the ingredients in food processor and blend into a fine powder. Store the seasoning in a well-sealed jar in a cool, dry location. Place a portion in a shaker for easy use.

OLD-TIME SCOURING POWDER FORMULA

You will need the following ingredients:

1 Ounce of baking soda (fresh)
1 Ounce of prepared chalk (powdered chalk will do)
1 Ounce of powdered pumice stone
1 Ounce sifted wood ashes

Place all the ingredients into a jar and mix well. It works best to use this scouring powder with a piece of raw potato. The starch tends to increase the effectiveness and the potato adds just enough moisture.

THE INCAS INVENTED JERKY

A South American tribe called the Quechua, which was originally a tribe of the Inca empire, prepared the first beef jerky in the mid-1800's. The jerky was called "ch'arki" and was prepared by drying strips of beef, salting them, and pounding them flat between two large stones. The American Indians also made a jerky-like food called pemmican from buffalo meat. They dried the meat, then crushed it into a powder before adding wild cherries and hot fat. They then placed the mixture into a casing made from the waterproof animal hide. The pemmican would last for quite some time and would be used as their food source on long hunts. This old recipe is now called "kippered" jerky.

GRANDPA'S SECRET JERKY FORMULA

You will need the following ingredients:

1 Pound sirloin steak (lean, no visible fat)
1 Tablespoon of tomato sauce
1 Tablespoon of apple cider vinegar
1/4 Cup of Worcestershire sauce
1/4 Cup of low-salt soy sauce
1 Teaspoon of granulated sugar
1/4 Teaspoon of garlic powder
1/4 Teaspoon of onion powder
1 Teaspoon of table salt
1/4 Teaspoon of cayenne powder (optional)

Place the steak in the freezer until it is firm enough to slice. Then, making sure to cut against the grain, slice into very thin (one-inch wide) strips. Arrange the strips on a baking sheet. Place the remaining ingredients in a large bowl and mix thoroughly, then pour over the strips of beef and refrigerate for about 10 hours. Remove the strips from the marinade and arrange them on an cake rack that has been placed over a cookie sheet. Bake in a 140° F. oven for about 15–20 hours or until they are cooked through and dried out. Splintering on the edges is normal, depending on how thin the strips were cut. Store the jerky in well-sealed plastic bags. Jerky prepared in this manner can be stored for about 3–4 weeks.

GLOW-IN-THE-DARK INK
You will need the following ingredients:

1   Ounce of cinnamon oil (not extract)
$1/4$ Ounce of phosphorus (chemical supply house)

Place the ingredients in a well-sealed bottle and immerse in a very warm water bath until the ingredients have melted together. Dip a pen in the ink and write, then go into a dark room to see the results.

GRANDMA'S NATURAL DISINFECTANT
You will need the following ingredients:

$1/2$ Cup of cheap vodka (not grandpa's)
$1/2$ Teaspoon of tea tree oil
$1/2$ Teaspoon of essential lime oil (lemon is OK)
$1/4$ Teaspoon of essential grapefruit oil
$2 1/4$ Cups of cold tap water

Place all the ingredients into a spray bottle and spray the counters, etc. Also excellent as an air freshener, mouthwash, and deodorant.

1905 AIR PURIFIER & ODOR REMOVER
You will need the following ingredients:

$1 1/2$ Tablespoons of chlorophyll
1   Quart of cool tap water
1   Quart of denatured alcohol
$2 1/2$ Cup of formaldehyde (35–40% solution)
4   Drops of essential lavender oil
1   Small kerosene lamp (from hardware store)

Place the water, alcohol, and chlorophyll in a bucket and mix well, then add the formaldehyde and the essential oil and mix. ***Store this mixture in a safe container—some of these chemicals are harmful and flammable.*** This formula will work just as well as store-bought ones (if not better). Place the mixture in a kerosene lamp and allow a small portion (about an inch) of the wick to show. Once a week, cut off the exposed wick and pull up another inch.

GRANDPA'S DENTURE SOAK #1

You will need the following ingredients:

1 Cup of isopropyl alcohol
1 Teaspoon of citric acid
7 Drops of peppermint oil

Place all the ingredients in a small bowl and mix well, then soak the dentures for 20–30 minutes. Rinse the dentures in cold water.

GRANDPA'S DENTURE SOAK #2

You will need the following ingredients:

1 Tablespoon of baking soda (fresh)
1 Tablespoon of powdered laundry detergent (no bleach)
1 Cup of cool tap water

Place all the ingredients in a small bowl and mix well, then soak the dentures for 20–30 minutes. This will clean and freshen the dentures. Rinse them well with cool water.

ADHESIVE FOR GRANDPA'S DENTURES

You will need the following ingredients:

$1/2$ Cup of powdered tragacanth (from pharmacy)
2 Tablespoons of powdered acacia (from pharmacy)
$1^1/2$ Teaspoons of boric acid

Place all the ingredients in a small dish and mix well, then sprinkle a small amount on a wet dental plate.

THIS WILL BREAK YOUR TOOTH

Rock candy dates back to about the 1200's in Persia. An English reference to the candy dates to about the late 1500's when it was prescribed for excess phlegm. Even Shakespeare made reference to the candy as being good for a sore throat. Basically, rock candy is a highly refined form of pure cane sugar with no impurities. The actual refining process is called crystallization, which involves breaking the sugar molecules apart and allowing them to re-form into larger, purer, sugar crystals.

ROCK CANDY FORMULA

You will need the following ingredients:

1 Cup of cold tap water
2 Cups of granulated sugar (more if desired)
  Food coloring

Place the water in a small saucepan and bring to a boil, then dissolve the sugar in the boiling water. Pour the water into a drinking glass.

Tie a piece of cotton string to the center of a pencil, then attach a paper clip to the end of the string to weigh it down. Dampen the string very slightly, then roll it in a very small amount of sugar. Place the pencil with the string hanging down into the drinking glass. When the water cools (from the sugar being added), additional sugar can be added to produce larger crystals if desired.

For larger crystals, bring the water back to a boil and add as much sugar as you can while still maintaining a solution. Add the food coloring (if desired), mix, and pour the solution into the water glass, holding the pencil with string attached. Allow it to remain undisturbed for 2–3 days or until the sugar crystals have sufficiently covered the string. Crystals should start to form after 2–3 hours. To produce different colors of rock candy, divide the solution or make additional solutions and use glasses with different colors.

S.BEAN

MAKING CHEESE WAX—OLD-FASHIONED PRESERVATIVE

You will need the following ingredients:

> 3 Cups of beeswax (grated)
> 3 Cups of paraffin wax (grated)

Place the ingredients in a double boiler and slowly melt. Tie a string around a block of cheese and lower it into the wax solution. Remove and allow the wax to harden. Repeat the step 2–3 times until you have a thick wax coating. Store the cheese in a cool, dry location. This will stop insects and mold from attacking the cheese.

FORMULA FOR GRANDPA'S EGG PRESERVATIVE

You will need the following ingredients:

> 1 Quart of waterglass (sodium silicate)
> 2 Gallons of cold tap water

Place the water in a large pot and bring to a boil, then remove from the heat, cover, and allow the water to cool. Add the waterglass and stir well. Place eggs in a large crock, cover them with the solution and store in a cool, dry, dark location. Eggs should stay fresh for at least 2–3 months, maybe more. If an egg goes bad, it will be very easy to tell which one by the smell of hydrogen sulfide (rotten eggs).

SOLVING THE STICKY IRON PROBLEM

You will need the following ingredients:

1 *Teaspoon of silicon oil emulsion*
1 *Quart of cool tap water*

Place the ingredients into a medium bowl and mix well, then fill a spray bottle and spray the bottom of the iron. Rub the bottom of the iron after you spray and heat until the solution steams off.

GRANDMA'S JAR-SEALING WAX

You will need the following ingredients:

1 *Pound of paraffin wax*
4 *Tablespoons of stearic acid*

Place the ingredients in a double boiler and melt together, mixing well. This is an excellent sealer for jams and preserves. The stearic acid increases the density of the paraffin providing a better seal.

CLEANING GRANDPA'S GOLF BALLS

You will need the following ingredients:

$1/4$ *Cup of household ammonia*
1 *Cup of cool tap water*

Place the ingredients in a medium container and mix well. Soak the golf balls in the solution for 8-10 hours. Rinse with cold water and hit away.

KITCHEN FIRE EXTINGUISHER

You will need the following ingredients:

2 *Cups of soda ash*
1 *Cup of alum*
1 *Cup of borax*
$1/4$ *Cup of potash (from the nursery or feed store)*
3 *Pints of sodium silicate (waterglass)*

Place all the ingredients in a container and mix well until all the dry ingredients are dissolved. Store in a sealed container. Place 3 cups of this concentrated mixture into a small bucket with 1 gallon of cool tap water and mix well, then fill a large spray bottle and keep in a handy location. Spray at the base of a grease fire for best results.

NO MORE DRIPPING CANDLE WAX

You will need the following ingredients:

    3   Teaspoons of magnesium sulfate
    3   Teaspoons of Dextrin
    20 Teaspoons of cool tap water

Place the water in a medium container and dissolve the ingredients. Dip candles in the solution and allow them to dry thoroughly before using. This will cause the wax to burn completely with no drips.

SHOE LEATHER TOPS PRESERVATIVE

You will need the following ingredients:

    1   Cup of Neat's foot oil
    1   Cup of mineral oil

Place the ingredients into a small container and blend very well. Warm the oil slightly before rubbing it onto shoes or other leather items with a clean, soft cloth. This treatment should be done every 4–6 months to keep leather in top condition. Do not use on suede unless you wish to ruin the item.

TEST FOR REAL VS. CULTIVATED PEARLS

You will need the following ingredients:

        Methyl iodide solution
    5   Drops of monobromide naphthalene

Place the ingredients into a small beaker and drop the pearl in. If the pearl is real it will float. If the pearl is cultivated it will sink to the bottom.

GRANDPA'S BAROMETER

You will need the following ingredients:

    2   Ounces of cobalt chloride
    1   Ounce of table salt
    1/2 Ounce of gum acacia
    150 Grains of calcium chloride
    6   Ounces of cool tap water
    1   Sheet of white blotting paper

Place the water in a medium bowl and dissolve the dry ingredients into the water. Soak the white blotting paper in the solution and hang it up to air dry. The blotting paper will change colors depending on the level of dampness in the air. The following colors will appear:

COLOR	INDICATES
Blue	Dry
Lavender Blue	Almost dry
Bluish Red	Damp
Pink	Very Damp
Rose Red	Rain

SLEEPYTIME TEA

You will need the following ingredients:

S. BEAN

- 1 Tablespoon of powdered valerian root
- 1 Tablespoon of lemon verbena
- 1 Tablespoon of lemon peel

Place all the ingredients into a small container and blend well. Place 1 tablespoon of the mixture into an infuser and place into a cup of hot water. Let it steep for 4 minutes, strain, and drink.

MAKING IVORY SOFTENER

You will need the following ingredients:

- 1 Ounce of spirit of niter
- 5 Ounces of cool tap water

Place the water in a glass container and stir well to dissolve the spirit of niter. Then place the ivory item into the solution and allow it to remain for 5 days. This will make the ivory flexible.

MAKING PAPER AS SOFT AS CLOTH

You will need the following ingredients:

- 1 Pint of glycerin
- 10 Parts of cool tap water

Place the water in a large container and dissolve the glycerin. Dip the paper in the solution, then remove it and let it dry. When dry, the paper will be as soft as a piece of cloth.

PENCIL WRITING FIXATIVE

You will need the following ingredients:

- 1 Ounce of shellac
- 1/2 Ounce of sandarac
- 23 1/2 Ounces of spirits of wine

Place the spirits of wine in a container and dissolve the shellac and sandarac into the spirits. Mix very well; then quickly dip the paper into the solution and allow it to dry.

Another solution can be prepared by combining a small amount of bleached shellac with some milk and placing the solution in an atomizer to be sprayed on the pencil writing.

WHITEWASH FOR FENCES AND BARNS

You will need the following ingredients:

$2^1/_2$ *Pounds of casein*
   5 *Gallons of water*
$1^1/_2$ *Pounds of trisodium phosphate (TSP) or borax*
  25 *Pounds of hydrated lime*
$1^1/_2$ *Pints of formaldehyde*

This old whitewash formula may be harmful if consumed. Place the casein in one gallon of hot water until it is softened, then dissolve the TSP in another container containing $1/_2$ gallon of water and mix well. Mix both solutions together to blend well. In another container, place the hydrated lime in $3^1/_2$ gallons of hot water and stir rapidly until it becomes thick and pasty. In another container, dissolve the formaldehyde in $1^1/_2$ gallons of water and mix well. When the casein and lime solutions have cooled, combine them and stir well. Add the formaldehyde solution to the whitewash just before you are going to paint and blend thoroughly to be sure that the paint is mixed uniformly. The white wash will not keep and must be used up in one day's work. It is better get a few Toms and Hucks to help. If you do decide to use borax, the formula will not be as weather-resistant as using the TSP.

HARD WATER SOFTENER

You will need the following ingredients:

  1 *Pound of sodium carbonate (or sal soda)*
  1 *Quart of cool tap water*

Place the water in a container and mix the sodium carbonate in well. Just two tablespoons of this solution will soften 1 gallon of hard water. Be sure that the sodium carbonate is fully dissolved or particles will adhere to fabrics if used in the washing machine.

GLOVE CLEANER

You will need the following ingredients:

  1 *Ounce of white soap shavings*
  1 *Ounce of talcum*
  4 *Ounces of cool tap water*

Place the soap shavings and the water in a saucepan and place on low heat until the soap is dissolved, then add the talcum and continue stirring until the solution looks uniform. Apply the cleaner to gloves with a soft bristle brush, then wipe with a damp cloth. Be sure that all soap residue has been removed.

REJUVENATING GRANDPA'S STRAW HAT

The following ingredients will be needed by weight:

Solution One
- 10 Parts of sodium hyposulfite
- 5 Parts of glycerine
- 10 Parts of ethyl alcohol
- 75 Parts of cool tap water

Solution Two
- 2 Parts of citric acid
- 10 Parts of ethyl alcohol
- 90 Parts of cool tap water

Place all the ingredients for Solution One into a container and blend well. Sponge a generous amount of the solution onto the straw hat and allow the hat to rest in a relatively damp location for about 24 hours. Place the ingredients for Solution Two into a container and blend well, then sponge the straw hat with Solution Two. Allow the hat to dry, then press with a hot iron (if necessary) or use a stiff gum water to help return it to its original shape.

GRANDPA'S HARNESS DRESSING

You will need the following ingredients:

- 100 Parts of ox blood (purified and fresh)
- 20 Parts of glycerine (technical)
- 30 Parts of turpentine oil
- 50 Parts of pine oil
- 20 Parts of ox gall
- $1^1/_2$ Parts of formalin

Place the ingredients into a container one at a time in the order they are listed, mixing as each one is added. Filter the mixture through a piece of thin linen, then apply with a rag. This mixture will leave a permanent glossy finish on the harness.

HARNESS OIL

You will need the following ingredients:

 10 *Ounces of Neat's foot oil*
  2 *Ounces of oil of turpentine*
  4 *Ounces of petrolatum*
 1/2 Ounce of lampblack

Place the lampblack, turpentine, and Neat's foot oil in a container and mix thoroughly. Place the petrolatum in a double boiler and melt, then pour it into the turpentine mixture and mix. Be sure that the hot petrolatum has cooled somewhat before adding it to the other mixture.

GRANDPA'S SHAVING STUFF

LATHER-UP AND SHAVE 'EM OFF

Since many men still use old-fashioned shaving methods, some of the following formulas were designed to be used with these methods. Traditionally, shaving soaps were used to lather the face with a wet brush and were typically used with a straight razor, while brushless creams were generally applied with the fingers. The type of cream and method used depended on the type of beard and how difficult it was to shave. When using these preparations, first wash your face to remove any trace of oiliness for the best results. The shaving creams must come into full contact with facial hair to soften it properly before removal.

OLD BELT RAZOR SHARPENER

You will need the following ingredients:

  1 *Ounce of prepared putty powder*
 1/4 Ounce of powdered oxalic acid
 20 *Grains of powdered gum arabic*

Place all the ingredients into a small container and mix well with enough cool tap water to form a paste. Apply a thin coating of the paste to the razor strop and cover the other side with a layer of grease.

NO-LATHER SHAVING CREAM

You will need the following ingredients:

  1 *Teaspoon of white mineral oil*
  1 *Teaspoon of glycosterin*
  5 *Teaspoons of boiling water*

Place the mineral oil and the glycosterin in a saucepan and heat to 150° F. while stirring well. Add the boiling water and again stir very well. Remove from the heat and stir continually until the mixture is cool. Pour into a sealed porcelain jar.

OLD-FASHIONED LATHER SHAVING CREAM
You will need the following ingredients:

  2 Ounces of cetyl alcohol
  2 Ounces of caustic potash pellets
  1/2 Ounce of boric acid
  2 Ounces of glycerin
  10 Ounces of stearic acid
  4 Ounces of coconut oil
  2 Ounces of virgin olive oil
  1 Ounce of sodium lauryl sulfonate
  1 Ounce of carbitol
  1 Pint of cool tap water

Place the water in a medium saucepan and dissolve the potash pellets, boric acid, and glycerin. Place the saucepan over medium heat and boil the mixture for 15–20 minutes. In another saucepan, combine the stearic acid, coconut oil, olive oil, and sodium lauryl sulfonate and heat until the ingredients are well blended. Add the oil mixture to the potash pellet mixture along with the cetyl alcohol, mix well and remove from the heat. Continue to stir as the mixture cools. Add the carbitol when the shaving cream mixture is almost cold, stir well and pour into jars with lids.

SOAP FOR SHAVING
You will need the following ingredients:

  2 Ounces of caustic potash pellets
  4 Ounces of very hot tap water
  7 Ounces of lard
  5 Ounces of tallow
  1 1/2 Ounces of stearic acid
  1/2 Ounce of ethyl alcohol
    Perfume spray or essential oil (if desired)

Place the potash pellets in a bowl of very hot tap water and allow them to dissolve. Place the lard, tallow, and stearic acid in a double boiler and allow it to melt, then add the potash pellet mixture to the lard mixture and continue stirring until the ingredients are all well blended. Remove from the heat and add the alcohol and any perfume or essential oil that you desire and continue mixing until the soap is cool. Pour the soap into a dish or shaving mug to harden.

BRUSHLESS SHAVING CREAM FOR DRY SKIN

You will need the following ingredients:

2^1/$_2$ Ounces of stearic acid
  3 Ounces of mineral oil
  2 Teaspoons of triethanolamine
  2 Teaspoons of borax
^{1}/$_2$ Ounce of carbitol
14 Ounces of cool tap water
  4 Drops of essential lavender or rose oil
  3 Containers/saucepans

Place the mineral oil in the first small saucepan and place on low heat. Place the stearic acid in the second saucepan and melt on low heat, then add it to the mineral oil. Place the water, borax, and triethanolamine in the third saucepan, stir well, and heat on low heat. Then pour it into the mixture of mineral oil and stearic acid and stir well until it becomes smooth and uniform in appearance. Remove from the heat and add the carbitol and any perfume or essential oil if so desired. Mix until the cream is almost completely cool, then pour it into a glass jar with a lid.

GRANDPA'S BRUSH SHAVING SOAP

The following ingredients will be need:

^{1}/$_4$ Cups of cold tap water
  5 Cups of Castile soap (grated)
  2 Ounces of a dark rum
  1 Tablespoon of ground allspice
  1 Tablespoon of finely ground cinnamon
  1 Ounce of bay essential oil
  1 Ounce of sweet orange essential oil
  3 Ounces of vitamin E

Place the essential oils, rum, cinnamon, and allspice in a sealed jar and mix thoroughly, then allow it to stand for 2 days. Strain the mixture through a piece of cheesecloth. Place the water and rum mixture into a double boiler and heat to 180° F., then add the grated soap and stir just until the soap melts. Add the vitamin E as soon as the mixture looks clean and all the ingredients have been well blended. Stir and place the soap into molds. When the soap cools and has a thick skin, remove it from the molds and allow it to mellow for about 5 weeks.

BRUSHLESS SHAVING CREAM FOR OILY SKIN

You will need the following ingredients:

  5 *Ounces of stearic acid*
  1 *Ounce of anhydrous lanolin*
  1 *Teaspoon of triethanolamine*
  1 *Teaspoon of borax*
  2 *Teaspoons of carbitol*
14 *Ounces of cool tap water*
  4 *Drops of essential lavender or rose oil*
  3 *Container/saucepans*

To prepare this formula, use the directions provided for the Brushless Shaving Cream for Dry Skin, but substitute the anhydrous lanolin for the mineral oil.

BERGAMOT COLOGNE

You will need the following ingredients:

$1/2$ *Teaspoons of oil of lavender (fine)*
$1/2$ *Teaspoons of oil of cloves*
$1^1/2$ *Ounces of oil of bergamot*
  2 *Teaspoons of oil of lemon*
  1 *Teaspoon of oil of sandalwood*
$1/2$ *Pint of ethyl alcohol*
$1/2$ *Pint of cool tap water*

Place all the ingredients except the water in a medium bowl and blend well, then add the water and mix thoroughly. Pour into a sealed glass bottle and shake before each use.

BAY RUM FACE SPLASH

You will need the following ingredients:

$1^1/2$ *Teaspoons of oil of bay leaves*
$1/4$ *Teaspoon of oil of orange peel (very fresh)*
$1/2$ *Ounce of magnesium carbonate*
  1 *Ounce of tincture of orange peel*
$1/2$ *Pint of ethyl alcohol*
$1/2$ *Pint of cool tap water*

Place the magnesium carbonate and the oils into a medium bowl and mix thoroughly. Place the tincture of orange peel, alcohol, and water into another bowl and mix thoroughly, then slowly add this mixture to the oil mixture and stir well. Pour into a well-sealed glass bottle and shake before each use.

REMEDIES FROM THE OLDEN DAYS

GRANDPA'S ARTHRITIS RELIEF
You will need the following ingredients:

  4   *Tablespoon of pure orange juice*
  1   *Tablespoon of cod liver oil*

Place the cod liver oil in a small glass and mix with the orange juice. Complete your evening meal no later than 6:00 P.M. Do not eat anything for 3–4 hours, then drink the orange juice mixture just before going to bed. The stomach must be empty so that the digestive system is quiet and no bile is flowing. This will allow the oil to be absorbed by the joint and possibly alleviate the problem. This is an old historical remedy that was used in the 1800's. Many people claimed that they achieved excellent results. The author does not recommend this formula as a treatment for a disease. It is included for informational purposes only.

PHYTO (NOT FIDO) TO THE RESCUE

While modern science just recently identified hundreds of phytonutrients in fruits and vegetables, it seems that grandpa must have known something a long time ago. The following combination of fruit juices provides a person with an excellent blend of the phytonutrients that are presently being studied in relation to reducing the risk of heart disease and lowering cholesterol levels.

GRANDPA'S CHOLESTEROL LOWERING SECRET FORMULA
You will need the following ingredients:

  1   *Cups of purple grape juice*
  2   *Cups of pure cranberry juice (from concentrate)*
  2   *Cups of pasteurized apple juice*
  1/3 *Cup of apple cider vinegar*

Place all the ingredients in a sealed pitcher and mix thoroughly. Drink one eight-ounce glass of the juice twice a day to lower cholesterol.

SOME STATES ARE POISON-PLANT FREE

Three state—Alaska, Hawaii, and parts of Nevada—do not have any poison oak, ivy, or sumac. All other states have at least one variety. The poison ivy plant gives off an oil called "urushiol," that can remain active for some time on clothing and even your pet could transfer the oil to your skin to cause the allergic reaction. Approximately 2 out of every 3 people are allergic to these poisonous plants. Reactions can occur in as little as 10 minutes and a rash will erupt, possibly blister, and almost always itch. It takes about 10 days for the rash and itching to subside. If you are very susceptible to poisonous plants you should consult your pharmacist for the latest preparation that will block the oil from penetrating your skin.

POISON IVY AND POISON OAK RELIEF

You will need the following ingredients:

2   *Ounces of potassium permanganate*
4   *Cups of cold tap water*

Place the ingredients in a medium bowl and mix thoroughly. Apply the solution to the affected area twice daily or as needed for relief of the symptoms. If a brown stain appears, it can be removed with a weak solution of oxalic acid and water.

PRICKLY HEAT/MOSQUITO BITE FORMULA

You will need the following ingredients:

2   *Teaspoons of calamine*
1   *Tablespoon of zinc oxide*
5   *Teaspoons of glycerin*
6$1/2$ *Tablespoons of lime water*
3$1/4$ *Ounces of rose water*

Place all the ingredients into a medium bowl and blend thoroughly, then apply to the affected area. Store in a well-sealed bottle and mix well before each use.

REMEDY FOR BOILS

You will need the following ingredients:

1   *Cup of white vinegar*
$1/4$ *Cup of turpentine*
1   *Fresh medium egg white only*

Place all the ingredients in a medium bottle and shake until well mixed. The solution should look milky. Apply a small amount to the boil and allow it to air dry. This should be done twice a day for the best results.

CORN FORMULA FOR PEOPLE WHO WEAR TOO SMALL A SHOE

You will need the following ingredients:

$1/2$ *Teaspoon of resorcin*
$1/2$ *Teaspoon of salicylic acid*
5   *Teaspoons of collodion elasticum*

Place the ingredients in a small bowl and mix well. Apply to the corn for 6 days. The foot should be bathed in very hot water. The corn should be easy to remove. Pressure from poor-fitting shoes is usually the cause of the problem.

DIGESTIVE AID

You will need the following ingredients:

> 2 *Tablespoons of apple cider vinegar*
> 2 *Cups of tepid tap water*

Place the ingredients in a tall glass and drink before each meal if you are having digestive problems. A small amount of pure honey can be added to improve the taste.

BROWN AGE SPOTS

You will need the following ingredients:

> 2 *Teaspoon of white onion juice*
> 2 *Teaspoons of white vinegar*

Place the ingredients in a small bottle and shake well to mix. Rub the solution into the spots twice a day until they disappear. This may have to be repeated if they decide to return.

GRAMPS ANTI-DIZZINESS FORMULA

You will need the following ingredients:

> 2 *Teaspoons of apple cider vinegar*
> 2 *Teaspoons of pure honey*
> *1/2 Cup of warm tap water*

Place the ingredients in a cup and mix well, then drink twice per day to relieve the symptoms.

SUNBURN RELIEF #1

You will need the following ingredients:

> 1 *Tablespoons of white vinegar*
> 2 *Tablespoons of virgin olive oil*

Place the ingredients in a small bowl and mix well. Use a cotton ball and dab on affected areas. Relief is almost instantaneous, but reapplication will be necessary when the discomfort returns.

SUNBURN RELIEF #2

You will need the following ingredients:

> 1   Cup white vinegar
> 5   Tablespoons of table salt
> 5   Tablespoons of plain yogurt
> 2^1/$_4$ Tablespoons of aloe vera gel

Place all the ingredients in a small bowl and mix thoroughly until the mixture is creamy. Store in a well-sealed jar in the refrigerator. Always shake before using and apply to affected areas every hour until relief has occurred. A cloth can be soaked in the solution and placed on the burned area as an alternative method of relief.

SUNBURN RELIEF #3

You will need the following ingredients:

> 2   Teaspoons of aloe vera (liquid)
> 15   Drops of calendula tincture
> 4   Drops of essential rose oil

Place all the ingredients in a small spray bottle and shake well. Use as needed to relieve the heat of sunburn. Store in a cool, dry location and shake well before each use.

SUNBURN RELIEF #4

You will need the following ingredients:

> 4   Parts of borax
> 2   Parts of potassium chlorate
> 10   Parts of glycerine
> 4   Parts of ethyl alcohol
> 90   Parts of rose water

Place all the ingredients into a container and mix well. Store in a well-sealed bottle and shake before each use.

COUGH SUPPRESSANT

You will need the following ingredients:

> 1   Cup of pure honey
> 3   Tablespoons of lemon juice
> 1/4   Cup of warm tap water

Place the honey and lemon juice in a small bowl and slowly add the water while mixing. The mixture should be stored in the refrigerator in a sealed jar and used as needed. One to two tablespoons is the normal dosage.

COLD RELIEF

You will need the following ingredients:

1   Cup of fresh cranberries
1/2   Tablespoon of pure honey
1   Tablespoon of potato starch
2   Cups of cold tap water

Place the cranberries and the water in a small saucepan and heat on medium until the cranberries pop open. Strain the mixture and add the honey to the liquid and bring to a boil. Remove from the heat and allow it to cool. Place the potato starch in a small bowl with 2 tablespoons of cold tap water and mix. Very slowly add the starch mixture to the cranberry mixture while stirring continually. Return the pan to the heat and bring to a boil. Keep stirring until it thickens and becomes almost transparent. Store in the refrigerator.

SORE MUSCLE RELIEF #1

You will need the following ingredients:

1 1/4   Teaspoons of peppermint oil (from health food store)
1   Pint of white vinegar
1   Pint of warm tap water

Place all the ingredients in a small container and mix well. Massage the solution into the area of the sore muscle for relief.

SORE MUSCLE RELIEF #2

You will need the following ingredients:

2   Teaspoons of cayenne pepper
2   Tablespoons of virgin olive oil
2   Drops of essential bay oil

Place the ingredients into a small bowl and mix well, then heat in the microwave until warm, not hot. Rub into sore area with a clean cloth. Do not use on open sores or wounds and discontinue use if a rash occurs.

OLD-FASHIONED MUSTARD PLASTER

You will need the following ingredients:

1   Tablespoon of dry mustard
1/4   Cup of all-purpose flour
Lukewarm tap water

Sift the mustard and flour together in a small bowl. Slowly add water to the mixture until a paste is formed. Spread the paste on a piece of muslin the size of a person's chest. Place the mustard plaster on the chest and place another piece of muslin on top of it. The skin must be dry before applying the plaster. If any allergic reaction, such as a rash, is observed, discontinue using the plaster and wash the area with warm soapy water. Leave the plaster on for only 20 minutes or until the skin turns red. This was traditionally used twice each day until the congestion subsided.

REMEDY FOR SORE THROAT
You will need the following ingredients:

$^1/_2$ Cup of apple cider vinegar
1 Teaspoon of cayenne pepper (from health food store)
4 Tablespoons of honey
$^1/_2$ Cup of cool tap water

Place all the ingredients in a small bowl and blend thoroughly. Store in a small, capped bottle. Take 2–3 tablespoons every 4 hours to relieve the discomfort of a sore throat. The cayenne will help increase the circulation and speed up the healing process.

GET ME A CRACKER, QUICK!

Morning sickness affects about 50% of all pregnant women in their first trimester. It may cause nausea in the morning, during the day, or at night. The sickness usually lasts through the first three months and is rarely a problem after that. The cause is related to the change in hormones and the associated problems that cause poor metabolism of carbohydrates. Usually, if you consume a few small meals during the day while in the first trimester, the problem will be minimal. Moving very slowly when you first arise also tends to help reduce the frequency of morning sickness. When it does occur, a cracker seems to help.

GRANDPA CURES MORNING SICKNESS (MOST OF THE TIME)
You will need the following ingredients:

$1^1/_4$ Tablespoon of fresh ginger root
1 Teaspoon of dried peppermint
2 Teaspoons of dried chamomile
1 Teaspoon of dried lemon balm
$3^1/_2$ Cups of cold tap water

Place the gingerroot in a small saucepan with enough water to cover and simmer for 15–20 minutes, then add the rest of the ingredients and allow the mixture to steep for 10 minutes. Strain the mixture through a piece of cheesecloth or a fine strainer and place into a covered glass for use the next morning. It is best to double or triple this recipe if you have problems every morning and just store the remainder in the refrigerator and place a cup next to the bed every night. It wouldn't hurt to have a saltine cracker next to the cup, just in case.

THERE'S A FUNGUS AMONG US—ATHLETES FOOT

You will need the following ingredients:

    25   *Cloves of fresh garlic (grated very fine)*
   $3^1/4$ *Teaspoons of ground cinnamon*
     3 *Teaspoons of powdered cloves*
     6 *Ounces of 100 proof cheap vodka*

Place the vodka in a jar (do not drink) and add the garlic and cinnamon, then shake to mix and store in a cool, dark location for 12 days. The mixture should be shaken (and not stirred) every 2 days. Strain the mixture through a piece of cheesecloth and place in a well-sealed bottle until needed. The solution can be applied to the affected area with a cotton ball, morning and night.

FACE IT, IT'S NO FUN

The majority of acne cases are heridtary and are related to the development of the sebaceous (oil secreting) gland in the skin. The problem has been related to excessive hormone secretion that seems to trigger the problem around puberty. However, acne can occur at almost any age, even during infancy. Treatment varies from individual to individual and is somewhat dependent on the person's overall hormonal functioning mechanisms. One treatment regimen is to prescribe the drug tetracycline, which reduces the fat enzyme (lipase) in the secretions from the gland.

ACNE SALVE

You will need the following ingredients:

  $^1/2$ *Teaspoon of helichrysum absolute (from drug store)*
   2 *Ounces of rose hip seed oil (from health food store)*

Place the ingredients in an opaque glass bottle and place in a water bath for 1 minute. Shake and apply a few drops to the pre-cleaned skin area.

QUICK, FILL THE TUB WITH TOMATO JUICE

There is an "old wives' tale" that says tomato juice will solve the problem of skunk smells. However, a number of studies have shown that tomato juice only masks the smell for a short period of time. The following formula will do a great job of removing the smell. An alternative would be to use hydrogen peroxide and bicarbonate of soda.

REMOVING SKUNK SMELL FROM PETS

You will need the following ingredients:

1   *Cup of apple cider vinegar*
6   *Ounces of baking soda (fresh)*
2   *Tablespoons of lemon juice*
$1/4$ *Cup of baby shampoo*
5   *Drops of vanilla essential oil (from health food store)*
   Enough warm water to bathe your animal

Place all the ingredients into a medium bowl and mix very gently. If you mix too violently, the shampoo will foam up. Pour the mixture into the bath water and place a clothespin on your nose, then wash the poor pet.

S. BEAN

1930's CHEST SALVE

You will need the following ingredients:

4   *Ounces of brown Vaseline*
4   *Ounces of paraffin wax*
1   *Tablespoon of eucalyptus oil*
1   *Teaspoon of menthol crystals*
$1/4$ *Teaspoon of cassia oil*
1   *Teaspoon of turpentine*

Place the paraffin and Vaseline in a double boiler and melt together, then add the menthol crystals and dissolve them by mixing well. Remove from the heat and allow the mixture to cool. While the mixture is cooling, add the turpentine and the oils and blend thoroughly. As soon as the salve thickens, pour it into a sealed container for storage. Apply the salve to the chest and cover with a warm towel.

AUNT EM'S NASAL INHALER

You will need the following ingredients:

  1   Very small amber or dark blue bottle
 $1/2$ Ounce of sea salt
 25 Drops of essential rosemary oil

Place the salt and oil in the very small bottle, close with a lid, and shake. One sniff of this and your nose will clear right up.

GRANDPA'S ANTACID RELIEF

You will need the following ingredients:

  1   Tablespoon of bicarbonate of soda
  1   Teaspoon of granulated sugar
  4   Drops of peppermint oil (or other flavoring)
  1   Cup of water

Place all the ingredients in a small container and mix well. Take one or two tablespoons to relieve indigestion or over-acidity.

GRANDPA'S SHAVING NICK RELIEVER

You will need the following ingredients:

 $1/2$ Tablespoon of glycerin
 $1^1/2$ Cups of cool tap water
  1   Tablespoon of alum

Place all the ingredients into a small bottle and shake well to mix. Apply with a cotton swab to the nick to relieve the discomfort and slight bleeding. Store in a well-sealed bottle and shake well before each use.

HOT, HOT, HOT

Capsicum is the compound that makes a hot pepper hot. About 80% of the compound can be found in the pepper's seeds and membrane and almost nothing will reduce its potency, including cooking and freezing. The hotness can be neutralized with either a dairy product or beer. When capsicum is used in preparations it has the ability to improve circulation and is a common ingredient in many herbal remedies.

CAPSICUM SALVE

You will need the following ingredients:

6 *Teaspoons of tincture of capsicum*
2 *Teaspoons of tincture of camphor*
3 *Teaspoons of ammonia water*
3 *Teaspoons of ethyl alcohol*
2 *Teaspoons of soap liniment*

Place all the ingredients into a small bowl and mix very well, then store in a sealed glass container. This is a traditional formula used for localized relief of pain.

CAPSICUM LINIMENT

You will need the following ingredients:

1 *Ounce of tincture of capsicum*
$1/2$ *Ounce of tincture of myrrh*
1 *Dram of menthol*
$1/2$ *Ounce of oil of sassafras*
1 *Ounce of oil of origanum*
1 *Ounce of camphor*
$1^1/2$ *Pints of rubbing alcohol*

Place all the ingredients into a medium container and blend thoroughly. Use as you would any other liniment. Capsicum has been used historically to increase circulation and speed healing.

1940's WART FORMULA

You will need the following ingredients:

2 *Teaspoons of sulfur*
1 *Teaspoon of acetic acid*
5 *Teaspoons of glycerin*

Place all the ingredients into a small bowl and mix well. To use, place the solution on the wart and keep covered. Repeat once each day until the wart is gone.

OLD INDIAN STYPTIC

American Indians used the herbs calendula and yarrow to make a styptic. The herbs were made into a paste, formed into stick shapes, and rubbed on a bleeding wound. Sometimes the paste was placed directly into the wound with excellent results.

STYPTIC PENCIL FORMULA

You will need the following ingredients:

5 *Ounces of potassium alum crystals*
2¹/₂ *Teaspoons of finely powdered French chalk*
2 *Teaspoons of glycerin*

Place the crystals in a small saucepan and heat on low heat until they liquefy, then remove any top scum leaving a clear liquid. In a small bowl mix the chalk and glycerin into a paste and add the paste to the liquid crystals; blend thoroughly. Remove from the heat and pour the mixture into a small, greased pan and allow it to cool enough to cut into pencil sized pieces. These pencils were used to stop bleeding from minor cuts made from shaving with a straight razor.

THE ORIGINAL SMELLING SALTS

The earliest record of the use of smelling salts goes back to the 1400's in China when people would carry a small bottle of rock salt ammonium carbonate whose pungent odor was said to revive a person who was not feeling well. If a woman felt faint, she would sniff the rock salts. Physicians and medical personnel now use a small ampoule that says "aromatic ammonia" to revive fainting victims.

OLD-FASHIONED SMELLING SALTS FORMULA

You will need the following ingredients:

5 *Minims of tincture of orris*
10 *Minims of oil of lavender*
30 *Minims of extract of violet*
2 *Ounces of ammonia water*

Place all the ingredients into a small bottle with a good seal and shake to mix. Shake before each use and only use when grandma faints.

NATURAL LAXATIVE

You will need the following ingredients:

¹/₂ *Cup of virgin olive oil*
¹/₂ *Cup of fresh orange juice*

Place the ingredients into a glass and mix well. Take just before bedtime.

1930'S ANTISEPTIC VAGINAL JELLY

You will need the following ingredients:

1^1/$_2$ Teaspoons of gum tragacanth
2^1/$_2$ Teaspoons of glycerin
25 Teaspoons of distilled water
1^1/$_4$ Teaspoons of boric acid

Place the gum tragacanth and the glycerin in a medium bowl, mix well, then very slowly add the water and boric acid while continually stirring. Allow the solution to remain at room temperature for 10 hours before using. Mix well before using.

PREVENTING MOSQUITO BITES

You will need the following ingredients:

1 Teaspoon of cinnamon oil
1 Teaspoon of patchouli oil
2 Teaspoons of sandalwood oil
1 Pint of rubbing alcohol

Place all the ingredients into a medium bowl and mix well, then apply to any exposed skin areas. Mosquitoes hate this stuff (your friends may too).

1950's SORE THROAT SPRAY

You will need the following ingredients:

4 Ounces of white mineral oil
5 Grains of menthol
10 Grains of camphor
5 Grains of eucalyptus

Place all the ingredients into a small bowl and mix thoroughly, then place into a small throat sprayer and spray while holding the tongue down.

DIAPER RASH POWDER

You will need the following ingredients:

2 Ounces of goldenseal powder
2 Ounce of dry clay

Place the ingredients into a small container and mix well. Store in a sealed bottle in a cool dry location.

GRANDPA'S OINTMENT FOR BARBER'S ITCH

You will need the following ingredients:

30 Grains of ichthyol
12 Grains of salicylic acid
45 Drops of mercury oleate (10%)
 1 Ounce of lanolin

Place all the ingredients into a container and mix well. Apply to the affected area.

GRANDMA'S NIPPLE OINTMENT

You will need the following ingredients:

24 Grams of white wax
80 Grams of sweet almond oil
40 Grams of clarified honey
25 Grams of balsam Peru

Place all the ingredients into a container and blend well, then apply a small amount.

IMPROVE THE EFFICIENCY OF YOUR SEPTIC TANK

You will need the following ingredients:

1 Quart of warm tap water
1 Pound of brown sugar
1 Envelope of dried yeast (fresh)

Place the ingredients into a medium bowl and gently mix well. Allow the mixture to stand for 10 minutes, then flush down the toilet. This will initiate the growth of anaerobic bacteria.

HOMEMADE TALLOW FOR SOAP-MAKING

You will need the following ingredients:

> 5 *Pounds of beef fat*
> *Tap water as required*

Place the beef fat in an old large pot and melt on low heat, stirring occasionally to make sure that the fat does not burn. After the fat has melted, cook the fat for 45 minutes, then allow it to cool for a few minutes before pouring through a sieve into another pot. Discard any solid residue. Make sure that the fat has cooled enough to accept water without splattering. Add half the volume of cool tap water and bring to a boil, then reduce the heat to low, cover, and allow the mixture to simmer for 3–4 hours. Remove from heat and allow the fat to cool somewhat before pouring through a sieve again into a plastic container to cool. Place the container in the refrigerator or in a very cool location for about 24 hours until a layered mixture is formed. There will be three distinct layers, the top layer will be the pure tallow, the middle layer will be a mixture of fat and water with residues, and the bottom layer will be the heavier protein jelly.

Place the mixture in a large pan and carefully separate the tallow from the other layers, wrap it in plastic wrap and store it in a cool, dry location or in the refrigerator. The tallow should remain usable for about 4–6 weeks depending on storage conditions.

Chapter 4

Automotive-Related Formulas

ARE DOGS CHASING YOUR CAR?

In the early 1900s, paint on carriages and cars was protected with a thin coating of rendered beef fat (which is probably why dogs were always seen chasing cars). Car waxing is very important, since the paint and coatings are only about .007 of an inch thick. Almost all finishes will deteriorate if not polished regularly. Carnauba comes from a tree found in Brazil and is a common wax ingredient. It is the most natural of all wax ingredients and produces the hardest and clearest surface. Carnauba also has the ability to absorb the acid in acid rain. Most car enthusiasts recommend a pure wax coating product and not a cleaner and wax combined for the best results.

FORMULA FOR CAR WAX #1
You will need the following ingredients:

> 2 Cups of turpentine
> 2 Tablespoons of melted yellow beeswax (no debris)
> 1/2 Cup melted ceresin wax
> 1 Tablespoon of pine oil

Place the ceresin wax and the beeswax in a double boiler and heat until melted. Stir well and allow it to cool until it is semi-liquid. Add the turpentine and pine oil and mix well. Place in a sealed container and allow to cool and dry. The wax should be applied with a rag and polished after it dries with a soft cloth for the best results. Always remember to do a small area at a time to keep the wax from over-drying, which makes it harder to remove and shine.

FORMULA FOR CAR WAX #2
You will need the following ingredients:

> 1 Cup of linseed oil
> 4 Tablespoons of caranuba wax
> 2 Tablespoons of beeswax
> 1/2 Cup of white vinegar (fresh)

Place all ingredients into a double boiler and heat until melted and well blended. Remove from heat, stir well, and pour into a metal container. Place the container on a safe surface and allow the wax to cool. Apply the wax to the car with a soft lint-free cloth. After the wax dries, very lightly dampen a piece of cloth with white vinegar and polish—you will have a beautiful shine.

GREASE BUSTER

You will need the following ingredients:

> 1   *Teaspoon of glycerin (from pharmacy)*
> 2   *Tablespoons of liquid dishwashing soap*
> 3   *Tablespoons of cornmeal*

Place all the ingredients into a small bowl and mix thoroughly. Use on your hands to remove grease stains.

WINDSHIELD DEICER #1

You will need the following ingredients:

> $20^1/_2$ *Ounces of isopropyl alcohol 91%*
> $4^1/_2$ *Ounces of magnesium chloride hexahydrate*

Both items are available at a chemical supply house or through a pharmacy. Place the alcohol in a large jar and add the magnesium. The magnesium should easily dissolve into solution. A drop of perfume or color may be added if desired. Place some of the solution in a spray bottle and keep handy in the car. This solution will clear an iced windshield in seconds and keep it clear for your entire trip. Keep out of reach of children.

WINDSHIELD DEICER #2

You will need the following ingredients:

> 1   *Cup of propylene glycol (from pharmacy) or anti-freeze*
> $3^1/_2$ *Cups of rubbing alcohol*
> 2   *Quarts of cool tap water*

Place the ingredients into a large jar and mix well. Place into a spray bottle and keep handy. Keep out of reach of children.

WINDSHIELD WIPER FROST-FREE FLUID

You will need the following ingredients:

> 3   *Cups of white vinegar*
> 1   *Cup of cool tap water*

Place the ingredients into a container and mix well. Wipe the solution on the windshield weekly (more if it snows often) to keep the windshield free from frost.

METAL CLEANER #1

You will need the following ingredients:

> 3   *Tablespoons of diatomaceous earth*
> 3   *Tablespoons of baking soda*
> 1   *Teaspoon of lemon juice*

Place all the ingredients into a small plastic bowl or container and mix until a paste forms. Add just enough lemon juice to make the paste. Rub lightly into the metal, then rinse well with very warm water.

METAL CLEANER #2

You will need the following ingredients:

$1^1/_2$ Cups of trisodium phosphate (TSP)
6 Cups of soda ash
$2^1/_2$ Cups of bicarbonate of soda

Place all the ingredients in a large bowl or container (wear gloves) and mix well. Store in a well-sealed container. To use, place a small amount on a damp sponge, clean the metal surface, and rinse with cold water.

S. BEAN

HARD WATER SPOT REMOVER FOR CARS

You will need the following ingredients:

3 Tablespoons of lemon juice
1 Tablespoon of alum (from pharmacy)
2 Cups of very hot tap water
1 Spray bottle

Place all the ingredients in a spray bottle and shake to mix thoroughly. Spray on the affected area and allow the mixture to sit for a few seconds before wiping off. Do not allow the mixture to dry.

NATURAL FIBERGLASS CLEANER

You will need the following ingredients:

1   Cup of borax or baking soda
¼   Cup of white vinegar

Place the borax or baking soda in a small bowl and add the vinegar until the powder is good and damp. Sponge the solution on the area that needs cleaning and rub until clean. Sponge off with warm water, then rinse well.

MOTOR OIL CLEANUP

You will need the following ingredients:

1   Bag unscented kitty litter
2   Cups of washing soda

Spread the kitty litter on the oil spill and rub into the oil to absorb it. Brush up the kitty litter. Repeat until all the oil is gone. Any residue remaining can be cleaned by brushing again with the washing soda and a small amount of water.

DON'T LET YOUR VINYL HAVE A CRACK-UP

Deterioration of vinyl, especially that resulting from the heat from the sun shining through the windshield, is very common. Ultraviolet radiation will cause the vinyl to fade and crack. Water-based vinyl conditioners will provide a nicer finish than oil-based products and provide better protection against the sun.

UPHOLSTERY CLEANER FOR VINYL

You will need the following ingredients:

¼   Cup of washing soda
1   Cup of boiling water

The washing soda must be fully dissolved in the boiling water. Saturate a sponge and, wearing rubber gloves, clean the vinyl. Rinse the vinyl very well and dry. It may take a few rinsings to remove all the washing soda.

AUTO VINYL CLEANER

You will need the following ingredients:

1   Cup of whiting (calcium carbonate)
3   Cups of baking soda (fresh)

Place the whiting and baking soda in a container and blend well. Rub the mixture into the vinyl with a dampened sponge to remove soil and renew the appearance. Wash off the mixture with mild liquid hand detergent and warm water.

CLOUDY WINDSHIELD CLEANER

You will need the following ingredients:

4 *Ounces of household ammonia*
1 *Gallon of cool tap water*

Place the water in a bucket and add the ammonia and mix well. Wearing rubber gloves, clean the inside surface of the windshield. This solution will remove the haze that results from vinyl that gives off a plasticizer.

NATURAL ROAD TAR REMOVER

You will need the following ingredients:

1 *Cup of linseed oil (food grade)*
1 *Damp cloth*

Using the damp cloth, gently rub a small amount of linseed oil onto the tar until it disappears. This works as well as kerosene and is not as harsh.

CHROME CLEANER

You will need the following ingredients:

1 *Cup of baking soda (fresh)*
1/4 *Cup of cold tap water*

Place the baking soda into a small bowl and add just enough of the water to make a paste. Sponge the paste on the chrome, then rinse off. A small amount of lemon juice in the water will make it more effective.

BLACK TIRES ARE THE BEST

It takes a lot of care to keep tires from drying out and cracking from the combination of ozone and sunlight. Tire manufacturers protect the tires the best they can using a stabilizer called a "competitive absorber." These absorbers capture the UV rays from the sun and convert them to heat, which is then harmlessly dissipated. The most common of these "absorbers" is carbon black. Tires will eventually turn gray as the carbon black loses its ability to protect, thus turning the black tires gray over time. Higher quality tires have a wax compound added to the carbon black that extends the life of the tire and slows the rate of graying.

SIDEWALL CLEANER FOR TIRES

You will need the following ingredients:

> 1 Cup of baking soda (fresh)
> Cool tap water

Place the baking soda in a small bowl and add just enough water to prepare a loose paste. Wash the tires, then rinse with cool water until all the baking soda residue has been removed.

SEAL LEAKS IN OLDER TUBELESS TIRES

You will need the following ingredients:

> 1/2 Cup of sodium silicate (waterglass)
> 1 Cup liquid latex emulsion

Place the ingredients into a container and mix well. Jack up the car just enough to take the pressure off the tire. Remove the stem, which will deflate the tire, and pour 1/4 cup of the mixture into the tire using a small funnel. Be sure to wipe off the inside of the valve housing before reinserting the valve.

THE SMELL OF EVAPORATING OILS

Leather needs frequent cleaning and replacement of the oils lost through evaporation. The lost oils produce the leather smell that many people like (which is why they like to have leather seats). If you do not replace the oils every month or two, the leather will dry out and develop cracks. It is best to test leather cleaner on an inconspicuous location in case the leather is not colorfast for that particular cleaner and oil.

AUTO LEATHER MOISTURIZER #1

You will need the following ingredients:

> 2 Tablespoons of castor oil
> 1/4 Cup of wheat germ oil
> 1/8 Cup of almond oil (sweet variety)

Place the oils in a jar and shake well until well mixed. Apply the solution to the leather and allow it to remain on for 1 hour. Use a clean, dry soft cloth and buff the area. This will prevent cracking and keep the leather soft.

AUTO LEATHER MOISTURIZER #2

You will need the following ingredients:

2 *Cups of Neat's foot oil (from hardware store)*
2 *Cups of mineral oil*

Place the ingredients into a bottle and shake well before each use. Store in a well-sealed bottle in a cool location.

STOP MOTOR KNOCKING AND USE REGULAR GAS

You will need the following ingredients:

1   *Cup of denatured alcohol (flammable)*
1/2 *Cup benzene (flammable)*
1   *Tablespoon of hydrogen peroxide (use with caution)*

Place the ingredients into a container and mix well, then add 1 teaspoon to your tank for every 5 gallons of gasoline. This is an excellent anti-knock mixture.

ANTIFREEZE FOR GAS TANKS

You will need the following ingredients:

2 *Cups of rubbing alcohol*
3 *Drops of cinnamon essential oil*

Place the ingredients in a glass jar and mix well. In colder climates, add 1/3 cup to your gas tank twice a month to help remove moisture and stop the gas from freezing. Keep out of reach of children.

CLEANING ADDITIVE FOR CAR ENGINES

You will need the following ingredients:

1 *Cup of paraffin*
1 *Cup of SAE 30 motor oil*

Place the paraffin in a double boiler and allow it to melt, then add the motor oil and stir well. Remove from the heat and allow the mixture to cool to room temperature. Add 4 ounces to the gas tank with every 5 gallons of gas once every 3 months to keep the engine clean and the carbon deposits to a minimum.

MAKE SURE YOU HAVE A "COOL" CAR

Dirt and grime should never be left on a car for any length of time or they will scratch and dull the finish. The car should be washed when it is cool outside and never in direct sunlight or the car will dry too fast, leaving grease spots. The car should be thoroughly wet down to remove the particles of grime so that you don't rub them into the finish. A natural sea sponge is recommended since their many fine filaments tend to attract grime away from the car. Wash mitts are also excellent and, to dry the car, a chamois is recommended.

CAR WASH SOLUTION

You will need the following ingredients:

> 1 Gallon of cool tap water
> 1/2 Cup of liquid dish detergent
> 1/4 Cup of baking soda (fresh)

Place all the ingredients into a container and mix gently to prevent excessive sudsing. Place 1 cup of the mixture into a bucket of warm tap water and mix well before washing.

REMOVE SCRATCHES FROM WINDSHIELDS

You will need the following ingredients:

> 4 Ounces of household ammonia
> 1 Gallon of warm tap water
> Jewelers rouge (jewelry supply house or local jeweler)

Place the jeweler's rouge on a lamb's wool buffing pad attached to an auto electric buffer and buff the scratch. The scratch should disappear. Clean the area with the solution of ammonia and water (wear rubber gloves).

COATING TO PROTECT BATTERY TERMINALS

You will need the following ingredients:

> 1 Cup of sodium silicate
> 1 Cup of cold tap water

Place the ingredients into a container and mix well, then brush on the mixture to clean terminals and cable connections. This coating should prevent the buildup of corrosion and extend battery life.

GREASE STAIN REMOVER—SMALL AREA

You will need the following ingredients:

$^1/_2$ Cup of sodium aluminate
1 Quart of water

Place the ingredients into a medium jar and place in a water bath to warm. Soak the stained area in the solution for 5 minutes before cleaning with cool water.

SWEEPING COMPOUND FOR GARAGE FLOORS

You will need the following ingredients:

14 Cups of clean sawdust (no chunks or extraneous material)
4 Cups of rock salt
$3^1/_4$ Cups of mineral oil

Place all the ingredients into a bucket and mix well. Sprinkle the mixture on the floor to keep the dust down when you are sweeping.

RADIATOR CLEANER

You will need the following ingredients:

$2^1/_2$ Pounds of washing soda
3 Quarts of cool tap water

Place the water in a bucket, add the washing soda and mix well. Pour the mixture into the radiator and fill the radiator with water. Allow the engine to run for 20 minutes then flush with clean water for 5–7 minutes. Refill with your regular antifreeze mixture. A rust remover can be added if you are concerned about rust being present in your radiator.

RADIATOR SCALE REMOVER

You will need the following ingredients:

7 Ounces of trisodium phosphate (TSP)
$4^1/_4$ Gallons of warm tap water

Place the ingredients into a bucket and mix well. Drain the radiator and fill it with the TSP solution, then turn on the engine and run it just a little above idling for about 15 minutes. Drain the TSP solution and flush the radiator with clean water.

RADIATOR RUST REMOVER

You will need the following ingredients:

> 4 Ounces of oxalic acid (toxic)
> 4 Ounces of sodium bisulfite
> 2 Gallons of cool tap water

Place all the ingredients into a bucket and mix well, then drain the radiator and pour the solution into the radiator. Run the engine for about an hour before draining the solution out, then run clean water through the radiator. This is usually only needed if you actually see rusty water in the radiator.

INSIDE WINDSHIELD DEFOGGER

You will need the following ingredients:

> 2 Tablespoon silicon liquid emulsion (from chemical
>   supply house)
> 6 Cup of cool tap water

Place the ingredients in a small container and mix well, then dampen a soft cloth and wipe the inside surfaces of the car windows. This will prevent the windows from fogging up.

ANTI-FREEZE #1

You will need the following ingredients:

> 5 Pints of ethylene glycol
> 1 Gallon of cool tap water

Place the ingredients into a bucket and mix well, then pour into radiator. The 5 to 1 ratio will be effective for temperatures down to –10°F. For temperatures below that level and down to –20° F., use a 6 to 1 ratio.

ANTI-FREEZE #2

You will need the following ingredients:

> 5 Parts of denatured alcohol
> 1 Part of methanol
> 3 Parts of glycerin
> 1 Part of cool tap water

Place all the ingredients into a safe container and mix well.

ANTI-FREEZE #3

You will need the following ingredients:

3 Parts of carbonate potash
2 Parts of glycerin
4 Parts of cool tap water

Place all the ingredients into a safe container and mix well.

COATING FOR RUBBER HOSES

You will need the following ingredients:

5 Ounces of gum arabic
3 Ounces of molasses
15 Ounces of white wine
6 Ounces of ethyl alcohol

Place the white wine in a bowl and dissolve the molasses and gum arabic into it. Add the alcohol a little at a time, stirring constantly. The gum arabic will precipitate out unless the stirring is done very thoroughly. Apply the solution to a rubber hose with a small brush to prevent the escape of any gases.

RUSTPROOFING METALS

You will need the following ingredients:

9 Parts antimony trichloride
9 Parts of crystallized iron chloride
4 Parts tannic acid
18 Parts cool tap water

Place the water in a medium basin and dissolve the other ingredients into the water and mix well. Apply the solution to the metal with a soft cloth. Two applications are usually needed but allow the first application to dry thoroughly before applying the second coat. After the second coat has dried, clean the surface with warm tap water and rub the surface with linseed oil.

AUTO FIRE EXTINGUISHER

You will need the following ingredients:

23 Ounces of sodium carbonate
$1/2$ Ounce of oxide of iron

Place the ingredients in a sealed container and mix well. Keep in the car and throw the contents onto the fire. The chemicals will produce carbonic gas when they come into contact with the flames and quickly extinguish the fire.

AUTO PAINT REMOVER

You will need the following ingredients:

15 Parts of benzol (highly flammable)
4 Parts fusel oil
1 Part yellow wax

Place the benzol and wax in a safe container and dissolve the wax fully. Add the fusel oil and mix well. Make sure there are no flames or cigarettes around when preparing this formula since it is flammable. Use the same precaution you would when working with gasoline.

OLD-FASHIONED AUTOMOBILE POLISH

You will need the following ingredients:

1 Pound of cedar oil
1 Pint of turpentine
1 Pint of ammonia water
2 Ounces of Venice turpentine

Place the turpentine into a container and dissolve the Venice turpentine into it. Add this mixture to the other ingredients and blend well. Apply the mixture with a soft cloth, then polish with a clean cloth.

MECHANIC'S SOAP #1

You will need the following ingredients:

4 Ounces of almond meal
4 Ounces of precipitated chalk
1 Ounce of zinc oxide
1 Ounce of powdered orris root

Place all the ingredients into a container and mix with adequate water to prepare a paste. This is a soap-less formula.

MECHANIC'S SOAP #2

You will need the following ingredients:

6 Ounces of precipitated chalk
2 Ounces of finely powdered pumice
1 Ounce of corn meal
1 Ounce of kaolin

Place all the ingredients into a container and add sufficient witch hazel to prepare a paste. This should remove most grease stains without soap.

MECHANIC'S SOAP #3

You will need the following ingredients:

    3 *Ounces of soap flakes*
    1 *Pint of very hot tap water*
    4 *Ounces of silicate of soda*
  $1/2$ *Ounce of borax*
  $1/2$ *Ounce of raw linseed oil*
      Powdered pumice as needed

Place the hot water in a container and dissolve the soap chips, silicate of soda, and borax. While the solution is still hot, stir in the linseed oil. If necessary, some powdered pumice can be added to make a paste.

MECHANIC'S SOAP #4

You will need the following ingredients:

  $1^1/_2$ *Pints of cool tap water*
  10 *Ounces of white soap chips*
    1 *Ounce of glycerin*
  $2^1/_2$ *Ounces of borax*
  $1^1/_4$ *Ounces of dry sodium carbonate*
  14 *Ounces of powdered pumice*

Place 8 ounces of the water in a pot and dissolve the soap chips on low heat. In another container add the glycerin, borax, and dry sodium carbonate to the remaining water and mix well. Add the second solution to the soap solution and mix well. Continue mixing on low heat. When the mixture starts to thicken, add the pumice and stir until the soap is thick enough to pour into molds.

SQUEAK STOPPER

You will need the following ingredients:

    3 *Ounces of canola oil*
    1 *Quart of paraffin oil*

Place the ingredients into a container and mix well, then place a portion into a spray bottle and spray those squeaks away.

Chapter 5

Household Helper
Formulas

FORMULA FOR SILVERPLATING

You will need the following ingredients:

1   *Ounce of precipitate silver (chemical supply house)*
1/2 *Ounce of cynate of potash (chemical supply house)*
1/4 *Ounce of hyposulphite of soda (from a pharmacy)*
1/8 *Ounce of whiting (chemical supply house)*
1   *Quart of cold tap water*

Place the water in a small bucket and add all the ingredients except the whiting. Mix thoroughly, then add the whiting and mix. Clean the item to be plated with soap and water making sure to rinse very well and dry completely. Allow the item to air dry for another 15 minutes to be sure it is completely dry, then apply the plating mixture with a soft rag. Allow it to sit overnight.

PRESERVATIVE FOR OLD NEWSPAPER CLIPPINGS

You will need the following ingredients:

1   *Milk of magnesia tablet*
1   *Quart of club soda (fresh)*

Place the club soda in a medium bowl and dissolve the tablet. Allow the mixture to remain overnight, then blend well and pour into a shallow pan. Place the old, brittle newspaper clipping in the solution and let it soak for 2 hours. Very carefully remove the clipping and place it on a soft towel to dry. This preservation method will keep the paper in great shape for about 20 years before needing to be repeated.

ROOT ELIMINATOR FOR DRAINS

You will need the following ingredients:

3   *Cups of caustic soda*
1/4 *Cup of copper sulfate*

Place the ingredients into a cup and mix well, then pour it into a drain and flush with 2–3 quarts of very hot water. These chemicals will cause skin irritation and burns so use with caution.

EFFECTIVE DRAIN CLEANER #1

You will need the following ingredients:

1   *Cup of baking soda (fresh)*
1   *Cup of table salt*
1/4 *Cup of cream of tartar*
2   *Cups of boiling water*

Place all the ingredients in a well-sealed jar and shake to mix thoroughly. To clear a drain, pour $1/4$ to $1/2$ cups of the solution down the drain followed by the 2 cups of boiling water. Wait 1–2 minutes then run water in the drain to flush out.

EFFECTIVE DRAIN CLEANER #2
You will need the following ingredients:

$1/2$ Cup of baking soda
$1/2$ Cup of white vinegar
  2   Quarts of boiling water

Pour the baking soda down the drain, then pour the vinegar down the drain, cover and allow the mixture to stand for 5 minutes. Pour the boiling water down the drain.

EFFECTIVE DRAIN CLEANER #3
You will need the following ingredients:

$1/4$ Cup of pure lemon juice
$1/2$ Cup of baking soda
  1   Cup of white vinegar (fresh)
  1   Gallon of boiling water

Place the baking soda down the drain and pour in the vinegar and lemon juice. Wait for 10 minutes before pouring the boiling water down the drain to flush it out.

RUST REMOVER FOR HANDLEBARS AND HOUSEHOLD TOOLS #1
You will need the following ingredients:

  6   Tablespoons of table salt
  2   Tablespoons of lemon juice

Place the salt and lemon juice in a container and mix into a paste. Apply with a dry, clean cloth to handlebars or tools. Rub as needed and rinse thoroughly.

RUST REMOVER #2
You will need the following ingredients:

  2   Tablespoon of ammonium citrate crystals
  4   Cups of cool tap water

Place the ingredients into a small plastic bucket and mix well. To use, place the rusty tools or metal objects into the solution and allow them to remain for about 15 hours.

RUST REMOVER #3

You will need the following ingredients:

1 Part of muriatic acid
1 Part of cool tap water

Wear gloves. Place the acid and the water in a safe container and mix well, then place the rusted article in the solution. Flush thoroughly with cool water.

LEATHER POLISH AND CLEANER

You will need the following ingredients:

^{1}/$_2$ Cup of white vinegar
^{1}/$_2$ Cup of linseed oil (food grade)
1 Capsule of vitamin E (liquid insides only)

Place the ingredients in a jar and shake well. Saturate a piece of clean soft cloth and rub the solution into the leather. Test the solution on an inconspicuous area of the leather to be sure the leather will not change color. This solution should be safe for almost any leather.

SADDLE UP ON A SOFT SADDLE

Unless leather is oiled, it tends to get very brittle and crack easily. In the 1800's, a process, called "fatliquoring," was developed by a currier to soften leather and make it last longer by working special oils in to the leather. The actual "fatliquor," a blend of special oils in a soap base, was called "saddle soap," since it was primarily used on saddle leather. Saddle soap is not really a cleaner, but it provides the softness by forcing oils into the leather. The item to be saddle-soaped should be as clean as possible since the soap has the tendency to force dirt back into the leather.

SADDLE SOAP #1

You will need the following ingredients:

4 *Tablespoons of pure beeswax*
1/8 Cup of linseed oil (food grade)
1/4 Cup of white vinegar
1/8 Cup of liquid dish soap (vegetable source)

Place the beeswax and vinegar in a small saucepan and heat on low heat until the wax is melted. In a small bowl, combine the linseed oil and the liquid soap; mix well and add it to the wax mixture. Heat just enough to change the wax to a liquid form, allowing all the ingredients to mix together. Pour the mixture into a heat-resistant container and allow it to cool until it is solid. Use as you would use any other saddle soap.

SADDLE SOAP #2

You will need the following ingredients:

6 1/2 Parts of beeswax
1 Part of caustic potash
20 Parts of cool tap water
2 Parts of Castile soap (grated)
15 Parts of turpentine

Wear gloves. Place the beeswax, caustic potash, and 10 parts of water in a double boiler or medium pot and bring to a boil. Boil for 5 minutes while stirring well. In another pot, place the Castile soap and water and dissolve fully over low heat. Remove the pot from the heat and add the contents to the beeswax and blend thoroughly, then remove from the heat and stir in the turpentine. Mix the soap well, then allow it to cool somewhat before placing in molds if desired.

PLASTERBOARD & WALLBOARD HOLE PATCH

You will need the following ingredients:

2 *Tablespoons of table salt*
2 *Tablespoons of cornstarch*
5 *Teaspoons of cold tap water*

Place the salt and cornstarch into a small dish and add the water to make a paste (if it's too runny, it won't work). Fill the hole and allow it to fully dry, lightly sand any rough or raised spots. Finish it by going over the area with a damp sponge.

VARNISH REMOVER

You will need the following ingredients:

1 Cup of caustic soda (use with caution)
3/4 Cup of caustic potash (use with caution)
2 Cups of calcium carbonate
1 1/2 Cups of pumice powder

Place all the ingredients into a medium bucket (use gloves, a mask, and goggles) and mix well. To remove varnish and old paint put 1/2 cup of the mixture in a small container and add enough cold water to make a creamy substance. Apply the mixture to the area with a brush and allow it to stand for 5 minutes. Flush with cold water.

VINYL SIDING CLEANER

You will need the following ingredients:

4 Cups of chlorine bleach
2/3 Cup of trisodium phosphate (TSP)
1/2 Cup of borax
1 Gallon of cool tap water

Place all the ingredients into a bucket and mix well. Brush onto the siding, then rinse until all residue is removed. Keep out of the reach of children and pets.

REMOVE WATER MARKS FROM WOOD

You will need the following ingredients:

4 Tablespoons of virgin olive oil
3 Tablespoons of paraffin shavings

Place the ingredients in the top of a double boiler and heat until melted. Remove from the heat and allow to cool. Place a small amount on a clean soft cloth and rub the area in a circular motion with easy pressure. This works most of the time.

CONCRETE AND CEMENT CLEANER

You will need the following ingredients:

1 Gallon of very hot tap water
3 Pounds of metasilicate

Place the water in a bucket and add the metasilicate, then mix. Pour the solution on the stained area and use a broom to scrub.

CLEANER FOR TYPE

You will need the following ingredients:

$^1/_2$ Pint naphtha (from chemical supply house)
   1   Quart of carbon tetrachloride (from chemical supply house)

Place the ingredients into a medium container and mix well. Avoid breathing the fumes. This cleaning procedure should be done outside where there will be good ventilation. Handle these chemicals with extreme care.

WOOD REJUVENATOR

You will need the following ingredients:

   1   Cup of boiled linseed oil (from paint supply house)
   1   Cup of turpentine
   1   Cup of white vinegar

Place all the ingredients into a small bucket and mix well (wear rubber gloves). Dip a piece of #0000 steel wool into the solution and very lightly rub the surface, then clean off with a clean soft cloth.

WOOD TREATMENT FOR DECKS

You will need the following ingredients:

   1   Quart of boiled linseed oil
   1   Quart of turpentine

Place the ingredients into a bucket and mix well, then paint the surface with a paintbrush. Wear gloves and a mask.

INCREASE THE EFFICIENCY OF FUEL OIL

You will need the following ingredients:

   90   Ounces of naphthalene (from chemical supply house)
   10   Ounces of anthracene (from chemical supply house)

Place the ingredients into a container and mix well, then add 20 ounces of mixture to every 100 gallons of fuel oil when it is delivered. This should help to eliminate clogged burners and greasy deposits.

SPEEDY SNOW & ICE MELTING FORMULA

You will need the following ingredients:

   6   Cups of rock salt
   12   Cups of ammonium chloride
   6   Cups of magnesium sulfate

Place all the ingredients in a bucket and mix well, Sprinkle on sidewalks and driveways to melt ice and snow. This will even handle hard-packed snow.

STATIC-REDUCING SPRAY FOR CARPETS

You will need the following ingredients:

> 3 *Tablespoons of silicon oil emulsion (from chemical supply house)*
> 1 *Quart of cool tap water*

Place the ingredients into a container and mix well, then place a portion into a spray bottle with a fine spray setting and spray the carpet to reduce friction and eliminate the static problem. Store in a well-sealed container.

PLASTER CRACK FILLER

You will need the following ingredients:

> 8 *Parts of plaster of paris*
> 1 *Part of dextrin*
> 1 *Part of pumice powder*

Place all the ingredients into a container and mix well. Then add just enough cool tap water to produce the desired consistency.

FILLING CRACKS IN OAK

You will need the following ingredients:

> *Fine starch flour*
> *Thick brown shellac*

Place the ingredients into a container and mix well. Add enough of the brown shellac to the starch to make a paste. Apply paste to the crack and allow to dry. Once dry, sandpaper the surface and rub with a soft cloth dampened in oil and thin shellac.

THERE'S A STRANGE SMELL COMING FROM THE BATHROOM

If you have a septic tank, you are probably familiar with an occasional strange smell and know it's time to have the tank pumped or to add a special bacteria. However, if you do not use a septic tank and you smell a strange odor, it may be caused by "sewer gas," which contains methane. The odor is usually associated with sulfur and you should call your gas company or a plumber as soon as possible. Plumbers have special gas detectors and can locate the problem and correct it.

DETECTING SEWER GAS

You will need the following ingredients:

2 Ounces of lead acetate
1 Pint of distilled water or rain water

Place the ingredients into a container and mix well, then place a piece of unglazed white paper into the solution. Remove the paper immediately and allow it to dry. If the odor you smell is caused by a sewer gas leak, the paper will turn a dark color.

FILLING CRACKS IN MAHOGANY

You will need the following ingredients:

4 Ounces of beeswax
1 Ounce of red lead
Yellow ochre

Place the beeswax in a double boiler and melt, then add the red lead and enough ochre to produce the desired mahogany color. Remove from the heat and allow to cool. Use the mixture before it hardens and is warm enough to work with.

MAKING CLOTH FIREPROOF

You will need the following ingredients:

10 Ounces of borax
8 Ounces of boric acid
1 Gallon of cool tap water

Place the water in a large container and dissolve the borax and boric acid in the water. Place the cloth item into the solution and wring out very well, then allow to air dry. The material will smolder if burned but will not burst into flames.

MAKING CLOTH WATERPROOF

You will need the following ingredients:

10 *Ounces of white soap chips*
20 *Ounces of dextrine*
1 *Gallon of cool tap water*
6 *Ounces of zinc sulfate (white vitriol)*
2$1/4$ *Quarts of cool tap water*

Place the water, soap chips, and dextrine into a large pot and heat until the solids are dissolved. Then place the cloth item into the solution and allow it to remain for 2–3 minutes. Remove from the heat. In another container, place the zinc sulfate and the 2$1/4$ quarts of water and mix well, then place the cloth item in this solution and allow to remain for 2–3 minutes. Remove the cloth item and allow it to air dry.

Chapter 6

Home-Based
Business Products

ALL-AROUND METAL POLISH

You will need the following ingredients:

96 *Ounces of cold tap water*
1/2 *Pound of whiting*
1 *Pound of Tripoli (top quality only)*
1/2 *Pound of silica (top quality only)*
3 *Ounces of citric acid*

Place all the ingredients in a large white plastic pail and mix thoroughly. If you would like to color the mixture, use a water-soluble acid-proof color.

SUPER HAND CLEANSER

You will need the following ingredients:

4 *Quarts of cold tap water*
1 *Box borax soap chips or powder*
1 *Box of Lux*
3 *Pint of corn meal*

Place all the ingredients together in a medium bucket and mix thoroughly into a paste. Put the paste into jars with lids and label the jars as super hand cleanser.

SUPER COPPER & BRASS CLEANER #1

You will need the following ingredients:

1/2 *Cup of powdered laundry detergent (no bleach)*
3/4 *Cup of white vinegar (not apple cider)*
1/2 *Cup of all-purpose flour*
1/2 *Cup of table salt*
1/4 *Cup of lemon juice*
1/2 *Cup of very warm tap water*

Place the detergent, salt, and flour in a medium bowl and mix well. Add the rest of the ingredients and blend well. Dip a piece of clean cloth into the mixture and use it to clean your copper and brass. Store the remainder in a well-sealed jar.

SUPER COPPER AND BRASS CLEANER #2

You will need the following ingredients:

1/4 *Cup petroleum distillate (from oil company)*
2 *Teaspoons of caustic soda (handle with care, skin irritant)*
1 *Tablespoon of denatured alcohol (flammable)*
3/4 *Tablespoon of stearic acid*
Talc

Place the petroleum distillate in a container and add the stearic acid, then mix well. Add the remaining ingredients and just enough talc to produce a paste. Apply the paste with a clean, soft cloth and wipe off with another soft cloth to polish.

ALUMINUM POLISH

You will need the following ingredients:

> 1 Cup of alum
> 1 Cup of talc (from the drugstore)
> 1½ Cups of whiting

Place all the ingredients into a container and mix well (wear a dust mask). Store out of reach of children in a well-sealed container. Be careful not to inhale the talc. The solution should be applied with a soft, damp cloth.

GOLD POLISH

You will need the following ingredients:

> ½ Cup of household ammonia
> 1 Cup of diatomaceous earth
> ½ Cup of denatured alcohol
> ¼ Cup of cool tap water

Place the ammonia and alcohol in a bowl and mix well. Wearing a dust mask, gradually mix in the diatomaceous earth stirring the solution. Add the water and stir until the solution resembles a thick cream. Store in a well-sealed glass container.

FISHING BAIT—RUBBERY FROGS AND WORMS

You will need the following ingredients:

> 30 Ounces of Geon 202
> 20 Ounces of Good-rite GP 261
> 25 Ounces of hydrogenated terphenyl
> 25 Ounces of tin stabilizer

Mix all of the ingredients together using an electric mixer (or mix by hand). Pour into molds and place in a 350° F. oven to harden the plastic.

Supply Sources:
Geon 202 and GP 261 from:
B.F. Goodrich Chemical Company
3135 Euclid Ave. Cleveland, OH
Follow directions and precautions from B.F. Goodrich
when purchasing the supplies.

Hydrogenated terphenyl from:
   Harshaw Chemical Co.
   1945 E. 97th St. Cleveland, OH
Tin stabilizer from:
   Metal and Thermit Corp.,
   Rahway, NJ

BALLROOM FLOOR POWDER

You will need the following ingredients:

1   *Pound of hard paraffin*
7   *Pounds of powdered boric acid*
1   *Dram of essential lavender oil*
20 *Minims of oil of neroli*

Melt the paraffin in a double boiler. Remove from the heat and add the powdered boric acid and the oils and mix well. After the ingredients have been well blended, sift the solution through a fine sieve and allow it to cool.

BALLROOM FLOOR WAX

You will need the following ingredients:

5   *Ounces of yellow wax*
1   *Pound of stearin*
3   *Pounds of oil of turpentine*

Place all the ingredients into a double boiler and heat while stirring well. Remove from the heat and continue stirring until all the ingredients are blended and the mixture is almost fully cooled, then pour into cans.

ALL METAL SURFACES POLISHING CLOTH

You will need the following ingredients:

2   *Pounds of whiting*
2   *Ounces of oleic acid*
1   *Gallon of benzine (use with care, flammable)*

Place all ingredients into a bucket and mix well. Use new packages of lint-free rags or perfect-cut cloths. Soak the cloths, wring them out well (use rubber gloves) and allow them to air dry. These cloths are excellent for polishing silverware and most metal services.

Chapter 7

Formulas
For Pest Control

S.BEAN

GETTING RID OF ANTS

GIVING THE QUEEN HEARTBURN

Mix the following ingredients together in a small bowl:

$3^1/2$ Ounces of strawberry jam
$1^1/2$ Tablespoons of wet, canned cat food
1 Tablespoon of boric acid

This concoction is a treat for ants and the workers will bring the treat to their queen. The queen and the other ants will get excited and quickly gobble up the goody and, within a few hours, will die of heartburn. This works well on carpenter ants and termites. Make sure this treat is out of reach of children and animals that you wish to have around for a while. It will make them very sick. It doesn't take very much to do the job.

THE ANT TRAPPER

You will need the following ingredients:

6 Tablespoons of granulated sugar
6 Tablespoons of active dry yeast (fresh)
$1/2$ Cup standard grade molasses or honey
10 Small plastic lids or bottle caps

Place all the ingredients in a small bowl and mix thoroughly until smooth. Place the mixture into the lids or caps and place near an ant trail or near their mound. The mixture can also be spread on a piece of cardboard or a small stick and placed in their pathway or into a crevice.

ANT DUST

You will need the following ingredients:

$1/4$ Pound of dried peppermint (from health food store)
$1/4$ Pound rock dust (from nursery)
$1/4$ Pound seaweed powder
$1/4$ Pound alfalfa meal (organic, from health food store)
$1/4$ Pound cayenne pepper

Place all ingredients in a well-sealed jar or plastic container and shake well to mix. Avoid getting any of the powder on your hands or in your eyes. Place a small amount of the powder where the ants frequent. This will keep them away but will not kill them. Keep away from children and pets.

ANT SPRAY FOR THE GARDEN

You will need the following ingredients:

2   Tablespoons of flaked Ivory soap
1   Tablespoon of Tabasco sauce
5   Drops of sesame seed oil (from health food store)
5   Drops of Jungle Rain
1   Gallon spray bottle

Place all ingredients in the gallon bottle and shake to mix well. This can be sprayed directly on the ants or on their pathways. Keep away from children and pets.

FIRE ANT REMEDY

The following ingredients are needed:

1   Quart of cold
        tap water
1/4 Ounce of peppermint
        powder
5   Tablespoons of Jungle
        Rain (from a nursery)
1   Ounce of Citra Solve
        (from health food store)
2   Ounces of powdered Ivory soap
1   Spray bottle

Place all ingredients in a plastic bottle with a lid
and shake to mix. Spray the solution anywhere
you have seen ants and in their nest if you can find it.

GETTING RID OF ANT HILLS

You will need the following ingredients:

1/4 Cup of liquid hand soap
1   Gallon of cool tap water

Place the ingredients into a bucket and mix well. Pour 1–2 cups on the anthill and repeat after 1 hour to be sure that the mixture penetrates well into the chambers.

GETTING RID OF MOSQUITOES

KILL THOSE LITTLE BLOOD SUCKERS

In the United States alone there are over 150 species of mosquito and most can mature from an egg in one to two weeks. Mosquitoes need water to reproduce and can find standing water in pet dishes, drainage ditches, fish ponds, old tires, damp mulch, rain gutter lines, sewers, planters, leaks around spigots, etc. Mosquitoes like to live near your home and are smart enough to know that there are plenty of free meals there—namely you and your family. During the day they seek shelter from the sun but become more active in shady spots or when it cools down. They will never go very far from water. Getting rid of even the slightest amount of standing water should help to eliminate the problem.

MOSQUITO REPELLENT FOR ARMS AND LEGS
You will need the following ingredients:

> 4 Parts glycerin (from pharmacy)
> 1 Part eucalyptus oil

Mix the ingredients together in a small bowl. Place in a well-sealed container. Rub a small amount on arms or legs to keep mosquitoes from biting.

MOSQUITO REPELLENT #1
You will need the following ingredients:

> 3 Cups of rubbing alcohol
> 1½ Cups of red cedar wood shavings
> ½ Cup of eucalyptus leaves
> 1 Spray bottle

Place all the ingredients in a large bowl and mix well. Cover the bowl and allow it to stand for 6 days before straining the solution through a piece of cheesecloth. Place the liquid in a small spray bottle and spray on skin as needed.

MOSQUITO REPELLENT #2
You will need the following ingredients:

> 1 Ounce of oil of citronella (from health food store)
> 5 Drops of corn oil

Place the ingredients in a small bowl and mix well. Rub the mixture on your skin before going into mosquito-land.

MOSQUITO REPELLENT #3

You will need the following ingredients:

> 1 *Cup peanut oil*
> $1/2$ *Cup dried chamomile*
> $1/2$ *Cup of dried nettle*
> $1/2$ *Cup of dried pennyroyal*
> $1/4$ *Cup of sweet basil*
> $1/2$ *Cup of sweet orange oil*
> 1 *Teaspoon of boric acid*

Place all the ingredients in a double boiler and crush the herbs into the oil, then heat, stirring occasionally, for about 45 minutes. Cover the mixture, remove from the heat, and allow it to cool. Strain the mixture through a fine sieve, mashing the herbs to acquire the most fluid possible. Store in a well-sealed container in the refrigerator until needed. Rub on exposed areas. It will not take very much to do the job.

GETTING RID OF ROACHES

A ROACH BY ANY OTHER NAME IS STILL A ROACH

Roaches do not mind living outside but, given the chance, they and their whole family will move in with you. Roaches are known by a number of different names: water bugs, palmetto bugs, and, of course, cockroaches. They are bugs of the night and will seek out any drop of water or food that may be within their grasp, they are not fussy at all. Outside, they will take up residence almost anywhere—in a tree, a woodpile, a planter, under rocks, etc. In general, roaches will try to find a warm, damp location, which is where they prefer to breed. Cleanliness will reduce or eliminate most roach problems, but poison bait or frequent professional spraying by an expert helps. Roaches will not come back to an area where they are frequently poisoned.

THE ROACH EXTERMINATOR #1

You will need the following ingredients:

> $1/2$ *Pound of borax*
> 30 *Ounces of powdered sugar*
> $1/2$ *Ounce cocoa powder*
> 1 *Ounces of sodium chloride*

Place all the ingredients into a medium plastic container and mix thoroughly. The bug poison should be sprinkled around wherever the problem exists. This is harmful to pets and children and should be used with caution.

THE ROACH EXTERMINATOR #2

You will need the following ingredients:

$^1/_2$ Pound of borax
  2 Pounds of powdered sugar (10X)
$^1/_2$ Ounce of cocoa powder
  1 Ounce of sodium fluoride (from pharmacy)

Place all the ingredients in a small bucket and mix thoroughly. Sprinkle areas where the roaches frequent. Keep out of reach of children and pets.

THE ROACH EXTERMINATOR #3

You will need the following ingredients:

$^1/_2$ Cup of all-purpose flour
$^1/_8$ Cup of granulated sugar (any will do)
$^1/_4$ Cup of lard
  8 Ounces of boric acid
     Cool tap water

Place all the ingredients into a small bowl, blend thoroughly, and form into small balls of dough. Place 1–3 dough balls into a small plastic bag and place where the roach problem exists. This is toxic and needs to be kept out of reach of children and animals.

ROACH & ANT REPELLENT

You will need the following ingredients:

  1 Cup of borax
$^1/_4$ Cup of crushed fresh black pepper
$^1/_4$ Cup of crushed bay leaves

Place the ingredients in jar with a well-sealed lid and shake well. Sprinkle a small amount of the mixture in the corners of cupboards and drawers. You should never see another cockroach or ant ever again.

GETTING RID OF FLIES & FLEAS

FLY ELIMINATOR

You will need the following ingredients:

- 1¹/₂ Ounces of formalin
- 6 Ounces of granulated sugar
- 1 Gallon of cold tap water
- 1 Spray bottle

Place all the ingredients in a 1-gallon container and mix thoroughly. Fill a small spray bottle and spray the solution on the windowsills. Dead flies will start appearing very shortly. Keep out of reach of children.

FLYPAPER #1

You will need the following ingredients:

- 1 Tablespoon of brown sugar
- 1 Tablespoon of granulated sugar
- ¹/₄ Cup of an inexpensive maple syrup
- 1 Brown paper bag
- 1 Cookie sheet

Place all the ingredients in a small bowl and mix thoroughly. Cut 8-inch strips, (about 2 inches wide) from a brown paper bag and place them on the cookie sheet. Pour the mixture over the strips and allow them to soak overnight. Hang the strips where needed.

FLYPAPER #2

You will need the following ingredients:

- 9 Parts rosin
- 3 Parts canola oil
- 1 Part honey

Place all the ingredients into a saucepan and melt together, stirring well, and apply to the paper while still warm. Cut long strips of paper, fold them in half and staple the ends together so that they will be strong. Size the paper with shellac or varnish to prevent the mixture from spreading too far.

FLYPAPER #3

You will need the following ingredients:

    1 Ounce of Venice turpentine
    4 Ounces of rosin
    1 Ounce of castor oil
    1 Ounce of granulated sugar

Place all the ingredients into a double boiler and mix well, then apply to paper prepared in the same manner as in Flypaper #2. Using a brush, apply the solution while it is still warm.

FLYING INSECT POTPOURRI

You will need the following ingredients:

    $^1/_2$ Cup of pennyroyal
    1 Cup of southernwood
    $1^1/_2$ Cups of lavender flowers
    $1^1/_2$ Cups rosemary
    $^1/_2$ Cup of spearmint
    3 Tablespoons of orris root
    $^1/_2$ Cup of santolina
    $^1/_4$ Cup of tansy
    8 Yellow tulips (dried well)
    $^1/_4$ Cup of mugwort
    $^1/_4$ Cup of cedarwood chips (fresh as possible)

Place all the ingredients into a container and blend well and place into a few potpourri baskets around the house. The aroma is pleasant—except to flying insects.

FLEA CONTROL

You will need the following ingredients:

    1 Pound of diatomaceous earth (from nursery)
    8 Ounces of table salt
    2 Ounces of peppermint powder

Place the ingredients into a shaker. The shaker should have a sealed cap for mixing and another cap with holes for sprinkling. Sprinkle the powder (try not to inhale the mixture) on carpets where there may be a flea problem and allow it to stand for 1 hour before thoroughly vacuuming it up. Keep kids and pets off the carpet until it has been well vacuumed.

FLEA-ELIMINATOR FLOOR CLEANER
You will need the following ingredients:

1 *Tablespoon of liquid dish soap*
4 *Lemons (sliced thin)*
5 *Drops of pennyroyal (from health food store)*
1 *Gallon very warm water*

Place the sliced lemons in a medium saucepan, cover with cold tap water, and simmer on low heat for 1 hour. Remove the juice from the lemons and strain well. Place the juice into a bucket and add the soap, pennyroyal, and water. Mix the solution very well before applying with a damp sponge mop. Allow the floor to dry before rinsing with a clean, damp, sponge mop.

RODENT, GOPHER, & MOLE CONTROL

A TUNNELING NUISANCE

Moles are great at tunneling with the powerful claws on their front feet. They prefer to eat insects, but when the insects are intermingled with the root system of a plant, they will eat both the insect and the plant's roots. Their favorite bug is the grub, and if you can control the grub population in your yard, you will probably be able to control the mole population. Spraying your yard in early spring for fleas will eliminate the majority of the grub population and reduce the overall number of insects for the moles to feed on. Many different methods have been tried to remove moles including: smoke bombs, high-pressure water, poisons, rat bait, hand grenades, and dynamite. The following preparation works better than all of these put together.

MICE, GOPHERS & MOLES
The following ingredients will be need:

1 *Teaspoon of oil of peppermint*
1 *Teaspoon of chili powder*
$1/2$ *Ounce of Tabasco sauce*
1 *Pint of cold tap water*
Cotton balls

Mix together all ingredients (except the cotton balls) in a medium bowl. Place about 10 drops of the mixture on a cotton ball and place the cotton ball anywhere a rodent problem exists or drop it down a gopher or mole hole. Rodents are allergic to peppermint and spicy peppers.

WATCH 'EM RUN

You will need the following ingredients:

> 1   *Ounce of peppermint oil*
> $1/4$ *Ounce of cayenne pepper*

Place the ingredients in a small bowl and mix. Dip a cotton ball in the mixture and drop the cotton ball down the gopher or mole hole. You will never see those critters again.

GOPHER & MOLE KILLER

You will need the following ingredients:

> 4   *Ounce of powdered seaweed*
> 2   *Ounces of powdered vitamin D₃*
> 2   *Ounces of any vegetable powder*

Place all the ingredients in a small plastic container and mix well. Rodents have difficulty regulating their calcium absorption and the vitamin will eventually kill them off. To use, place a small amount of the mixture inside any vegetable (a potato, for example) by cutting out a small plug, inserting the mixture, and replacing the plug. Drop the vegetable down the gopher or mole hole.

PLUGGING UP THE MOUSE HOLE

You will need the following ingredients:

> $1^{1}/2$ *Cups of asphalt*
> $1^{1}/3$ *Cups of kerosene (flammable)*
> $1/2$ *Teaspoon cayenne pepper*

Place the asphalt and kerosene in a safe container and mix well, then add the cayenne pepper to form a smooth paste. Seal the hole with the mixture and the rodents will not use it ever again.

RODENT POISON THAT IS HARMLESS TO HUMANS
You will need the following ingredients:

    2   Ounces of barium carbonate
    1/2 Ounce of granulated sugar
    1/2 Pound of bread crumbs

Place all the ingredients into a bowl and mix well. Add a small amount of water to dampen the mixture and allow it to be made into small balls that can be placed out for the rodents.

GETTING RID OF MOTHS

MOTH-PAPER
You will need the following ingredients:

    4   Parts naphthalene
    8   Parts paraffin wax

Place the ingredients into a medium saucepan on low heat and melt the wax. Mix the solution thoroughly and brush it onto a piece of thick paper while the solution is still warm. The chemical will attract and kill moths. Keep out of reach of children and pets.

MOTH REPELLENT
You will need the following ingredients. (All herbs may be purchased at a health food store):

    4   Teaspoons of orris root powder
    1   Cup of wormwood
    1/2 Cup of lavender
    1 1/2 Cup of yarrow
    1   Cup of mint
    10   Drops of oil of cloves
    1   Cup cedar chips
    10   Bay leaves
    1   Tablespoon whole cloves
    3   Clothespins or bag clip
    1   Stainless steel fork

Place the orris root powder in a small bowl and add the oil of cloves, then mix well with the stainless steel fork, crushing all lumps. Place all the other herbs in a brown paper bag and shake to mix. Add the oil and orris root to the bag and shake well to mix. Seal the bag with the clothes-pins or a bag clip and place it in a dry, cool location for 2 weeks. After the herb mixture has mellowed, place a portion in a number of old socks and hang them up in the closets. You will never see another moth, they will be fighting to get in next door.

GETTING RID OF SNAILS

SLUGGING IT OUT WITH SNAILS

A snail's favorite plant is the pansy. They feed at night and are easy to track since they leave a trail of slime. Snails are hermaphrodites, which means that they contain both the male and female sex organs and do not need another snail to mate. Their breeding seasons are spring and fall. They love moist, dark places—this is where they breed. Plain beer seems to attract them and when they consume it, it dries them out, killing them.

SLIPPERY GUNK FOR SNAILS
You will need the following ingredients:

    10 Ounces Vaseline
     8 Ounces castor oil
     1 Ounce cayenne pepper
     1 Ounce Tabasco sauce

Place the Vaseline and the castor oil in a medium plastic container and mix. Add the pepper and Tabasco to give it a real boost. This mixture works great if placed on the trunk of a plant.

SNAILS LOVE BEER

You will need the following ingredients:

1¼ Tablespoons of brewers yeast
1 Quart of very cheap beer
1 Quart of apple cider vinegar
1 Tablespoon of Jungle Rain
1 Cup of warm tap water
2 Tablespoons of granulated sugar
One-gallon bottle

Place the cheap beer and vinegar in the gallon bottle and shake. Dissolve the sugar in the warm water. Add the sugar-water and the brewers yeast to the beer and vinegar solution and mix. Add the Jungle Rain, mix well, and pour into small lids or holders that can easily be placed where the snails frequent. This will attract every snail in the neighborhood and do them all in.

WORMS

CABBAGE WORM CURE

You will need the following ingredients:

½ Cup of table salt
1 Cup of all-purpose flour

Place the ingredients in a small dish and mix well. Sprinkle the powder on the plants early in the morning when the plants still have some dew on them.

MEALYBUG KILLER SPRAY

You will need the following ingredients:

2 Tablespoons of light corn oil
2 Tablespoons of liquid dish soap
1 Gallon of cold tap water

Place all the ingredients in a medium bucket and mix well. Place a small amount in a sprayer and spray the plants that have the mealy bugs on them. Give the bugs a good squirt or two.

JAPANESE BEETLES

AN UNWELCOME VISITOR

The Japanese beetle migrated to the United States around the turn of the century, probably in the root system of a plant. They are not fussy eaters and will consume almost any plant they come upon. Their favorites, however, are rose bushes, purple plum trees, cherry trees, and myrtle. Most beetles lay their eggs in the grass and one excellent method of reducing or eliminating the beetle problem is to treat the grass with a killer in early spring before they hatch.

BEETLE ELIMINATOR

You will need the following ingredients:

    2   Pounds of hydrated lime (use with caution)
    5   Ounces of alum
    10 Gallons of cool tap water

Place the water in a large bucket and slowly add the other ingredients while stirring. Place the solution in a sprayer and spray the tops and bottoms of leaves.

ANIMAL REPELLENTS

DEER DETERRENT #1

You will need the following ingredients:

    1   Tablespoon of cayenne pepper
    3   Tablespoons of kelp
    3   Tablespoons of liquid hand soap
    1/2 Teaspoon of oil of peppermint
    1   Pint of warm water

Place all the ingredients into a medium bowl and mix well. Be careful not to get the cayenne pepper in your eyes. Place the mixture into a spray bottle and spray the areas where the deer frequent. Do not use on plants that you will be consuming.

DEER DETERRENT #2

You will need the following ingredients:

1   *Tablespoons of dried blood (garden supply house)*
4   *Cloves of powdered garlic*
2   *Gallons of cool tap water*

Place the water into a bucket and add the dried blood; mix well. Place a portion of the mixture into a sprayer and spray the area that the deer frequent. Use sparingly, since this formula is high in nitrogen and may burn plants. This formula keeps rabbits away, too.

TERMITES

DOWN WITH THE QUEEN

Termites are really not bad insects. They are the best wood recyclers around and will turn a dead log into food for many other insects. Unfortunately, they are not fussy where they find their wood and your home is a handy source of food. The queen termite is the key to the termite "swarm." One method of killing the queen is to mix up a batch of her favorite delicacy—a small amount of grape jelly, some canned cat food, and a teaspoon of boric acid. The workers will not eat a delicacy of this magnitude, but bring it back to the queen as a treat.

TERMITE PROTECTION

You will need the following ingredients:

1   *Cup of paradichlorobenzene (moth crystals, very toxic)*
8   *Cups of denatured alcohol (any type)*

Place the ingredients into a container and mix well. This formula is for outside use only and should be mixed outside wearing a mask. Brush at least two coats onto exposed wood surfaces. There will be an odor, which cannot be helped. This treatment, however, is very effective.

Chapter 8

Formulas
For Pets

S. BEAN

FORMULAS FOR PETS

MY DOG HAS CAT FLEAS

The most common flea is the "cat flea," which can be found on your dog. It is best to treat areas that fleas may frequent before you have a problem, because afterwards it is very hard to get rid of them. The flea cycle is as follows: the fleas jump on your pet and have a warm blood meal (if your pet is not available, they'll take you); then they mate and lay eggs (they are not fussy about where they lay them); the hundreds of eggs hatch in 2–3 weeks, releasing small caterpillar-like larvae (which feed on almost any organic matter they find); then the larvae spin cocoons and enter the pupae stage (the flea cannot be killed while in the cocoon since no chemical spray can penetrate it.); the eggs hatch and you have more fleas. Treating your yard is one of the best methods of controlling a flea population. Professional help is usually needed for bad infestations.

FLEA SHAMPOO FOR PETS #1
You will need the following ingredients:

1 Cup Castile soap (liquid)
$1/8$ Ounce of essential oil of pine
$1/8$ Ounce of essential rose oil

Place all the ingredients into a jar with a lid and shake to mix well. Add the mixture to your pet's bath water and the fleas will be very unhappy.

FLEA SHAMPOO FOR PETS #2
You will need the following ingredients:

$1/2$ Cup oleic acid
$1/4$ Cup of triethanolamine (from pharmacy)
$4 1/2$ Cups of kerosene (flammable)

Place all the ingredients into a container and mix well. Use this solution in place of soap. Place the pet in a bath of water and shampoo the pet with a small amount of the solution.

PET'S BEDDING FLEA ELIMINATOR
You will need the following ingredients:

$1/2$ Cup of pennyroyal
2 Tablespoons of dried thyme
2 Tablespoons of dried wormwood
2 Tablespoons of dried rosemary

Place the herbs in a food processor and powder. Open a seam of your pet's pillow, insert the herbs, and sew up the seam, making sure that the powder is as evenly distributed as possible.

KEEP FLEAS OFF PETS

You will need the following ingredients:

 1   Tablespoon of mineral oil
 1   Cup of kerosene
 1   Tablespoon of castor oil
 2   Teaspoons of eucalyptus oil
 1   Cup of trichloroethylene

Place all the ingredients into a container and mix well. Mix the solution with an equal amount of water before placing into a spray bottle and spraying on the pet. Try $1/2$ cup of the solution in $1/2$ cup of water and mix well. This should be enough for most pets. Make sure to shake the solution well before each use.

BASIC PET SHAMPOO

You will need the following ingredients:

 $1/2$ Cup of Castile soap (grated)
 $2^1/2$ Tablespoons of glycerin
 3   Drops of pine oil or any scent your pet prefers
 2   Tablespoons of denatured alcohol
 $1^1/2$ Cups of warm tap water

Place the soap and water in a double boiler and warm to melt the soap into the water, then add the glycerin and mix well. Remove the pan from the heat and allow the mixture to cool. As it cools, add the alcohol and the pine drops and mix well.

DIGGING DOG SPRAY

You will need the following ingredients:

1   *Clove of garlic (crushed)*
1   *Teaspoon of Tabasco sauce*
$1/2$ *Teaspoon oil of peppermint*
$1/2$ *Teaspoon of cayenne pepper*
1   *Small yellow onion (chopped fine)*
1   *Quart of warm tap water*

Place all the ingredients into a large jar with a good lid and shake well. Allow it to sit for about 8 hours before placing the solution into a spray bottle. Spray the dog's favorite digging spot. The dog will dig no more, or sneeze a lot.

MAKING EARWAX REMOVER FOR PETS

You will need the following ingredients:

$1/4$ *Cup of isopropyl alcohol*
10   *Drops of glycerin*

Place the ingredients into a small bottle and shake to mix well, then place a small amount (at room temperature) on a cotton swab and clean the pets ears, very gently. The pet will probably shake its head, which will help clean out the wax. Be careful to remove the swab if the pet shakes its head to avoid damage to the eardrum.

DOG DEODORANT

You will need the following ingredients:

1   *Large size box of baking soda (fresh)*
2   *Pounds of cornstarch*
2   *Cups of dried pennyroyal*
2   *Cups of dried lavender*
$1^1/4$ *Cups of dried rosemary*
15   *Drops of essential lemon oil*
15   *Drops of citronella oil*
20   *Drops of essential rosemary oil*
25   *Drops of essential lemon oil*
25   *Drops of essential pennyroyal oil*

Place the dried herbs in a blender and powder. Place all the ingredients into a small bucket, mix, and allow to stand in a cool, dark location for 2–3 days. Mix well and sprinkle where needed.

ANIMAL DRY BATH FOR WINTER

You will need the following ingredients:

2   *Tablespoons of trisodium phosphate (TSP)*
2   *Tablespoons of borax*
4   *Tablespoons of sodium carbonate*
12 *Tablespoons of talc*
1¹/₂ *Cups of starch*

Place all the ingredients into a container and mix well. Rub the mixture on the animal against the direction of the hair; then brush well or vacuum to remove the dry shampoo. If you would like to leave your pet smelling sweet, just add a few drops of your pet's favorite essential oil to the mixture.

FOOT CONDITIONER FOR HUNTING DOGS

You will need the following ingredients:

¹/₄ *Cup of black tea*
1 *Tablespoon of tincture of benzoin*
1 *Teaspoon of alum*
1 *Cup of cool tap water*

Place the tea and water into a glass pot (or any other that will not stain from the tannins) and boil for about 15–20 minutes—this will remove most of the tannins. Boil until only about ¹/₄ cup of the liquid is left in the pot. Strain the mixture through a piece of cheesecloth, then add the alum and benzoin and mix very well (always shake well before using). Apply the mixture to the dog's pads every day for about 2 weeks before going on a hunting trip. This will make for a happier dog.

OINTMENT FOR ANIMAL SORES & CUTS

You will need the following ingredients:

8 *Ounces of lard*
4 *Ounces of beeswax*
4 *Ounces of rosin*
¹/₂ *Ounce of carbolic acid*

Place the beeswax, lard, and rosin in a double boiler and heat while stirring until melted, then add the carbolic acid and mix thoroughly. Remove from heat and allow the ointment to cool, then store in a well-sealed container until needed.

DOGGIE TREATS

You will need the following ingredients:

1 *Cup of chicken*
1 *Cup of whole wheat flour*
2 *Cups of standard oats*
2 *Large eggs*
1¹/4 *Tablespoon of garlic powder*
1 *Tablespoon of parsley*
2 *Tablespoons of soy sauce*
¹/4 *Cup of powdered whole milk*

Place the chicken in a medium saucepan and cook in chicken fat for 15 minutes, then add a small amount of water and simmer for 35 minutes. Remove from heat and allow the chicken to cool for about 20–30 minutes. Slice the chicken into small pieces and place it along with the rest of the ingredients into a food processor and blend, but do not liquefy. Place tablespoon-sized (or larger) globs on a cookie sheet and bake at 250° F. for 40–50 minutes. Set the biscuits in the sun (out of dog's reach) for a few hours to fully dehydrate. Allow the biscuits to cool for another 12 hours before allowing your pet to devour them.

HOMEMADE DOGGIE BISCUITS

You will need the following ingredients:

³/4 *Cup of rye flour*
1³/4 *Cup of whole wheat flour*
³/4 *Cup of bulgur*
¹/2 *Cup of cornmeal*
¹/2 *Cup of Brewer's yeast (fresh from health food store)*
1 *Teaspoon of dry yeast*
¹/2 *Cup of reduced fat dry milk*
¹/4 *Cup of warm tap water*
1 *Cup of de-fatted chicken or turkey broth*
¹/4 *Cup of dried parsley*
1 *Large egg (beat with 1 tablespoon of whole milk)*

Place the warm water and dry yeast in a bowl and stir until all the yeast dissolves, then add the chicken or turkey broth. Place the flours, Brewer's yeast, bulgur, dry milk, cornmeal, and parsley in another bowl and mix well. Stir the liquid mixture into the dry mixture and mix well into a stiff dough. If the dough is too difficult to work with, add a small amount of warm water to loosen it up. Roll the dough out on a floured surface to about ¹/4 to ¹/2 inch thickness, then cut into biscuits with a cookie cutter. Place the biscuits on a cookie sheet, lightly glaze with a beaten egg, and bake at 300° F. for 40 minutes. Leave the biscuits in the oven overnight to thoroughly dry out.

CANARY FOOD

You will need the following ingredients:

    2 Ounces of dried egg yolk
    1 Ounce of powdered poppy heads
    1 Ounce of powdered cuttlefish bone
    2 Ounces of granulated sugar

Place all the ingredients into a small bowl and mix well. Store the food in a well-sealed container in a cool dry location.

PARROT GRIT

You will need the following ingredients:

    1 Teaspoon of coarse, sharp sand
    1 Teaspoon of powdered charcoal (fine)
    1 Teaspoon of ashes (filtered and clean)
    1 Teaspoon of flowers of sulfur

Place all the ingredients into a sifter and sift together. Keep a portion of the mixture in the parrot's cage at all times.

MIXED BIRDSEED

You will need the following ingredients:

    6 Ounces of canary seed
    2 Ounces of rapeseed
    1 Ounces of Maw seed
    2 Ounces of millet seed

Place all the seeds in a jar and shake well. This formula is mainly for wild birds.

MOCKINGBIRD FOOD

You will need the following ingredients:

    2 Ounces of cayenne pepper
    8 Ounces of rapeseed
   16 Ounces of hemp seed
    2 Ounces of corn meal
    2 Ounces of rice
    8 Ounces of crushed cracker
    2 Ounces of lard oil

Place the first 6 ingredients into a bowl and crush into a powder, then add the oil and blend well.

CARDINAL FOOD

You will need the following ingredients:

      8 *Ounces of sunflower seed*
    16 *Ounces of hemp seed*
    10 *Ounces of canary seed*
      8 *Ounces of wheat*
      6 *Ounces of rice*

Place all the ingredients into a bowl and grind into a powder.

Chapter 9

Holiday
Formulas

SUGARY TEA OR COFFEE STIRRER

You will need the following ingredients:

> Vegetable oil spray
> 40 One-inch diameter pieces of flavored hard candy (crushed)
> 2¹/₄ Tablespoons light corn syrup
> 28 Heavy duty plastic spoons

Place a layer of waxed paper on a cookie sheet or jellyroll pan. Spray a small saucepan with the vegetable spray and place over low heat. Add the crushed candies and corn syrup to the saucepan, heat, and stir frequently until all the candy is melted. Place the spoons on the cookie sheet with the handles resting on the rim. Carefully pour the melted candy into the bowls of the spoons and wait for the candy to harden. The spoons should be stored in an airtight container.

FLOATING NUT CANDLES

You will need the following ingredients:

> Walnut half shells
> Pure white wax
> Colored birthday candles

Place the wax into a small saucepan and melt. Pour the warm wax into the nutshells (or halved oranges or lemons) then insert the small candle as it is hardening. If the candles are too large the shell will tip over. Place the nutshells into a fancy bowl with colored water (use food coloring) for an unusual centerpiece.

WINDOW FROSTING #1

You will need the following ingredients:

> 4¹/₂ Teaspoons of Epsom salts
> 1 Cup of cheap beer

Place the beer in a medium bowl and allow the Epsom salts to fully dissolve. The mixture will foam as the salt crystals are released and will be partially dissolved.

Use a 2–3 inch paintbrush to apply the mixture to your windows in any pattern you like. You can also use a dishtowel to dab the mixture on. When the mixture dries, it will leave crystals that look like ice formed on the windowpane. The window can easily be cleaned with a damp cloth.

WINDOW FROSTING #2
You will need the following ingredients:

 3 *Ounces of magnesium sulfate*
 1 *Ounce of dextrine*
10 *Ounces of cool tap water*

Place the ingredients in the water and allow them to dissolve, mix well, and apply the solution to the windows. When the solution dries, the magnesium sulfate will crystallize and look like fine ice crystals.

WINDOW FROSTING #3 (OPAQUE)
You will need the following ingredients:

 2 *Ounces of dextrine*
 8 *Ounces of zinc vitriol*
 3 *Ounces of sulfate of magnesia*
20 *Ounces of cool tap water*

Place all the ingredients into a large container and mix well, then apply to the window. The window will have a crystallized appearance and people will not be able to see in or out.

COLORED FLAME FROM LOGS
You will need the following ingredients:

$1/2$ *Pint of methanol (denatured alcohol)*
$1/4$ *Teaspoon strontium nitrate (red flame)*
$1/4$ *Teaspoon barium nitrate (green flame)*
$1/4$ *Teaspoon table salt (yellow flame)*
$1/4$ *Teaspoon copper sulfate (blue flame)*
$1/4$ *Teaspoon copper sulfide (purple flame)*

Place the methanol into a spray bottle and add one of the chemicals listed above and mix. Spray the logs to be used and allow them to dry before lighting the fire.

> **CAUTION:** Never spray the logs while the fire is lit.
> Methanol is also poisonous.

SPRINKLE ON COLORS

You will need the following ingredients:

> *Potassium sulfate mixed with potassium nitrate (violet)*
> *Strontium chloride (red)*
> *Calcium chloride (blue)*
> *Epsom salts (white)*
> *Borax (yellow/green)*
> *Blue vitriol (green)*
> *Table salt (yellow)*

Some of the ingredients can be easily obtained at the supermarket, while others may need to be ordered from a chemical supply house or your pharmacy. Just sprinkle the chemicals on the flames for the best results.

MAKING CHRISTMAS TREES FIRE RETARDANT

You will need the following ingredients:

> 1   *Cup of ammonium sulfate (from nursery)*
> 1/2 *Cup boric acid*
> 2   *Tablespoons of borax*
> 2   *Gallon of cold tap water*
> 1   *Spray bottle*

Place all the ingredients in a bucket and mix thoroughly. Place some of the mixture in a spray bottle and spray the tree well. Use the rest of the solution to fill the tree stand in place of water.

WINEMAKING WITH A BALLOON

You will need the following ingredients:

> 3 1/2 *Cups of granulated sugar*
> 24   *Ounces of frozen grape juice*
>   *concentrate (90% thawed)*
> 1/3 *Cake of yeast (fresh)*

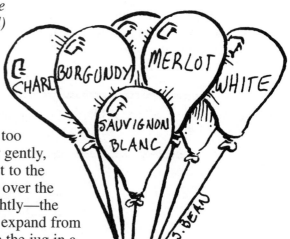

Place the slushy grape juice and the sugar in a medium bowl and mix thoroughly. Pour the mixture into a one-gallon jug. Place the yeast into a measuring cup of lukewarm water (not too hot or it will kill the little yeasties), stir gently, then add the cup of water with the yeast to the gallon of juice and sugar. Tie a balloon over the opening in the neck of the jug (very tightly—the seal must be airtight). The balloon will expand from the gas produced by fermentation. Store the jug in a cool location (not over 75° F.) for 3–5 weeks. If the balloon expands to the breaking point, release the gas and retie the balloon. When the balloon no longer expands, the wine is ready. If the wine is bottled before the balloon has finished expanding, the wine bottle may explode since the gas is still being formed. Be sure to strain the wine through a piece of cheesecloth as you pour it into the bottle to remove any residue. A cork, if available, is the best sealer. The bottle should be stored on its side in a cool, dark location.

FIREPLACE LOG STARTER

You will need the following ingredients:

> 5 Pounds of sawdust (clean)
> 1 Quart old auto oil

Place the ingredients in a safe container and mix well, then wait for at least an hour to allow complete absorption. Sprinkle a small amount around the smaller logs or twigs and then light.

DYEING EASTER EGGS

You will need the following ingredients:

> 1 Teaspoon of white vinegar per color
> 1/2 Cup of boiling water per color
> 1 Wax crayon
> 1+ Egg cartons
>   Hard-boiled eggs
>   Food coloring (different colors)

Place the boiling water in a cup with the vinegar and add the food coloring. Draw a design or name on the egg (if desired) with the wax crayon and use a spoon to place the egg in the water. Let the egg soak until the desired color is obtained. Store the eggs in the refrigerator in an egg carton lined with paper towels to absorb the excess moisture. To make different colored eggs, combine the following food colorings:

> Orange = 12 drops of yellow + 6 drops of red
> Purple = 10 drops of red + 4 drops of blue
> Rose = 15 drops of red + 5 drops of blue

HOLIDAY POTPOURRI

You will need the following ingredients:

$1^1/2$ *Cup of red rose petals*
$^1/2$ *Cup of white rose petals*
$^1/2$ *Cup of crushed blue statice*
$^1/4$ *Cup of chamomile flowers*
$^1/4$ *Cup of eucalyptus leaves*
$^1/4$ *Cup of oak moss*
15   *Drops of essential rose oil*
5   *Drops of essential lavender oil*

Place all the dried ingredients in a large bowl and gently mix. Place a portion of the mixture in a basket or sachet, then sprinkle the essential oils over the top of the mixture. All flowers and herbs should be very dry.

IT MAKES SENSE TO MAKE INCENSE

Records trace the use of incense back 5,000 years. Incense is found in four different forms: stick, cylinder, seeds, and loose. The primary scents used for incense are derived from berries, flowers, seeds, bark, leaves, and dried spices. Some herbs may smell good when fresh or dried, but may smell somewhat unpleasant when burned. Most incense is composed of five main ingredients: a base containing wood powder, a pleasant smelling substance (frankincense, cinnamon, etc.), a glue to hold it all together (usually gum arabic), potassium nitrate (the igniter), and a fragrant liquid, such as rosewater or a brandy.

INCENSE #1

You will need the following ingredients:

1   *Ounce of orris root*
5   *Ounces of charcoal*
$^1/2$ *Ounce of saltpeter*
$^1/2$ *Ounce of gum olibanum*
1   *Ounce of gum sandalwood*

Place all the ingredients in a bowl and mix with a small amount of mucilage to hold it all together, then form into a small cone and place the cone in an ashtray or incense burner and light the tip.

INCENSE #2

You will need the following ingredients:

$^1/_2$ Ounce of sassafras
$2^1/_2$ Ounces of benzoin
6 Ounces of charcoal
$^1/_4$ Ounce of potassium nitrate

The directions are the same as for Incense #1.

Chapter 10

Children's
Play Formulas

S.BEAN

> **CAUTION:** The following formulas should be made by adults or with adult supervision. Even though the following solutions are harmless, they may result in discomfort if they get into eyes or are consumed. Most formulas are non-edible and need parental or teacher supervision. Use these formulas at your own risk and take safety precautions.

GLUE FORMULAS FOR USE BY CHILDREN

LONG-LASTING, ALL-PURPOSE PASTE

You will need the following ingredients:

> 1 *Cup of granulated sugar*
> 1 *Cup of all-purpose flour*
> 4 *Cups of boiling water*
> 1 *Cup of cold tap water*
> 1 *Tablespoon powdered alum (from pharmacy)*

Place the all-purpose flour and the granulated sugar in a medium pot and slowly add the cold water making a paste solution. Then slowly add the boiling water and stir continually, making sure there are no lumps. Bring the mixture to a boil while stirring until the mixture is thick and clear. Remove the mixture from the heat, continue stirring, and add the powdered alum. Blend well before using. If the mixture will be stored, add 1/2 teaspoon of cinnamon oil to the glue. After storage, thin with hot water to re-harden.

PLAY GLUE

You will need the following ingredients:

> 2 *Tablespoons of Karo syrup*
> 3/4 *Cup of cool tap water*
> 3/4 *Cup of ice water*
> 1/2 *Cup of cornstarch (fresh)*
> 1 *Teaspoon of white vinegar (5%)*

Place the Karo syrup, white vinegar, and cool water in a saucepan and mix well, then heat on medium until the mixture begins to become somewhat solid (rolling ball state). In a medium bowl, blend the cornstarch and ice water together, then slowly add this mixture to the syrup mixture while stirring continuously. Remove from the heat and allow the glue to cool for at least 8–10 hours before using it. Store the glue in a well-sealed container. If the glue becomes too hard, just heat for a short period of time.

STANDARD PAPER PASTE

You will need the following ingredients:

  2/3   *Cup all-purpose flour*
  2   *Cups tap water*
  4   *Tablespoons granulated sugar*
  1/2   *Teaspoon of cinnamon oil*

Place the all-purpose flour and the granulated sugar in a medium saucepan and gradually add the water while continually stirring to avoid lumps. Continue cooking over low heat until the mixture is clear. Remove the mixture from the heat and slowly add the cinnamon oil while continuing to stir. This paste does not need to be refrigerated and will keep for 2–3 weeks.

COLLAGE AND PAPIER MÂCHÉ PASTE

You will need the following ingredients:

  1/2   *Cup of granulated sugar*
  1/2   *Cup of all-purpose flour*
  3 1/2   *Cups of tap water*
  1   *Teaspoon powdered alum*
  1/2   *Teaspoon of cinnamon oil*

Place the flour, sugar, and alum in a medium saucepan and gradually add 1 3/4 cups of water while continually stirring to eliminate lumps. The mixture should be boiled until it is clear and lump-free. Add the remaining water and the cinnamon oil and continue to stir until smooth and blended well. Will store for 3–4 months at room temperature.

GLUE FOR PAPER LABELS

You will need the following ingredients:

  1   *Ounce unflavored gelatin*
  1   *Tablespoon cold tap water*
  3   *Tablespoons boiling water*
  1/2   *Teaspoon white peppermint extract (or other flavor)*
  2   *Drops boric acid in solution*

Place a small pot on the stove and boil the 3 tablespoons of water. Place the cold water in a small bowl and sprinkle the gelatin on top. Pour the gelatin mixture into the boiling water and stir continually until it completely dissolves. Add the flavoring and the boric acid solution and blend all the ingredients together. Apply the glue with a small brush to the back of any paper item or stamp, allow it to dry and just moisten when you wish to use it. The glue should be stored in a jar with a good sealing lid. If the glue becomes hard, just warm slightly until it softens.

PAINTS

SIMPLE FINGER PAINTS

You will need the following ingredients:

    1   Cup of quality liquid starch
    2   Cups of powdered tempera
        Cold tap water

Place the starch and tempera in a medium bowl and mix thoroughly until the mixture is smooth and creamy. Slowly add enough water to make a somewhat thick solution, mixing continuously. Place the mixture into dishes and add additional color if desired.

FINGER PAINT FROM SALT AND FLOUR

You will need the following ingredients:

    2   Cups of all-purpose flour
    2   Teaspoons of table salt
    3   Cups of cold tap water
    2   Cups of very hot tap water
        Food coloring

Place the salt and flour in a medium saucepan and gradually add the cold water. Use an eggbeater to blend the mixture until it is very smooth, then add the hot water and place over medium heat until the mixture is boiling and appears smooth. Remove the mixture from the heat and stir in the food coloring.

PAINTING ON CEMENT

You will need the following ingredients:

    $1/2$ Cup of cold tap water
    $1/2$ Cup of cornstarch (fresh)
    5–7   Drops of food coloring

Place the ingredients into a container and blend well. This paint can be used on any type of smooth, solid surface and can easily be removed with cold tap water or a garden hose.

FINGER PAINTS FROM JELL-O

You will need the following ingredients:

> 1   *Package of Jell-O*
>   *Boiling water*

Prepare the Jell-O according to the directions but add only enough water to make a loose goo that can be used for finger painting.

FINGER PAINTING GOO

You will need the following ingredients:

> $^1/_2$ *Cup all-purpose flour*
> 2 *Cups cold tap water*
> 1 *Tablespoon glycerin*
> 5 *Small jars*
>   *Food coloring*

Place the flour and $^1/_2$ cup of water in a medium saucepan and mix until it becomes a paste. Add the remaining water and heat slowly, stirring continuously, until the mixture becomes thick and clear. Allow it to cool, then add the glycerin. If the mixture is too thick, add additional water as needed. Pour the mixture into the small jars, then add a few drops of food coloring to each jar and stir. Poster paint may be used instead of food coloring if you so desire.

FINGER PAINTS FROM KOOL-AID

You will need the following ingredients:

> 2 *Cups of all-purpose flour*
> 2 *Packages of unsweetened Kool-Aid (any flavor)*
> $^1/_2$ *Cup of table salt*
> 3 *Cup of boiling water*
> 3 *Tablespoons of corn oil (any vegetable oil)*

Place the salt, flour, and Kool-Aid into a bowl and slowly add the oil and boiling water while mixing well.

RADIANT POSTER PAINT

You will need the following ingredients:

> 1 *Teaspoon of household liquid starch*
> 2 *Cup of cool tap water*
> $^1/_2$ *Cup of all-purpose flour*
> 5 *Tablespoons of tempera paint (powder)*
> 4 *Tablespoons of cool tap water*

Place the 2 cups of water and the flour into a saucepan and heat on low while stirring until the solution has been blended smooth. As soon as the solution thickens, remove it from the heat and allow it to cool. Then place the solution into a medium bowl. In another bowl combine the tempera paint, 4 tablespoons of water, and the liquid starch and blend well, then add the mixture to the flour solution and blend well. Store the paint in a well-sealed container in a cool, dry location.

VANILLA PUDDING FINGER PAINT
You will need the following ingredients:

> 1 Package of vanilla pudding
> Food coloring (if desired)

Prepare pudding according to the directions on the package; then add food coloring as desired. Finger painting may be done on a plate and then consumed.

DETERGENT PAINT
You will need the following ingredients:

> 1 Cup of powdered tempera paint
> 4 Tablespoons of a quality liquid starch
> 2 Teaspoons of liquid dishwashing detergent
> Cold tap water

Place the powdered tempera, liquid starch, and liquid dish detergent in a medium bowl and mix well. Slowly add the water mix until the mixture appears creamy and has a smooth texture.

STANDARD FINGERPAINT
The following ingredients are needed:

> $1/2$ Cup cornstarch (fresh)
> 1 Cup cold tap water
> 1 Envelope of unflavored gelatin
> 2 Cups of very hot water
> $1/2$ Cup of liquid detergent
> Food coloring

Combine $1/4$ cup of the cold water and the gelatin in a small bowl and mix well, then allow it to stand. Place the cornstarch and the rest of the cold water in a small saucepan and cook on low heat until fully dissolved. Add the very hot water and cook on medium heat, stirring continually, until the mixture is clear and starts to boil. Remove the mixture from the heat and add the gelatin mixture and the liquid detergent. Continue stirring until there are no lumps. Allow the mixture to cool completely. Place the finger paints in 4–5 small jars or containers and add food coloring to each.

WATER COLOR PAINT WITH SCRATCH & SNIFF KOOL-AID AROMA

You will need the following ingredients:

$1^1/2$ Tablespoon of unsweetened Kool-Aid (5 different colors)
$1^1/2$ Tablespoon of warm tap water
   5 Small baby food jars or small plastic containers

Place the water into the 5 jars or small plastic containers, then add the Kool-Aid and mix well. Use the solution to paint pictures, then allow the pictures to dry at least 6–8 hours. When the painted areas are scratched, the aroma of that flavor will be released.

WATER COLOR PAINT

You will need the following ingredients:

   1 Tablespoon white vinegar
   1 Tablespoon of cornstarch (fresh)
   2 Tablespoons of baking soda (fresh)
$1/4$ Teaspoon glycerin
      Small metal or plastic pans or trays
      Food coloring

In a medium bowl, mix the white vinegar with the baking soda. The mixture will bubble. When the bubbling stops, add the cornstarch and the glycerin, mix well then pour the mixture into the small containers. Add food coloring to each jar—colors may be mixed to form different colors.

ALL-PURPOSE FLOUR PAINT

You will need the following ingredients:

   2 Cups of all-purpose flour
$3/4$ Cup of cold tap water
   2 Tablespoons of liquid dish washing soap
      Food coloring or powdered tempera paint

Place the all-purpose flour, liquid dish soap, and water in a medium bowl and blend until the mixture is the consistency of thick paste. Add the food coloring or powdered tempera to color the paint.

STARCH PAINT

You will need the following ingredients:

   1 Cup of dry laundry starch
   1 Cup of a mild hand soap powder
   1 Cup of cold tap water
   2 Tablespoons of powdered tempera

Place the starch, soap powder, and powdered tempera in a medium bowl and add the water until the mixture has medium consistency. More water may be added if needed—if the mixture is too thick it will not be useable.

HIGH-GLOSS MILK PAINT

You will need the following ingredients:

> 3/4 Cup of canned condensed milk
> 1 1/4 Tablespoon of tempera paint (liquid)

Place the ingredients into a container and blend well. This produces a very shiny and reflective color when dry. Food coloring may also be used if desired, however, the paint will not be quite as glossy.

SOAP CHIP FINGERPAINT

You will need the following ingredients:

> 1 Cup of liquid laundry starch
> 1/2 Cup of Castile soap (grated)
> 6 Cups of warm tap water
>   Food coloring

Place just enough warm water in a bowl to dissolve the soap, making sure there are no lumps. Add this mixture to the starch and remaining water and mix well, then store the mixture in a covered plastic container. Food coloring may be added as desired.

ANYWHERE ON THE BODY PAINT #1

You will need the following ingredients:

> 1/4 Cup baby lotion
> 2 Tablespoons of liquid detergent
> 1–2 Tablespoons of tempera paint

Place the lotion, detergent, and tempera paint in a small bowl and mix thoroughly. Additional tempera may be needed to achieve the level of color desired. This paint washes off very easily.

ANYWHERE ON THE BODY PAINT #2

You will need the following ingredients:

> 4 Tablespoons of cornstarch (fresh)
> 2 Tablespoon of cold cream
> 2 Tablespoon of warm tap water
> 4 Drops of red food coloring

Place the cornstarch and cold cream into a small container and blend well, then slowly add the water, mixing continuously, until the solution is blended smooth. Add the food coloring and mix. If desired, place a smaller portion into different containers and add different food colors.

SOAP PAINT

You will need the following ingredients:

    1   *Cup of laundry soap (flakes)*
  1/4 *Cup of cool tap water*
  1/3 *Cup of laundry starch (liquid)*

Place all the ingredients into a container and blend thoroughly for at least 3–4 minutes. Food coloring may be added if desired.

INDIAN FACE PAINT

You will need the following ingredients:

   3 *Teaspoons of solid shortening*
 2^1/$_2$ *Teaspoons of cornstarch*
   1 *Teaspoon of all-purpose flour*
   4 *Drops of glycerin*
   5 *Cold cream cotton swabs*
      Food coloring

Place the shortening, cornstarch, and all-purpose flour into a medium bowl and blend thoroughly, forming a paste. Add the glycerin while stirring continually until the solution is spreadable and has no lumps. Slowly add the food coloring until the desired color is achieved. The cold cream swabs should be used to trace a design on the child's face before painting. The paint will be easy to remove with a mild soap and water solution.

FUN FACE PAINT

You will need the following ingredients:

1¹/₂ Teaspoons of cold cream
1 Teaspoon of cornstarch
¹/₂ Teaspoon of warm tap water
    Glitter as desired
    Food coloring as desired

Place all the ingredients into a small container and blend well, then add enough water to prepare a thin paint that can be applied with a small paintbrush. Glitter may be applied while the paint is still damp.

PUFFER-UPPER PAINT

You will need the following ingredients:

1 Cup of all-purpose flour
1 Cup of table salt
1 Cup of cool tap water
    Tempera paint as desired

Place all the ingredients into a bowl and mix well, then add enough tempera paint to color as desired. Place the mixture into a plastic squeeze bottle and squeeze a design and allow it to dry. The paint will puff up when dry.

PAINT FROM POWDERED MILK

You will need the following ingredients:

¹/₂ Cup of powdered non-fat milk
¹/₂ Cup of cool tap water
    Tempera paint (powder)

Place the milk and the water into a container and mix until the milk dissolves, then add only as much tempera as needed. This paint does not keep well and should be stored in a well-sealed jar in the refrigerator. It will dry quickly and produce a glossy, somewhat opaque finish. After you mix the powdered milk and water, allow the mixture to stand in the refrigerator for 3–4 hours or it may be somewhat grainy.

WORKABLE PUTTY

You will need the following ingredients:

2 Tablespoons of white school glue
1 Tablespoon of a liquid starch
    Food coloring

Place the liquid starch in a small bowl and add the white glue. Allow the mixture to stand for about 5 minutes before adding the food coloring.

Blend all the ingredients thoroughly, making sure all the starch has been absorbed and the color is evenly dispersed. Allow the mixture to set overnight. This will produce putty that will pick up pictures and even bounce.

GELATIN PUTTY

You will need the following ingredients:

0.3 *Ounce package of unsweetened gelatin*
2 *Cups of all-purpose flour*
1 *Cup of table salt*
4 *Tablespoons of cream of tartar*
2 *Cups of boiling water*
2 *Tablespoons of corn oil*

Place the flour, gelatin, salt, and cream of tartar in a saucepan and mix well, then add the boiling water and the corn oil and mix thoroughly. Place the pan over medium heat and stir until the mixture forms a ball. Allow the mixture to cool slightly then remove the ball and place it on a piece of waxed paper. Let the ball cool completely before making objects. Store the leftovers in a well-sealed container.

CHILDREN'S DOUGH RECIPE

You will need the following ingredients:

3 *Cups of cornstarch (fresh)*
4 *Cups of baking soda (fresh)*
2^1/$_2$ *Cups of cold tap water*

Place the cornstarch and baking soda into a medium saucepan and blend well. Add the cold water and place over medium heat for 5–7 minutes or until the mixture starts to thicken. Remove the pan from the heat, cover the pan with a piece of damp paper towel, and allow the mixture to cool before using.

OIL FUNDOUGH #1

You will need the following ingredients:

4 *Cups of all-purpose flour*
1 *Cup of table salt*
3 *Tablespoons of corn oil*
1 *Cup of cold water*

Place the flour and salt in a medium bowl and mix well. Blend in the corn oil and water to make dough with a pliable consistency. Add more water, a small amount at a time, if needed. Store the dough in a well-sealed plastic container in the refrigerator.

OIL FUNDOUGH #2

You will need the following ingredients:

2 Cups of all-purpose flour
1 Cup of table salt
2 Cups of cold tap water
2 Tablespoons of corn oil
1 Package of Kool-Aid powder

Place all the ingredients into a medium saucepan and place on low heat, stirring continually until the mixture forms a semi-solid mass. Remove from heat and allow it to cool. Store in a well-sealed container in the refrigerator.

CORNMEAL FUNDOUGH

You will need the following ingredients:

$1^1/2$ Cups of cornmeal (fresh)
1 Cup of table salt
$1^1/2$ Cups of all-purpose flour
1 Cup of cold tap water

Place all the ingredients in a medium bowl and blend them together into a dough. Additional water may be added if the mixture is not pliable enough. The dough will keep for 4-6 weeks if stored in an airtight plastic container.

REAL SIMPLE DOUGH

You will need the following ingredients:

4 Cups of all-purpose flour
1 Cup of table salt
$1^1/2$ Cups of warm tap water

Place the all-purpose flour and the salt in a large bowl and slowly add the warm water while mixing the solution with your hands. Lightly flour a piece of waxed paper and place it on the counter. Knead the dough for about 10 minutes or until it is pliable and smooth. Wrap the dough in the waxed paper and place it in a well-sealed plastic container. Use as needed.

FROSTING FUNDOUGH

You will need the following ingredients:

1 Can of white frosting mix
$1^1/2$ Cup of powdered sugar (10X)
1 Cup of smooth peanut butter

Place all the ingredients into a medium bowl and blend well into dough that can be used for modeling.

COOKED FUNDOUGH

You will need the following ingredients:

  1   Cup of all-purpose flour
  1   Cup of granulated sugar
  1   Cup of cold water
  5   Cups of boiling water

Place the sugar, flour, and water into a medium saucepan and mix. Add the boiling water slowly and cook for 6 minutes while stirring constantly. Allow the mixture to cool before using. This is very pliable dough, but will not keep well.

SUPER FUNDOUGH

You will need the following ingredients:

  $1/4$ Cup of corn oil
  3   Cups of all-purpose flour
  1   Cup of cold tap water
  1   Cup of table salt
  3   Tablespoons of white
         vinegar

Place all the ingredients into a large bowl and blend well. More water may be added if needed to provide a workable consistency. This dough will keep for 2–3 months if stored in a plastic bag. Dampen the dough occasionally keep the dough workable.

EXPERIMENTAL GUNK

You will need the following ingredients:

  $1^1/2$ Cups of cornstarch
  $2/3$ Cup of cool tap water
  2   Drops of red food coloring

Place the water and the food coloring in a container, then very slowly sprinkle in the cornstarch without mixing. Allow the solution to remain still for about 3 minutes, then grab a handful and form it into a ball. The heat and friction from your hands will cause the solution to become a solid. When you release it, it will return to a liquid state.

COFFEE GROUNDS DOUGH

You will need the following ingredients:

> 2 Cups of dry coffee grounds
> 1¹/2 Cups of cornmeal (fresh)
> ¹/2 Cup of table salt
> Warm tap water

Place the coffee grounds, cornmeal, and salt in a medium bowl and add just enough warm water to moisten well. Work the mixture with your hands until it becomes a workable dough. Store in a well-sealed plastic container.

EDIBLE FUNDOUGH

You will need the following ingredients:

> 1 Cup of peanut butter (not chunky or natural)
> 1 Small can of ready-to-use frosting
> 1¹/2 Cups of powdered sugar (10X)

Place all the ingredients into a medium bowl and mix thoroughly. If the mixture becomes too thick and not workable, add a small amount of cold water to loosen it up. Store in the refrigerator in a plastic container. Molds may be used to make different shapes and figures. All items made will be edible.

MILK AND HONEY FUNDOUGH

You will need the following ingredients:

> 1 Cup of pure honey
> 2 Cups of powdered low-fat milk
> 1 Cup of smooth peanut butter (not natural)

Place all the ingredients in a medium bowl and mix thoroughly by hand until a workable dough is formed. If needed, powdered milk can be added if the dough is too thin, or a small amount of cold water if it is too thick. Corn syrup can be used to replace the honey.

OATMEAL FUNDOUGH

You will need the following ingredients:

> 1 Cup of all-purpose flour
> 2 Cups of cooked instant oatmeal
> ¹/4 Cup of cold tap water

Mix all the ingredients together in a medium bowl, forming an easily molded dough. While this dough is edible, the taste leaves a lot to be desired and may not appeal to all children.

GRANOLA FUNDOUGH

You will need the following ingredients:

1   *Cup of plain granola*
1/4   *Cup of smooth peanut butter (not natural)*
1/4   *Cup of brown sugar*

Place the peanut butter and brown sugar into a small bowl and mix with your hands. If the mixture is too sticky, add more brown sugar to reduce the stickiness. If the mixture becomes too dry, add a little more peanut butter. Add as much granola as desired.

HONEY OF A FUNDOUGH

You will need the following ingredients:

1   *Tablespoon of pure honey*
1   *Cup of non-fat skim milk*
1/2   *Cup of creamy peanut butter (no chunks)*
1   *Quart-sized plastic zip-lock bag*

Place the honey, dry milk, and peanut butter into the plastic bag, seal the bag well, and knead the ingredients into a workable dough. After playing with the dough, it is best to discard it, since the peanut butter will not keep when mixed with dry milk.

GLUE FUNDOUGH

You will need the following ingredients:

1   *Cup of cornstarch (fresh)*
1   *Cup of all-purpose flour*
1/2   *Cup of white liquid school glue*
   Cold tap water
   Food coloring as desired

Place all the ingredients into a medium bowl and mix thoroughly, adding the water as needed to produce workable dough. This dough can be worked and molded and will dry into a hard solid.

MICROWAVE FUNDOUGH

You will need the following ingredients:

2   *Cups of all-purpose flour*
1   *Cup of table salt*
1/2   *Cup of cornstarch*
1   *Tablespoon of baking soda (fresh)*
2   *Cups of cool tap water*
1   *Tablespoon of corn oil*
3   *Drops of food coloring (any color)*

Place the dry ingredients in one bowl and the wet ingredients into another bowl and mix each separately. Combine the contents of the two bowls into one large bowl and mix well. Place the bowl in the microwave and heat on high for 3–4 minutes, stirring the mixture once every minute. Place the mixture on a board and knead into a workable dough.

JEWELRY-MAKING CLAY

You will need the following ingredients:

$^1/_2$ *Cup of table salt*
$^3/_4$ *Cup of all-purpose flour*
$^1/_2$ *Cup of cornstarch (fresh)*
    Warm tap water

Combine the salt, flour, and cornstarch in a medium bowl, then slowly add the warm water while stirring until the solution turns into an easily moldable dough. Shape the dough into small balls and pierce each ball with a toothpick to form string-able beads and allow the beads to dry completely. The beads can then be painted different colors.

GREATEST MODELING CLAY

You will need the following ingredients:

$^1/_2$ *Cup of table salt*
  1 *Cup of all-purpose flour*
  2 *Tablespoons of cream of tartar (fresh)*
$^1/_2$ *Tablespoons of corn oil*
  1 *Cup of cold tap water*
    Food coloring

Combine all the ingredients in a medium saucepan and heat over medium heat for 3 minutes. Do not overcook the mixture or allow it to burn on the bottom of the saucepan. Remove from the heat and allow the mixture to cool until it can be kneaded. Knead the clay until it is smooth; then store it in a plastic bag.

CLAY FROM DRYER LINT

You will need the following ingredients:

$^1/_2$ *Cup of all-purpose flour*
  1 *Cup of cold tap water*
$1^1/_2$ *Cups of dryer filter lint (fine, no large pieces)*
  1 *Day old newspaper*
  2 *Drops of wintergreen oil flavoring*
    Non-toxic paint

Place the dryer lint and water into a medium saucepan (make sure it is completely submerged in the water) and allow it to become fully saturated. Add the flour and stir the mixture until it is very smooth before adding the wintergreen oil flavoring. Continue to stir until the solution forms peaks and can be lifted with a spoon—this is the best consistency for modeling. Place the mixture on a piece of newspaper to cool. When the clay is cool, model the clay into any shape and allow the sculpture to dry for 3–4 days before painting it.

SAND CLAY FOR MODELING

You will need the following ingredients:

    2   Cups of clean sandbox sand
    1   Cup of cornstarch (fresh)
    1^1/$_2$ Cups of household liquid starch

Place the cornstarch and the sand in a container and mix well, then add the starch and blend. Place the mixture in a saucepan and place on medium heat while stirring continually until the mixture becomes a thick mass. Remove the saucepan from the heat and allow the modeling clay to cool before using. Knead the dough to make it more pliable before starting to work with it.

FLUBBER DUBBER #1

You will need the following ingredients:

    2^3/$_4$ Cups of warm tap water
    4   Teaspoons of borax
    2   Cups of Elmer's glue (no substitutes)
        Food coloring (as desired)

Place the glue and 1^1/$_2$ cups of warm water into a medium bowl and add food coloring as desired. In another bowl, place the borax and 1^1/$_3$ cups of warm water and mix well. Pour the glue water into the borax water—DO NOT mix. Just remove the flubber dubber and store in plastic bags. The result is a little like silly putty.

FLUBBER DUBBER #2

You will need the following ingredients:

    ^{1}/$_2$ Cup of laundry starch (liquid)
    ^{1}/$_2$ Cup of Elmer's Glue (no substitutions)
        Food coloring as desired

Place the glue in a small container and slowly add the starch while kneading with your fingers. The more you mix, the better the mixture will gel up. Add color as desired.

COTTON BALL FUNDOUGH

You will need the following ingredients:

1   Cup of all-purpose flour
2^1/$_3$ Cups of cool tap water
3   Cups of cotton balls or puffs
4   Drops of food coloring

Place very small pieces of the cotton into a small saucepan and add the water while mixing. Heat over low heat and slowly add the flour while stirring continually. When the mixture has become semi-solid remove from the heat and place the cotton fundough on a double thickness of dishtowel with one layer of paper towel underneath. As soon as the fundough has cooled, make your objects, then allow them to dry and harden for about a day. This is a common kindergarten fundough for making snowmen in the wintertime.

MISCELLANEOUS FUN STUFF

GIANT BUBBLE MIX #1

You will need the following ingredients:

1   Cup quality dishwashing liquid (a real grease-cutter)
3   Tablespoons of glycerin (from pharmacy)
10   Cups of cold tap water

Place all the ingredients in a small plastic bucket and blend well with a wooden spoon. An old bubble wand with a large opening will create ideal bubbles. If you don't have a bubble wand, you can make one by bending a hanger into a circle. The bubbles you make will be the largest you have ever seen and will retain their shape longer than the bubbles produced by most commercial products. Be careful not to make bubbles in an area where they might drift into traffic.

GIANT BUBBLE MIX #2

You will need the following ingredients:

2   Cups of Karo syrup
1   Cup of warm tap water
4   Tablespoons of liquid dishwashing soap

Place all the ingredients into a container and mix well. If the solution is too thick, add a small amount of water to thin it out.

STANDARD BUBBLE MIX

You will need the following ingredients:

1/2   *Cup of liquid dish soap*
1/2   *Cup of warm tap water*
  1   *Tablespoon of corn oil*

Place all the ingredients into a container and blend very slowly, otherwise it will bubble up too much and be hard to use.

LONG, FAT BUBBLES

You will need the following ingredients:

  1   *Cup of warm tap water*
1/4   *Cup of liquid dishwashing soap*
  1   *Teaspoon of table salt*

Place all the ingredients into a container and blend well. Make sure that all the salt is dissolved before using.

DISAPPEARING INK

You will need the following ingredients:

  1   *Laxative tablet (X-Lax or any other will do)*
  1   *Tablespoon of rubbing alcohol*
  2   *Cotton balls*
  1   *Tablespoon of household ammonia*
  1   *1 1/2–2 Tablespoon measuring spoon*

Place the laxative tablet into a very small bowl and mash it into powder using the back of a teaspoon. Place the tablespoon of alcohol into the measuring spoon and add the powdered laxative. Mix until the laxative tablet is fully dissolved then use the solution to write a message using a small, thin paintbrush. When the solution dries, the message will disappear. To read the message, slightly dampen a cotton ball in household ammonia and dab it on the area that was written on.

FLOATING APPLE SEEDS

You will need the following ingredients:

2/3   *Teaspoons of baking soda*
  1   *Tablespoon of white vinegar*
1/2   *Cup of cold tap water*
5+   *Apple seeds*

Place the water into a thin, tall glass, then add the baking soda and stir until it is dissolved. Add the apple seeds and the white vinegar and mix the solution gently. The apple seeds will rise to the top of the glass propelled by carbon dioxide bubbles. When the bubbles hit the top they will break and the apple seeds will fall down.

CHALK FOR DRAWING ON CONCRETE

You will need the following ingredients:

$3/4$ Cup of warm tap water
  3   Tablespoons of powdered tempera paint
$1^1/2$ Cups plaster of paris
      Toilet paper, gift-wrap, or paper towel cardboard tubes

Place the warm water in a medium plastic container or bowl and slowly sprinkle plaster of paris into the water until it will no longer dissolve. Blend well until the mixture is very thick. Add the tempera to the mixture and blend well. Pour the mixture into the cardboard tubes (cut the longer tubes into small ones) and gently tap the sides all the way down to get rid of any air pockets. Let the tubes dry for about 2 days. Remove the cardboard and you will have pieces of sidewalk chalk.

NEW CRAYONS FOR THE MILLENNIUM

Researchers have developed a new crayon that is made from soybeans instead of paraffin, which is a petroleum waste product. There has always been the possibility of toxic compounds in paraffin and soybean oil is an excellent substitute. Over a period of 8 years, the average child uses more than 700 crayons. There are more than two billion crayons produced every year and, up till now, none were truly biodegradable. Within five years, most paraffin-based crayons will be the crayons of the past.

CRAYONS FROM SOAP #1

You will need the following ingredients:

$1^3/4$ Cups of Ivory Snow Powder (works the best)
$1/4$ Cup of cold tap water
      Small candle molds
      Food coloring

Place the Ivory soap powder and water into a medium bowl and mix thoroughy. Add the desired food coloring (use a separate bowl for each color) and the soap powder until a pasty consistency is achieved. The mixture can then be poured into the candle molds to harden, which should take about 5–7 days. Remove the soap crayons from the molds and allow them to dry an additional 3 days before using.

CRAYONS FROM SOAP #2

You will need the following ingredients:

1   *Cup of Castile soap (grated)*
1/4   *Cup of warm tap water*
4   *Drops of food coloring*

Place all the ingredients into a container and blend until somewhat stiff, then place the mixture into a bowl with a rounded bottom and knead into a dough. Place the dough into cookie cutters or other molds and freeze for 8–10 minutes, then remove the crayons and allow them to dry until they are hard, usually 8–10 hours.

BALLOON FILLER-UPPER

You will need the following ingredients:

4   *Tablespoons of white vinegar*
1   *Teaspoon of baking soda (fresh)*
2   *Tablespoons of cold tap water*
1   *Clean plastic soda bottle*

Place the baking soda and the water in the bottle, then add the vinegar and very quickly fit the balloon over the top of the bottle. The carbon dioxide that is produced when the baking soda and vinegar combine will easily inflate the balloon. **NOTE:** Stretch a good-sized balloon a few times to make it more pliable before you add the ingredients.

HORROR MOVIE SLIME

You will need the following ingredients:

$1^1/2$ *Teaspoons of borax powder*
8   *Ounces of white school craft glue*
1   *Cup warm water*
1   *Cup cold water*
  Tempera paint, green

Place the glue and cold water into a large bowl and mix until well-blended. Add the paint gradually—just a few drops should do. Different colors may be used to make a number of weird-colored slimes.

Mix the warm water and the borax powder in a small bowl until the borax dissolves. Add the borax solution to the glue mixture and stir for 2 minutes. Knead the "slime dough" until it stretches easily and is very smooth to the touch. It is best to store the slime in an airtight container, since it dries out easily.

NO-BAKE CRAWLIES

You will need the following ingredients:

2 Tablespoons of white glue
2 Tablespoons of hot tap water
1 Envelope of unflavored gelatin
$1/2$ Tablespoon of tempera paint

Place the gelatin and hot water into a small bowl and mix well, then allow the gelatin to sit until dissolved. In another bowl, place the paint and glue and mix well. Mix the gelatin into the paint mixture and blend until the mixture is good and thick. Pour into cookie molds that resemble insects or worms and put the molds into the freezer for about 4–6 minutes or until firm. After removing the crawlies, allow them to fully dry before storing them in a plastic bag. The crawlies should have a rubbery texture.

THE DANCING WORMS

You will need the following ingredients:

5 Strands of cooked spaghetti (cut into 10–15 worms)
1 Cup of white vinegar
1 Cup of cool tap water
2 Tablespoons of baking soda
2 Drops of red food coloring
2 Drops of blue food coloring
1 Medium clear glass bowl

Mix the vinegar and water together in the bowl, then mix in the food coloring. While mixing, slowly add the baking soda. Place the spaghetti worms into the solution and watch them come to life and wiggle around in the water as if they were real worms. The bubbles released from the reaction of the vinegar and baking soda move the worms. When the worms reach the top and the gas is released, they fall back to the bottom and may pick up more gas and head for the top again.

CHALK FROM EGGSHELLS

You will need the following ingredients:

7 Large egg shells (clean and dry)
1 Teaspoon of all-purpose flour
1 Teaspoon of very hot tap water

Place the eggshells in a small plastic bowl and crush them into a fine powder with the back of a tablespoon (a mortar and pestle would be great). You will need 1 tablespoon of powder to produce 1 stick of chalk. Remove any pieces that would not grind up leaving only the finest powder. Place the water and flour into a small bowl and blend well into a paste, then add the tablespoon of eggshell and mix thoroughly. Use the back of a tablespoon to crush the mixture into a thick paste. Shape the paste into a cylinder and wrap it up in a piece of paper towel. Allow the chalk to dry out at room temperature for 2–3 days or until very hard. This eggshell chalk is best used on cement surfaces not chalkboards unless you like the screeching.

OCEAN WAVES IN A BOTTLE

You will need the following ingredients:

1	2-liter plastic soda bottle (empty)
1	Cup of corn oil
1/2	Tablespoons of powder tempera paint (any color)
1	Funnel

Combine the corn oil and tempera powder in a medium bowl. Allow the mixture to sit for 5–7 minutes. Slowly pour the mixture into the bottle using the funnel to avoid spillage. Add cool tap water until the bottle is full, then seal the bottle and place on its side to watch the ocean waves.

MAKING A VOLCANO ERUPTION

You will need the following ingredients:

1	Small juice glass
1/4	Teaspoon of liquid dish soap
4	Ounces of white vinegar
1	Tablespoon of baking soda
2	Drops of red food coloring

Place the white vinegar and food coloring into the juice glass and place outside on a thick piece of newspaper or other safe surface. Place on a volcano-shaped mound of sand for the most dramatic results. Add the baking soda and dish soap to the vinegar and watch the eruption. This project needs adult supervision.

KIDS' LIP GLOSS

You will need the following ingredients:

> 2 *Tablespoons of Crisco solid shortening*
> 1 *Tablespoon of flavored Kool-Aid (powder)*
> 1 *Small plastic tube (such as a film canister)*

Place the Crisco and powdered Kool-Aid in a small microwavable container and blend until smooth. Place the container in the microwave and heat on high for 30 seconds or until the mixture becomes a liquid, then pour the liquid gloss into the small container and refrigerate for 30 minutes or until solid. Use sparingly as a lipgloss.

SQUIRT & COLOR

You will need the following ingredients:

> 4 *Tablespoons of cornstarch*
> 1 *Cup of warm tap water*
> 4 *Drops of food coloring*
> 1 *Spray bottle*

Place all the ingredients into the spray bottle and shake well before each use. This makes a great paint spray when used on clean snow. If used on cement, it will easily wash off with a garden hose.

HAVE A TAFFY PULL

You will need the following ingredients:

> 1 *Cup of granulated sugar*
> 2/3 *Cup of cool tap water*
> 3/4 *Cup of light Karo syrup*
> 1 *Tablespoon of cornstarch*
> 2 1/4 *Tablespoons of butter (unsalted)*
> 1 *Teaspoon of table salt*
> 2 *Tablespoons of vanilla extract (pure)*
> 1 *Candy thermometer*

Place all the ingredients except the vanilla in a medium saucepan and heat until boiling on medium heat, stirring continuously. Stop stirring and cook until the thermometer reads 256° F. or until a hard ball is formed when dropped in cold water.

S.BEAN

Remove the mixture from the heat, stir in the vanilla, and pour into a buttered, square 8-inch pan with 2 inch sides. Allow the mixture to cool until the taffy is workable and not too hot to the touch. Pull the taffy into long strips about $1/2$ inch wide and cut into pieces with a scissors. Wrap the taffy in individual pieces in plastic wrap and keep in a cool, dry location.

HALLOWEEN BLOOD

You will need the following ingredients:

$5^1/2$ *Tablespoons of clear corn syrup*
$2^1/2$ *Tablespoons of cool tap water*
60   *Drops of red food coloring*
10   *Drops of yellow food coloring*
2   *Drops of blue food coloring*

Place the food coloring and the water in a medium bowl and mix well, then slowly add the corn syrup, stirring continually until the mixture becomes thick, but not too solid. The fake blood can be smeared on any part of your body, but the solution may stain some garments, so wear old clothes.

COLOR COPIER FOR COMICS

You will need the following ingredients:

1   *Teaspoon of real vanilla extract (do not use imitation)*
1   *Teaspoon of liquid dishwasher soap*

Place the ingredients into a small bowl and mix well. Place the cartoon on a solid surface or board and brush a thin layer of the solution on the picture, then cover it with a sheet of white bond or copy paper. Gently rub the back of the paper until the picture has been transferred. Remove the paper. The picture will be transferred to the white paper.

CRYSTAL FLOWER GARDEN

You will need the following ingredients:

$1/2$ *Cup of cool tap water*
4   *Tablespoons of liquid bluing*
4   *Tablespoons of table salt*
4   *Teaspoons of household ammonia*
  Food coloring

You will need the following supplies:

Cotton swabs (cut in half)
Pipe cleaners (cut in 2-inch pieces)
Several pieces of oil-based clay
Plastic margarine tubs or similar containers

The day before you start the garden, soak the ends of the cotton swabs in food coloring and place a few drops of the food coloring on the pipe cleaners. Make sure the cotton swabs are dry before continuing.

Place a piece of clay on the bottom of the plastic tub and insert 3 cotton swabs or pipe cleaners about $1/2$ inch into the clay. Mix the solution of bluing, salt, ammonia, and water in a bottle and blend well. Pour a small amount of the solution into the plastic containers, making sure that the solution covers up to about $1/2$ inch up the cotton swabs or pipe cleaners. Your garden will begin to "grow" in a few days.

SALT ART

You will need the following ingredients:

$1/2$ Cup of table salt
1 Stick of colored chalk
1 Baggie (good closure)
1 Baby food jar

Place the salt in the baggie, add the piece of chalk and seal the baggie well. Rub the bag between your hands until all the salt is colored. This may be done with any number of colors. Place the colored salt in the jar in layers or make a design. Make sure the jar is filled to the top before gluing the cover on.

SAND ART

You will need the following ingredients:

$1/2$ Cup of tempera paint (dry)
1 Cup of clean sandbox sand

Place the ingredients into a container and mix well. The amount of tempera paint can vary. Spread a small layer of glue on a picture and sprinkle on the colored sand. Smaller amounts can be made to produce different colors as needed.

THE EGGSPERIMENT

You will need the following ingredients:

1 Large egg, fresh
2 Drops of yellow food coloring
1 Medium bowl, deep
2 Cups of very hot tap water

Place the hot water in the bowl, then place the egg gently on the bottom with a spoon (don't burn your hand). To prove that eggs contain air, watch closely as tiny air bubbles are forced to escape from the egg because of the heat of the water. The heat makes the air expand and literally forces the air out. An egg is very porous and not an airtight compartment for the chick. It has about 6,758 small openings or pores in the shell to allow the air to escape. The food coloring allows you to see the bubbles more easily.

MAKING BUTTER

You will need the following ingredients:

> 1   *Cup heavy whipping cream (cold)*
> 1   *Metal mixing bowl (chilled)*
> 1   *Measuring cup*
> 1   *Hand mixer (electric)*

Place the heavy cream into the chilled bowl and mix until you see small clumps of yellow (about 8–10 minutes). The yellow clumps should be in a liquid, which must be poured off at regular intervals. Keep pouring the liquid off, allowing the yellow clumps to remain. Cream consists of butterfat and water and all you are doing is separating the two. Whipping allows the fat molecules to clump together, forming the recognizable butter. This butter does not have a long shelf life and must be refrigerated and used within 3–5 hours—discard the unused portion.

PLAIN OLD GUNK

You will need the following ingredients:

> 1   *Cup of cornstarch*
> 1   *Cup of cool tap water*

Place the ingredients into a small bowl, mix well, then play with the gunk.

COLORED GUNK

You will need the following ingredients:

> ¹/₃   *Cup of granulated sugar*
> 1   *Cup of cornstarch*
> 4   *Cups of cold water*

Place all the ingredients in a small saucepan and cook on low heat until thick, then remove from heat and cool. Place the mixture into a well-sealed plastic baggie, add some food coloring, and allow the child to experience the weird mixture.

KIDS' GLITTERING GEL

You will need the following ingredients:

$1^{1}/_{4}$ Teaspoon of glycerin
$^{1}/_{2}$ Cup of aloe vera gel
$^{1}/_{4}$ Teaspoon of a quality polyester glitter (hobby shop)
  3 Drops of essential rose oil
     Food coloring as desired

Place the aloe and glycerin in a small bowl and mix well, add the glitter, essential oil, and food coloring if desired. The glittering gel can be placed on arms or legs.

PET CELERY FEEDING TIME

You will need the following ingredients:

  1 Stalk of celery (with leaves)
  1 Teaspoon of red food coloring

Place the celery stalk in $^{3}/_{4}$ of a glass of water, add the food coloring, and mix well. The leaves of the celery stalk will turn red showing how plants feed by absorbing food from the soil and water.

SALVAGING LESS-THAN-PERFECT FRUIT

Making fruit leather can be a fun way to preserve fruit that has over-ripened or is not very appealing. Most of the nutrients are retained and the fruit leather is fun to eat. There are many methods of preparing fruit leather, including using a dehydrator, but a few of the easiest methods are described below. Fruits that turn brown easily such as bananas and pears are not recommended.

LEATHER YOU CAN EAT #1

You will need the following ingredients:

  8 Ounces of flavored applesauce
     Plastic wrap

Place the applesauce on a flat plate and place the plate into the micro-wave for about 5 minutes depending on the wattage. Keep an eye on it and do not allow it to burn. The applesauce will dehydrate and become a solid mass that can then be placed between two pieces of plastic wrap and consumed like a fruit roll.

LEATHER YOU CAN EAT #2

You will need the following ingredients:

4   Cups of fresh fruit (no bananas) cleaned well, no stems
1   Envelope of unflavored Knox Gelatin
2   Teaspoons of apples or berries for additional flavor
1   Cookie sheet with sides

Place a piece of plastic wrap on the cookie sheet and lightly spray it with oil. If you are using a citrus fruit, it will need to be peeled. Place the fruit into a blender and puree until it is good and smooth. Pulp is okay and will give the leather a little texture. Place the puree into a small saucepan and place over low heat until it just begins to bubble. Add the gelatin and a small amount of sugar if desired. Remove from the heat and pour on the cookie sheet. Refrigerate overnight. It will take 3–4 days before you see drying around the edges telling you that it is done. Make sure that it is spread evenly and always watch for mold. If any appears, discard the batch. Roll the leather and use kitchen shears to cut the strips, then roll up.

MAKING ICE CREAM IN A BAGGIE

You will need the following ingredients:

1   Tablespoon of granulated sugar
1/2   Cup of whole milk (reduced-fat is okay)
1/4   Teaspoon of real vanilla (no imitation)
6   Tablespoons of rock salt
1   Gallon-sized plastic bag with good closure
1   Pint sized plastic bag with good closure
     Ice cubes as needed

Fill the gallon-sized plastic bag half full of ice cubes, then add the rock salt, and seal the bag tight. Place the milk, sugar, and vanilla into the smaller plastic bag and seal it tight. Open the gallon bag and place the smaller bag inside, leaving the smaller bag sealed tight. Shake for 5–7 minutes or until you observe the ice cream forming, then remove the ice cream bag and wipe the closure well before opening to be sure that no rock salt residue gets into the ice cream. A small amount of chocolate syrup, food coloring, or small candies may be added.

MAGICAL GLITTER

You will need the following ingredients:

Karo syrup
Cold tap water
Small plastic bottle with screw cap
Drop of food coloring (if desired)
Metallic glitter strands (confetti-style)

Fill the plastic bottle about 3/4 full of Karo syrup, then add about 1 1/2 tablespoons of the metallic glitter strands and fill the bottle with cold tap water and seal well. Slowly turn the bottle upside down 2–3 times and watch it sparkle.

TELLING THE IDENTITY OF SALT & SUGAR

You will need the following ingredients:

     1 *Tablespoon of table salt*
     1 *Tablespoon of granulated sugar*
     2 *Drops of red food coloring*
     2 *Drops of blue food coloring*
     2 *Cups*
     1 *Ice-cube tray (with metal or plastic divider)*
        Cool tap water

Fill the cups half full with water, then add the red food coloring to one glass and the blue to the other. Place the salt into one cup and the sugar in the other cup and allow them to dissolve fully. Pour the solutions in opposite ends of the ice-cube tray and place into the freezer. The water with the sugar will freeze and the water with the salt will not freeze.

THE SECRET HIDING PLACE

You will need the following ingredients:

     1   *Cup of all-purpose flour*
     1   *Cup of used coffee grounds*
    1/2 *Cup of table salt*
    1/4 *Cup of sanitized sandbox sand*
    3/4 *Cup of cool tap water*

Place the flour, coffee grounds, salt, and sand in a container and blend well. Very slowly add the water while continually mixing until it reaches the consistency of a workable dough. Roll the dough out in a cylinder about 1–2 inches thick, then cut into even pieces about 3 inches long. Roll each piece between your hands as if preparing meatballs, which is what they will look like. Make a hole in each one and insert a small prize or toy, then seal the hole with leftover dough. Allow the balls to harden for about 3 days at room temperature or bake in the oven if you are in a hurry at 140° F for about 20 minutes.

MAKING COLORED PASTA FOR CRAFTS

You will need the following ingredients:

     8 *Ounce bag of pasta*
     8 *Drops of food coloring*
     1 *Teaspoon of rubbing alcohol*

Place all the ingredients into a plastic bag and shake well, then place the pasta on a cookie sheet and allow it to dry for about 15 minutes. Do not eat the pasta.

THE MAGICAL MOVING COIN

You will need the following ingredients:

> 1 *Cup of cold tap water*
> 1 *2-liter soda bottle*
> 1 *Quarter*

Place the quarter in the cup of water at room temperature, then place the empty 2-liter plastic bottle in the freezer for 5–6 minutes. Remove the bottle from the freezer and place the quarter over the mouth of the bottle to cover the opening completely. The quarter will jump up and down and make a weird chattering noise.

The quarter moves as a result of the expansion of the air as it warms up. When the bottle is in the freezer, the air in the bottle cools down and contracts, taking up less space in the bottle. When this occurs, air rushes in from the outside to occupy the empty space. When the bottle is removed from the freezer, the air starts to warm up and expand, thus causing the quarter to jump up and down as the warm air escapes.

MAKING A FROZEN DESSERT WITH NATURAL HEAT ENERGY

You will need the following ingredients:

> 1/2 *Cup of apple juice (pasteurized)*
> 1 *Tablespoon of pure lemon juice*
> 1/2 *Cup of rock salt*
> 6 *Cups of crushed ice*
> 1 *Medium mixing bowl*
> 1 *Small jar with screw top lid*

Place the apple juice and lemon juice into the small jar then seal and shake to mix. Remove the lid, place the jar in the center of the mixing bowl, and pour the ice around the jar almost up to the top. Sprinkle the rock salt on top of the ice (not in the juice), then wrap a few dish towels around the bowl to insulate it and place it next to an object that will hold the dishtowels firmly against the bowl. In about 2 hours, the juice will turn into a slushy treat. The salt and ice has the ability to draw the heat from the juice, bringing it near freezing point.

EASTER EGG DYE

THE OLD-FASHIONED WAY

The directions are the same for all dyes. Place all the ingredients in a medium bowl and mix well. Dip the eggs in the dye and allow them to dry in an egg container. Polish the eggs with a small amount of olive oil to make them shine.

You will need the following ingredients:

GREEN
- $1/4$ Ounce of brilliant green dye
- $2^3/4$ Teaspoons of citric acid
- 1 Ounce of dextrin
- 1 Pint of warm tap water

YELLOW
- $1/4$ Ounce of napthol yellow or yellow onion skins
- 5 Teaspoons of citric acid
- $1^1/4$ Ounces of dextrin
- 1 Pint of warm tap water

BLUE
- $1/2$ Teaspoon of marine blue
- 5 Teaspoons of citric acid
- $1^1/4$ Ounces of dextrin
- 1 Pint of warm tap water

BROWN
- $1/2$ Ounce of vesuvin
- $5^1/4$ Teaspoons of citric acid
- $1/2$ Ounce of dextrin
- 1 Pint of warm tap water

RED
- $1/2$ Teaspoon of diamond fuchsin
- $2^1/2$ Teaspoons of citric acid
- $1^1/4$ Ounces of dextrin
- 1 Pint of warm tap water

ORANGE
- 1 Teaspoon azo orange
- $2^1/2$ Teaspoons of citric acid
- $1^1/4$ Ounces of dextrin
- 1 Pint of warm tap water

VIOLET
- $1/2$ Teaspoon of methyl violet
- $2^1/2$ Teaspoons of citric acid
- $1^1/4$ Ounces of dextrin
- 1 Pint of warm tap water

Chapter 11

Stain
Removal

There are a few basic rules to remember before attempting to remove stains:

1. Never launder a garment before you attempt to remove the stain or the stain may be permanently set into the fabric.

2. The stain needs to be treated or at least reduced in severity as soon as the stain occurs and fully removed if possible.

3. Old stains may need more than one treatment to remove. Many old stains are still removable if the proper stain removal ingredients are used.

4. Non-washable garments should be taken to the cleaners as soon as possible or the stain may be permanent.

5. Always point out the stain to the cleaner and identify it if possible.

OLD GRASS STAINS

Supplies needed:

> 1 Egg white
> Glycerin *(from pharmacy)*

Old grass stains are very difficult to remove but this formula should do the trick. Mix equal parts of egg white with glycerin in a small bowl and dab on the grass-stained area. Allow it to remain for a few minutes, then wash the area with a carpet cleaner. Test the solution on an inconspicuous area to be sure the fabric is colorfast.

STUBBORN GRASS STAINS

You will need the following ingredients:

> 1/8 Cup of glycerin
> 1/4 Cup of warm tap water
> 1/4 Cup of isopropyl alcohol *(rubbing alcohol)*

Place all the ingredients in a small bowl and mix well. Place the garment in a bowl and pour the solution on the grass stain. Allow it to soak for 15 minutes. Wash the garment in warm, soapy water or launder as usual.

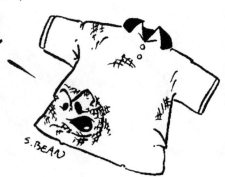

GETTING RID OF GRAVY STAINS
You will need the following ingredients:

> 1   *Teaspoon of household ammonia*
> *1/2* *Teaspoon of table salt*
> 1   *Cup of cool tap water*

Place all the ingredients into a small bowl and mix well. Allow the mixture to remain on the stained area for 10 minutes before laundering as usual. Persistent stains need a longer soak period.

ALUMINUM POT, BURNED-ON FOOD REMEDY
You will need the following ingredients:

> 1   *Tablespoons of baking soda*
> *1/4* *Cup of warm tap water*

Place the warm water over the burnt area; then pour the baking soda on top of the water. Allow the solution to sit for 12 hours before cleaning off.

MILDEW IN CLOTHING REMOVER #1
You will need the following ingredients:

> *1/4* *Cup of chlorine bleach*
> *1/4* *Cup of white vinegar*
> 2   *Cups of cold tap water*
> 2   *medium-sized containers.*

In the first container, mix together the bleach and one cup of water. Soak the mildew stain in the bleach water for 10 minutes. Remove the garment and place it in another container that has the vinegar mixed with 1 cup of water and allow it to soak for another 10 minutes. Wash the garment as usual.

MILDEW IN CLOTHING REMOVER #2
You will need the following ingredients:

> 4   *Tablespoons of hydrogen peroxide*
> 1   *Tablespoon of ammonium chloride*
> *2¹/₂* *Tablespoons of denatured alcohol*
> 1   *Cup of cool tap water*

Place the water into a medium bowl and, while stirring, add the other ingredients. Soaked the stained garment in the solution for 5–6 minutes, then rinse well in cold water. This process may have to be repeated as many as 2–3 times to remove stubborn mildew stains.

REMOVING RUST FROM FABRICS

You will need the following ingredients:

1 *Teaspoon of lemon juice*
1 *Teaspoon of sour milk*
1 *Teaspoon of cream of tartar*
1/2 *Teaspoon of baking soda (fresh)*

Place all the ingredients into a small bowl and mix thoroughly into a paste. Rub the paste into the rust stain and allow it to remain for 1 minute before washing the garment. Never allow the paste to remain more than 3 minutes or you may damage the fabric.

REMOVING NAIL POLISH FROM FABRICS

You will need the following ingredients:

3 *Teaspoons of glycerin*
3 *Teaspoons of apple cider vinegar*
3 *Tablespoons of very hot tap water*

Place all the ingredients in a small bowl and mix well. This may remove the fabric dye so first test on an inconspicuous area to make sure the garment is colorfast. You could try straight vinegar first or nail polish remover, but these may also remove the dye. Launder immediately after cleaning.

REMOVING TAR FROM CLOTHING

You will need the following ingredients:

1 *Tablespoon of butter*
1 *Tablespoon of orange essential oil*

Place the ingredients into a small bowl and mix thoroughly. Place the solution on the tar and allow a few minutes to melt it away (if the garment has already been washed, the tar cannot be removed) then wash immediately.

SUPER ALL-AROUND GOOD STAIN REMOVER

You will need the following ingredients:

1/2 *Cup white vinegar*
1/2 *Cup of household ammonia*
1/4 *Cup of baking soda (fresh)*
2 *Tablespoons of liquid hand detergent*
2 *Quarts of warm tap water*

Place all the ingredients in a container that has a lid and shake well. Pour the solution into a spray bottle. Spray on the stain and allow the solution to remain for 3–5 minutes before laundering the garment.

REMOVING COFFEE STAINS—EVEN MOST OLD ONES

You will need the following ingredients:

2 *Tablespoons of glycerin*
2 *Tablespoons of isopropyl alcohol*
6 *Tablespoons of cool tap water*
1 *Tablespoon of ammonium chloride*

Place all the ingredients into a bowl and mix thoroughly until they are dissolved. Saturate the stain with the solution and allow it to remain on the stain for 6–7 minutes before rinsing in cool tap water. If the stain does not disappear, repeat the steps and allow the mixture to remain for 10 minutes before rinsing. In almost every instance the stain will disappear in 2–3 minutes.

IRONING TIPS

If you need to remove melted plastic or fabric residues from a garment, just heat the area with an iron set on low temperature until the foreign material softens, then scrape it off with a piece of wood. Baking soda and water made into a paste will also work well. If a steam iron clogs from lint, just fill the iron and allow it to steam until it runs out.

REMOVING IRONING SCORCHES

You will need the following ingredients:

$1/2$ *Cup of hydrogen peroxide (3% solution)*
$1/2$ *Cup of cool tap water*

Place the ingredients into a small bowl and mix, then allow the scorched area of the garment to soak in the solution for about 10 minutes. Rinse the garment in cold water. This works better with natural fibers than with synthetics.

REMOVING RUST FROM CLOTHING

You will need the following ingredients:

> 2   *Tablespoons of alum (from drugstore)*
> 2   *Tablespoons of tartaric acid*

Place the ingredients into a small bowl and mix well. Sponge the mixture on the rust spot and allow it to sit for 5 minutes, then launder the garment.

REMOVING EGG YOLK

You will need the following ingredients:

> 1   *Tablespoon of glycerin*
> $1/4$ *Cup of isopropyl alcohol*
> $1/4$ *Cup Castile soap (powdered)*

Place the ingredients into a small bowl and mix well, then apply the mixture to the stained area and allow it to remain for about 5–7 minutes before rinsing the area with clean cool tap water.

GLASS OBJECT CLEANER

You will need the following ingredients:

> 1   *Cup of calcium carbonate*
> 4   *Tablespoons of ground quassia (from chemical supply*
>   *or pharmacy)*
> 4   *Tablespoons of ammonium carbonate (mix wearing gloves*
>   *and mask)*

Place all the ingredients into a container and mix thoroughly. Apply with a damp sponge or toothbrush depending on the type of surface to be cleaned. Rinse with cool water after cleaning. Store in a sealed container and mix before each use. Keep out of reach of children and pets.

PERSPIRATION STAIN REMOVER

You will need the following ingredients:

> 3   *Tablespoons of sodium perborate*
> $2 1/4$ *Cups of warm tap water*

Place the ingredients in a container and mix well. Mix before each use. Place a small amount of the mixture on an area that won't be seen to test for colorfastness before using on the stain. Saturate the stain and allow it to stand for 5 minutes before laundering as usual.

MAKING JAVELLE WATER FOR COTTONS AND LINENS

You will need the following ingredients:

4 *Ounces of washing soda*
8 *Ounces of boiling water*
2 *Ounces of chloride of lime*
1 *Pint of cold tap water*

Place the washing soda in the boiling water and dissolve fully. In another container dissolve the chloride of lime into the cold water, mix well, then combine the two solutions. Store in a dark bottle in a cool, dark location. This is an excellent stain remover for old cottons and linens but cannot be used on silk or wool. To use, apply the Javelle water to the stain or soak the garment in $1/4$ cup of the water mixed with 3 quarts of cool tap water. Soak for about 30 minutes if you use hot water, and 3 hours with cold water.

CARPET CLEANING

SPECIAL GUIDELINES FOR STAIN REMOVAL

1. Always test a spot remover in an inconspicuous location before applying on a stain.

2. Scrape away any residues with a blunt knife before starting.

3. Never use a hard-bristle brush on a stain, use a soft brush only.

4. Blot up any liquid using a paper towel.

5. Vacuum after all liquid is gone to remove any residue.

6. Try cleaning the area with clear water before using a spot remover.

7. Never over-wet the area.

REMOVING LIGHT CIGARETTE SCORCH MARKS

You will need the following ingredients:

1 *Cup white vinegar*
$2/3$ *Cup unscented talcum powder*
1 *Large finely chopped white onion*

Blend the ingredients in a small saucepan and bring to a boil, then allow the mixture to cool before spreading on the stained area. Allow the mixture to dry thoroughly then brush off with an old toothbrush. Most slight scorch marks can be removed with this method.

OLD IODINE STAINS

Mix together the following ingredients in a small plastic bowl:

*¹/₂ Teaspoon photographic hyposulfite
        (from photographers supply)*
3   Cup warm water

Use rubber gloves when handling the hyposulfite. Dab the solution on an area of the carpet in an inconspicuous location to see if it is colorfast. If the carpet is colorfast, dab the area with the solution until lightly saturated and allow it to stand for a few minutes. Wash the area with carpet shampoo immediately afterwards.

GETTING RID OF ANIMAL ODORS

You will need the following ingredients:

¹/₂ Cup of baking soda (fresh)
1   Cup of cornmeal
1   Cup of borax

Place the ingredients in a plastic container and mix thoroughly. Sprinkle on the affected area and allow it to remain for 6–8 hours before vacuuming.

CARPET FRESHENER

You will need the following ingredients:

²/₃ Cup of baking soda (fresh)
40   Drops of essential lime oil
25   Drops of essential tangerine oil
*   Drops of essential patchouli oil*

Place all the ingredients into a plastic container and mix well, then allow the freshener to stand for 24 hours before sprinkling on the carpet from a can with holes in the top. Let stand for 20 minutes, then vacuum up.

FABRIC SOFTENER

WASHING MACHINE FABRIC SOFTENER

You will need the following ingredients:

1   Cup of white vinegar
2   Cups of baking soda (fresh)
4   Cups of cold tap water

Place all the ingredients in a small bucket and mix well. Store in small plastic or glass sealed jars. Shake well before using. Add 1/4 cup of the softener to the final rinse for the best results. Keep out of reach of children.

DRYER FABRIC SOFTENER

You will need the following ingredients:

1/2 *Cup of baking soda (fresh)*
1 *Tablespoon of cornstarch*
1 *Tablespoon of arrowroot powder*
2 *Drops of essential rose oil (optional)*

Place all the ingredients into a small bowl and mix well. Place a small amount in a small cloth bag that can be well tied or secured with a drawstring and place it into the dryer with the load. Be sure the bag is well sealed or it will become a bit messy.

SUPER SOFT FABRIC SOFTENER

You will need the following ingredients:

1 *Tablespoon of unflavored gelatin*
1 1/2 *Cup of boiling water*

Completely dissolve the gelatin in the boiling water. Add the softener to the final rinse after the washing cycle is completed.

LAUNDRY DETERGENTS

LIQUID LAUNDRY DETERGENT

You will need the following ingredients:

1 *Cup of soap flakes (grated)*
1/2 *Cup of washing soda*
1/2 *Cup of borax*
4 *Tablespoons of glycerin*
4 *Cups of very warm tap water*

Place all the ingredients in a large bottle and mix well. Be careful not to mix too rapidly or you will get too many suds. Add 1/2–3/4 cup to your tub in warm water and then use a cold water rinse. This makes about 24 ounces and can be reduced or increased as desired.

1920'S LAUNDRY POWDER & HOUSEHOLD CLEANER

You will need the following ingredients:

4   Cups of powdered Castile soap (grated)
4   Cups of ammonium carbonate

Place the ingredients into a small bucket and mix very thoroughly in a well-ventilated area. Dilute using 2 tablespoons of the mixture to 1 quart of water for general cleaning purposes. Works great in a spray bottle in place of most household cleaners.

CLOTHES COLOR BRIGHTENER

You will need the following ingredients:

1   Pint of cool tap water
1   Tablespoons of gum acacia
1   Ounce of borax
1   Tablespoon of glycerin

Place the gum acacia in the water in a small container and allow it to soak for 8–10 hours. Place the gum solution and the other ingredients into a saucepan and boil while mixing occasionally. Remove from heat and allow the mixture to cool, then strain through a piece of cheesecloth or fine strainer. Store in a sealed glass bottle and add 1 tablespoon of the solution to every pint of starch.

LAUNDRY BLUING FOR WHITER WHITES

You will need the following ingredients:

$1/4$ Teaspoon of ultramarine blue
$1^3/4$ Cup of sodium bicarbonate
$1/2$ Cup of corn syrup

Place all the ingredients into a container and mix well. Place $1/4$–$1/2$ teaspoon in a wash load of whites for whiter whites. Grandmother did this all the time.

HELP FOR HEAVILY SOILED WORKCLOTHES

You will need the following ingredients:

3   Cups of soda ash
5   Cups of masonry sand

Place the ingredients into a container and mix well, then store in a cool, dry location in a well-sealed container. Place 2 tablespoons of the dry mixture into each load along with your regular detergent.

JEWELRY CLEANING

DIAMONDS
- Chlorine bleach will discolor the setting.
- Have the prongs holding the stone checked annually.
- When storing your jewelry, make sure the pieces don't touch each other.
- Diamonds will scratch other pieces of jewelry very easily.
- Clean your diamonds regularly with a milk detergent and warm water.

COLORED GEMSTONES
- Never expose gemstones to salt water or harsh chemical solutions.
- Check with your jeweler for cleaning methods for colored stones.
- Emeralds need special care, check with your jeweler.
- Hairspray will dull gemstones.
- Wipe gemstones with a soft cloth after each wearing.

10–24 KARAT GOLD JEWELRY
- Gold scratches easily, keep pieces away from other jewelry.
- Do not wear gold jewelry while bathing or showering with soaps and shampoos.
- Use a soft bristle brush when cleaning.
- Grease is easily removed with rubbing alcohol.
- Try not to get makeup and powders on the gold.

SILVER
- Store silver in a cool, dry location.
- Only rub silver with a soft cloth. Paper towel and tissues will scratch it.
- Never wear silver in a chlorinated swimming pool.

PEARLS
- Put on pearls after applying cosmetics, perfume, and hair spray.
- Quality pearls should be re-strung annually with knots between each pearl if worn regularly.
- Store pearls in a chamois bag or wrapped in tissue.
- Never use harsh chemical to clean pearls.
- Clean pearls with special pearl formulas or mild soap and warm water.

JEWELRY CLEANER
You will need the following ingredients:

> 2 *Tablespoon of household ammonia*
> 1 *Tablespoon of washing soda (from supermarket)*
> 1 *Tablespoon of liquid dishwashing detergent*
> 3 *Cups of very warm tap water*

Place all the ingredients in a medium bowl and mix thoroughly. Store the solution in a sealed glass jar. When you want to clean your jewelry, just soak the pieces in the solution for 5–7 minutes and brush with a soft-bristled toothbrush. Rinse the jewelry in warm water and dry well.

CAUTION: Do not place pearls or emeralds in this solution and never add chlorine bleach to these chemicals. Keep out of the reach of children.

SILVER JEWELRY CLEANER

You will need the following ingredients:

- $^{1}/_{2}$ *Cup of white vinegar*
- 2 *Tablespoons of baking soda*

Place the ingredients in a small bowl and mix well. Place the jewelry in the bowl and allow it to stand for 2 hours before rinsing with cold water and drying with a soft dry cloth.

GOLD CLEANER

You will need the following ingredients:

- 1 *Cup of Fuller's earth*
- 1 *Cup of calcium carbonate*
- 2 *Tablespoons of ammonium sulfate*
- 1 *Tablespoon of aluminum powder*

Place all the ingredients in a container and mix well. Apply the cleaner to oxidized gold jewelry with a damp sponge, then rinse with cool water. Store the mixture in a well-sealed container in a cool, dry location.

RESTORING TARNISHED GOLD

You will need the following ingredients:

- 20 *Ounces of sodium bicarbonate*
- 1 *Ounce of chlorinated lime*
- 1 *Ounce of table salt*
- 16 *Ounces of cool tap water*

Place all the ingredients into a container and mix well, then apply with a soft bristle brush. The solution may be applied either cold or lukewarm.

JEWELRY POLISH

You will need the following ingredients:

5 *Tablespoons of ferric oxide*
2 *Tablespoons of calcium*
    carbonate
Cool tap water

Place the ingredients into a small bowl
and mix well using just enough water to
produce a paste. Rub on the jewelry with
a soft cloth and then buff with another clean
soft cloth.

MISCELLANEOUS

BASIC 1940'S LAUNDRY SOAP

You will need the following ingredients:

16 *Parts of tallow*
 3 *Parts of coconut oil*
14 *Parts of soda lye (35° Baume)*
9$^1/_2$ *Parts of silicate of soda*
 2 *Parts of pearlash lye (32° Baume)*

Place the tallow and the coconut oil in a large pot and heat to 140° F.,
then add the other ingredients and mix well. Allow the mixture to remain
still for 1$^1/_2$ hours, then slowly stir until the mixture looks uniform in
appearance. Pour into a cake tin and allow to cool until almost firm
before slicing into bars. Leave the bars at room temperature for 2 days
to dry out before using the soap.

LAUNDRY SOAP FOR HARD WATER

You will need the following ingredients:

1 *Cup of baking soda (fresh)*
1 *Cup of washing soda*
1 *Cup of Castile soap (grated, fine)*
1 *Cup borax*

Place all the ingredients in a large container and mix well. Store in a
sealed container and use about $^1/_2$ cup of the laundry soap per full load.

DELICATE FABRICS SOAP

You will need the following ingredients:

8 *Ounces of thin soap shavings*
1 *Quart of boiling water*

Place the soap shavings in a saucepan and carefully pour the boiling water over them. Boil the mixture until the soap is fully melted and well-stirred. Remove from the heat and pour into a safe container to cool. A stiff gel will be produced that will easily dissolve in warm water and can also be rubbed directly on the flannel or delicate fabric.

OLD-FASHIONED SPRAY STARCH

You will need the following ingredients:

3 *Tablespoons of cornstarch*
4 *Cups of warm tap water*
2 *Drops of rose water (optional)*

Place all the ingredients into a spray bottle and shake well. Always shake well before using. The starch will last about 4–6 months in a well-sealed jar or spray bottle.

BASIC LAUNDRY STARCH

You will need the following ingredients:

2–6 *Tablespoons of cornstarch*
$1/3$ *Cupful of cold tap water*
$1/2$ *Teaspoon of lard or paraffin*
1 *Quart of boiling water*

Place the boiling water in a double boiler. In another container mix the cornstarch and the cold water and blend well. Stir the mixture into the boiling water and mix well, then add the lard and cook for 20 minutes. If lumps are present the mixture will need to be strained. The starch can be diluted with hot water to produce the degree of stiffness desired.

BLEACH CAN BE A DANGEROUS CHEMICAL

Bleach should never be mixed with any other household chemical, especially ammonia, or deadly chlorine gas may form. Whenever bleach is used, the area or item should be thoroughly rinsed with clean water to remove all traces of bleach. A general rule of thumb when cleaning with bleach or using it as a disinfectant is to mix 2 cups of bleach to one gallon of water.

GRANDMA'S HOMEMADE BLEACH

You will need the following ingredients:

> 1   *Cup of hydrogen peroxide*
> 3   *Tablespoons of lemon juice*
> 15   *Cups of cool tap water*

Place all the ingredients in a medium bucket and mix well. Use as you would ordinarily use bleach. Store in a well-sealed jar in a cool, dry, dark location and it will last about 4 months.

INK ERADICATOR

You will need the following ingredients:

> 1   *Part of citric acid*
> 2   *Parts of borax*
> 16   *Parts of distilled water*

Place the citric acid and water in a medium bowl and mix well, then add the borax and mix well. Saturate the spot with the mixture and allow it to stand for 2–3 minutes before removing and laundering the garment. This formula is for the old type of inkwell ink, but may work on newer versions of fountain pen ink as well.

GENERAL INK REMOVER #1

You will need the following ingredients:

> 1/4   *Cup of citric acid*
> 1/4   *Cup of alum*
> 1   *Cup of cool tap water*

Place all the ingredients into a small container and mix well. Place a small amount on the stain and allow the mixture to stand for 2–3 minutes before removing and laundering the garment.

GENERAL INK REMOVER #2

You will need the following ingredients:

> 10   *Parts of oxalic acid*
> 2   *Parts of stannic chloride*
> 5   *Parts of acetic acid*
>   *Cool tap water to make 500 parts*

Place all the ingredients into a container and mix well. Store in a well-sealed glass bottle and shake before each use.

VASE AND BOTTLE CLEANER #1

You will need the following ingredients:

1/4 Cup of white vinegar
3 Tablespoons of uncooked rice

Place the rice and vinegar into the bottle and shake vigorously. The rice provides just enough abrasive action, while the vinegar is cleansing.

VASE AND BOTTLE CLEANER #2

You will need the following ingredients:

1 Teaspoon of sodium aluminate
4 1/2 Tablespoons of caustic soda (handle with care, causes burns)
1 Gallon of very hot tap water

Place the ingredients into a container and mix well. Use a bottlebrush to scrub the inside of any bottle that will be used for food and rinse very well. This is an excellent method of sterilizing bottles for canning.

DRY CLEANING CAN BE DANGEROUS

The chemical of choice for most dry cleaners is perchloroethylene (perc). This is a highly toxic chemical and even the residues from dry cleaned clothes can irritate your eyes and nose. Perc is a carcinogen and has harmful effects on the nervous system and major organs. The safe level is 100 parts per million, but if you just picked up a load of dry cleaned clothes from the cleaners, your car may acquire a level of 350 parts per million in just 15 minutes. Even low levels in closets containing dry cleaned clothes may affect your memory and mood. To avoid most of the associated problems, be sure and remove all clothes from the plastic bag and allow to air outside before hanging them in a closet.

BASIC DRY CLEANING FORMULA

You will need the following ingredients:

2 Teaspoons of glycol oleate
7 1/2 Ounces of carbon tetrachloride
2 1/2 Ounces of naphtha
2 1/4 Ounces of benzene

Place all the ingredients into a safe container and mix well. Some of the ingredients are flammable and need to be handled with care.

DRY CLEANING SOLUTION #2

You will need the following ingredients:

2   *Ounces of kerosene*
6   *Ounces of carbon tetrachloride*
2   *Teaspoons of oil of citronella*

Place all the ingredients into a container and mix well. This cleaner will remove most grease spots from most materials.

REMOVING STUBBORN PAINT STAINS FROM GARMENTS

You will need the following ingredients:

2   *Parts of ammonia water*
1   *Part of spirits of turpentine*

Place the ingredients into a container and mix well. Soak the paint stain in this solution and the paint should liquefy. If the fabric is strong and the color fast, straight turpentine or benzene will remove most paint stains.

SUGAR-BASED SAP REMOVER

You will need the following ingredients:

1   *Cup of liquid dish detergent*
1   *Tablespoon of liquid car polish*
2   *Cups of very hot tap water*

Place the ingredients in a small bucket and mix well but do not over-mix or the solution will suds up too much. If the sap has hardened, press a smooth object on the sap to break the outer shell. Place a cloth into the hot mixture (wear rubber gloves) and place it on the sap with moderate pressure. Continue applying fresh hot solution on the sap as soon as it starts to cool. Wash the area and apply a coat of wax.

Chapter 12

Handyman Formulas

S.BEAN

WOOD FURNITURE RENEWAL

You will need the following ingredients:

6 *Parts linseed oil*
1 *Part turpentine*

Place the ingredients into a small bowl and mix well. Using a woolen rag, rub a light coating on the furniture that needs restoring. Immediately dry off with another woolen cloth.

CLEANER FOR CONCRETE

You will need the following ingredients:

3 *Pounds of metasilicate*
1 *Gallon of hot tap water*

Place the ingredients in a bucket and mix well. Use a broom to scrub when applying. For stubborn areas, allow the mixture to sit for 15–20 minutes before scrubbing. A more concentrated solution may be needed in bad areas.

CANNED HEAT

You will need the following ingredients:

2 *Small cans with screw-on lids*
$1/8$ *Cup of stearic acid*
2 *Cups of denatured alcohol (flammable)*
$1^1/2$ *Teaspoons of caustic soda (skin irritant)*

Place the stearic acid in 1 cup of denatured alcohol in a cooking container and mix well. In another container, place the caustic soda and 1 cup of denatured alcohol and mix well. Heat the mixtures separately to 140° F., remove from the heat and mix the two together, allow the mixture to cool. Place into the screw-top cans and use as you would any other canned heat product.

MAKING CLOTH FIRE RETARDANT

You will need the following ingredients:

1 *Cup of ammonium chloride (from pharmacy)*
$1/2$ *Cup of ammonium phosphate (from nursery)*
3 *Pints of cold tap water*

Place the ingredients into a medium plastic bucket and mix thoroughly. Place the cloth, clothing, tent, or other textile material into the solution, soak well then allow to air dry. The cloth will stand relatively high heat before catching fire.

MAKING WOOD FIRE RETARDANT
You will need the following ingredients:

$^1/_2$ Cup zinc chloride (from feed dealer)
$^1/_4$ Cup ferric chloride (from pharmacy)
3 Tablespoons boric acid
3 Tablespoons ammonium phosphate (from nursery)
2 Quarts warm tap water

Place all the ingredients in a bucket and mix thoroughly. The solution can be sprayed or brushed on the wood surface. For the best results, 2–3 coats should be applied after each one dries.

WATERPROOFING TENTS
You will need the following ingredients:

3 Cups of soybean oil (from health food store)
$1^1/_2$ Cups of turpentine

Place the ingredients in a medium container and mix well. Paint the solution on any cloth surface such as a tent, a canvas awning, or a boat cover.

MAKING LEATHER WATERPROOF
You will need the following ingredients:

$2^1/_2$ Ounces Neat's foot oil (from shoe shop)
$^3/_4$ Ounces of mineral oil
$^1/_2$ Ounce of tallow (from butcher)
Double boiler

Place the ingredients into a double boiler and stir, while cooking until well blended. Remove from heat and allow to cool before placing in a bottle for storage. The solution can be applied with a soft cloth to any leather shoe or boot.

> **CAUTION:** Neat's foot oil and tallow are both flammable and should be handled with caution. Do not place next to open flame.

WATERPROOF YOUR CONCRETE
The following ingredients will be need:

$1^1/_4$ Pound of ammonium sterate (from pharmacy)
4 Gallons of hot tap water

Place the ingredients in a large pan and mix thoroughly. Apply immediately to concrete walks, driveways, or cement walls.

OAK FURNITURE REVIVER

You will need the following ingredients:

$^1/_2$ Cup of soda ash
1 Quart of warm tap water

Place the ingredients into a small bucket and mix well, then clean the furniture with a soft bristle brush and rinse with cool water. Dry well with a clean, dry, soft cloth.

DEGREASING METALS

You will need the following ingredients:

1 Quart of triethanolamine
4 Tablespoons of boiled linseed oil

Place the ingredients into a bowl and mix well. Apply the solution to the metal surface and allow it to stand for 10 minutes before wiping clean.

J. BEAN

OIL FOR GUN CLEANING

You will need the following ingredients:

1 Cup mineral oil
1 Teaspoon of denatured alcohol
1 Tablespoon of triethanolamine

Place all the ingredients into a container and mix well, then place just a few drops on a clean, soft cloth and wipe the gun.

INEXPENSIVE LUBRICANT FOR GUNS

You will need the following ingredients:

$3/4$ Cup of petrolatum
$1/4$ Cup light machine oil

Place the ingredients into a double boiler and heat until they can easily be mixed together. Remove from heat and allow it to cool, then pour into a container before it hardens too much.

BLUING FOR GUNS

You will need the following ingredients:

$1/2$ Cup of antimony chloride
$1/2$ Cup of tannic acid
$3/4$ Cup of ferric chloride
$1^1/2$ Cup of cool tap water
  2 Tablespoons of boiled linseed oil

Place the water in a medium container and add the tannic acid, ferric chloride, and antimony chloride. Mix these ingredients well, then apply the solution to the pre-cleaned, smooth surface of the metal with a very fine brush. After it has dried, reapply the solution for a second coating. When the second coating is dry, rub the area with a clean cloth soaked in the boiled linseed oil and allow it to dry.

PENETRATING OIL TO REMOVE RUSTY SCREWS

You will need the following ingredients:

  1 Tablespoon of butyl alcohol (flammable)
  2 Tablespoons of kerosene (flammable)
  7 Tablespoons of mineral oil

Place all the ingredients into a jar with a lid and mix well. Place a small amount on the rusty screw or bolt and allow the mixture to remain for about 5 minutes, then remove the screw or bolt. Store in a cool, dry location.

SHELLAC UNDERCOATING

You will need the following ingredients:

  1 Teaspoon of boric acid
  4 Tablespoons of shellac

Place the ingredients into a container and mix well, then brush on the surface before you shellac or apply a coat of varnish. This will seal the surface and give you a more professional look to your project.

CHARCOAL LIGHTER FLUID

You will need the following ingredients:

$1/4$ Cup of kerosene
$2^3/4$ Cups of mineral oil

Place the ingredients into a container and mix well, then store in well-sealed container. Pour on the charcoal and allow it to penetrate before lighting. Never pour on a fire that is already started to avoid a flare-up.

SKI WAX FROM SOYBEANS

A new ski wax that does not use a petroleum product such as paraffin has been invented. The new wax uses soy beans and canola oil. All tests verify that the new wax is just as effective as paraffin-based waxes. Soybeans are being used to replace a number of products that relied on paraffin or other waxes for their base, such as crayons and candles. The soy wax is about 30% soybean oil and costs about 25 cents to produce one package.

SKI WAX

You will need the following ingredients:

$1^3/4$ Cups of wood tar
$1/2$ Cup of diglycol stearate
$1/4$ Cup of carnauba wax

Place all the ingredients in a double boiler and heat until all the ingredients are melted, then stir well and remove from the heat. Allow the mixture to cool, then pour the mixture into molds before it hardens too much.

BRICKS FOR KINDLING

You will need the following ingredients:

6 Ounces of dark rosin
1 Ounce of thin petroleum oil
13 Ounces of clean sawdust

Place all the ingredients into a container and mix well, then form into a small brick to use for kindling. The petroleum oil can be omitted if so desired.

ARTIFICIAL FIELDSTONE

You will need the following ingredients:

>   1   *Part of cement*
>   4   *Parts of sand*
>   1   *Part of sodium silicate (powdered)*

Place all the ingredients into a medium container and mix well using enough cool tap water to prepare a damp paste. Pour the mixture into a mold and allow it to set before removing.

ACID-RESISTANT PUTTY

You will need the following ingredients:

>   2   *Parts of gum elastic*
>   4   *Parts of linseed oil*
>   1   *Part of litharge*
>   *White bole*

Place all the ingredients into a container with enough white bole to produce a putty. This putty will be resistant to nitric and hydrochloric acids.

WATERPROOF PUTTY

You will need the following ingredients:

>   3   *Parts powdered graphite*
> $1^1/_2$ *Parts slaked lime*
>   4   *Parts of heavy spar (barytes)*
>   4   *Parts of thick linseed oil varnish*

Place all the ingredients into a container and mix very well. This putty will even repair a boiler leak. Store in a well-sealed container.

ARTIFICIAL GRANITE

You will need the following ingredients:

>   5   *Parts of lime*
> $1^1/_4$ *Parts of sodium silicate (42° Baume)*
>   6   *Parts fine quartz sand*
>   9   *Parts of coarse sand*

Follow the directions for making artificial fieldstone.

ARTIFICIAL MARBLE

You will need the following ingredients:

20 *Parts of alum*
 1 *Part of barium sulfate*
10 *Parts of cool tap water*

Place the water in a medium pot and dissolve the alum by bringing the water to a boil. Add the barium sulfate and mix well. When the mixture starts to thicken, remove it from the heat and continue stirring until the solution is semi-liquid. Pour the solution into a mold that is coated with 4 coats of collodiom and allow it to cool.

COLORING ARTIFICIAL STONE

You will need the following ingredients:

Blue	.......Breman blue	Green	......Chrome green
Yellow	......Chrome yellow	Black	.......Graphite
Red	........Colcothar	White	.......Zinc white
Brick Red	....Cinnabar	Orange	......Red lead

Mix the colored pigment with wet cement and place into molds to harden. Colors can be altered by varying the amount of pigment used.

ANTI-RUST VARNISH FOR TOOLS

You will need the following ingredients:

1 *Pint of alcohol solution of shellac*
1 *Pint of denatured alcohol*

Place all the ingredients into a container and mix well, then brush the varnish on the tools and allow each coat to dry before adding another coat. Apply 2–3 coats for the best results.

METAL VARNISH

You will need the following ingredients:

5 *Ounces of common shellac*
$1/2$ *Ounce of thick turpentine*
9 *Ounces of alcohol*

Place the alcohol into a container and dissolve the shellac and turpentine in the alcohol. Follow the directions for the anti-rust varnish.

STAIN FOUNDATION FOR NEW WOOD

You will need the following ingredients:

>   1   *Part raw linseed oil*
>   1   *Part turpentine*

Place the ingredients into a container and mix well, then apply and allow it to dry fully before applying stain. This is a great foundation for stain.

BASIC OIL STAIN

You will need the following ingredients:

>   2   *Quarts of raw linseed oil*
>   2   *Quarts of turpentine*
>   1   *Quart of Japan drier*

Place all the ingredients into a container and blend well to form the base for the oil stain. To color the stain, grind the following pigments with a small amount of linseed oil and add to the base mixture.

Light Oak

>   2   *Pounds of raw sienna*
> $1/2$ *Pound of raw umber*

Dark Oak

>   2   *Pounds of raw sienna*
>   12   *Ounces of raw umber*
>   *Small amount of burnt sienna as desired*

Mahogany

>   2   *Pounds of burnt sienna*
>   1   *Pound of rose lake*
>   4   *Ounces of drop black*

Cherry

>   2   *Pounds of burnt sienna*
>   1   *Pound of raw sienna*

WATER-BASED STAINS

You will need the following ingredients:

Fully dissolve the pigments in the hot water before using the stain. The directions will be the same for all the water-based stains.

Light Walnut

>   2   *Ounces of Pylam Black*
>   2   *Ounces of Acid Orange*
>   1   *Gallon of hot tap water*

DARK WALNUT

$2^1/2$ Ounces of Pylam Black
$^1/2$ Ounce of Acid Orange
$^1/2$ Ounce of Pylam Yellow
1 Gallon of hot tap water

BROWN MAHOGANY

2 Ounces of Azo Rubine
2 Ounces of Pylam Red
$1^1/4$ Ounces of Nigrosine Powder
$2^3/4$ Ounces of Acid Orange
1 Gallon of hot tap water

RED MAHOGANY

2 Ounces of Azo Red
2 Ounces of Pylam Red
14 Ounce of Pylam Black
$1^3/4$ Ounces of Acid Orange
$1^1/2$ Gallons of hot tap water

OAK

$^1/4$ Ounce of Pylam Black
$1^3/4$ Ounce of Metanil Yellow
1 Gallon of hot tap water

EBONY

2 Ounces of Nigrosine (water-soluble)
$1^3/4$ Ounces of oxalic acid
$4^3/4$ Quarts of hot tap water

OIL STAIN FOR WALNUT

You will need the following ingredients:

5 Pounds of burnt umber
$3^3/4$ Pints of linseed oil
$^1/2$ Pint of drier
6 Quarts of turpentine

Place all the ingredients into a container and blend thoroughly. Allow the first coat to dry fully before applying additional coats.

ACID-PROOF WOOD STAIN

The following ingredients will be needed for solution one:

1 Part of copper sulfate
1 Part of potassium chlorate
8 Parts of tap water

Place all the ingredients into a pot and heat to the boiling point. Apply 2 coats of the solution while it is still very hot. Do not apply the second coat until the first one is fully dry.

The following ingredients will be needed for solution two:

1¼   *Parts of light aniline oil*
2¼   *Parts of concentrated hydrochloric acid (use with care)*
12½ *Parts of cool tap water*

Place all the ingredients into an acid-safe container and blend well, then apply 2 coats, allowing the first coat to dry fully before applying the second coat. Wash the surface with a mild solution of soap and cool water. When dry, rub the surface with linseed oil.

ANTIQUE FINISH FOR WOODS
You will need the following ingredients:

3   *Teaspoons of dark chrome green*
2   *Teaspoons of Vandyke brown*
2   *Teaspoons of lampblack*
1   *Pint of turpentine*
1   *Pint of boiled linseed oil*
3   *Drops of Japan drier*

Place the turpentine and linseed oil in a container and mix well, then add the chrome green, Vandyke brown, and lampblack and dissolve fully. Add the Japan drier and blend well. Apply the finish to the entire surface and wipe off areas that may have a high spot when it starts to dry. After it is dry, wipe with a clean soft cloth.

CLEAR WOOD FILLER
You will need the following ingredients:

1½   *Ounces of Japan drier*
2½   *Ounces of turpentine*
5   *Ounces of linseed oil*
15½   *Ounces of silica*
9   *Ounces of asbestine (use with care)*

Place the Japan drier, turpentine, and linseed oil in a container and mix well, then add the silica and asbestine while mixing well until a paste is formed.

This mixture can be thinned by adding turpentine: add 20 ounces of the paste filler to 1 pint of the turpentine. Wood fillers are used on woods such as oak, walnut, mahogany, ash, and rosewood, which are considered open-grained woods and need to be sealed before varnish is applied. This will provide an even surface for the varnish. Filler should be applied across the grain with a stiff bristle brush for the best results. Allow the filler to remain for about 30 minutes before wiping off the excess with a soft cloth, rubbing across the grain. Allow the filler to become very hard before using very fine sandpaper to remove the excess. Dust well before applying varnish.

WOOD BLEACH

You will need the following ingredients:

    16 Ounces of oxalic acid
    1   Gallon of hot tap water

Place the water in a large container and dissolve the oxalic acid into it. Apply the solution while it is still very hot. Scrub the wood well with soap, sal soda, and water before bleaching. If the wood has any traces of grease, clean with alcohol to remove. This bleach is capable of removing stains that have been caused by weathering or sap leakage. Depending on the condition of the wood, a number of applications may be required to produce the desired results.

The following treatment is also need to return the wood to a state in which it can easily be worked with, since bleaching tends to raise the grain of the wood.

AFTER-BLEACHING TREATMENT FORMULA

You will need the following ingredients:

    2   Pounds of shellac gum
    1   Gallon of denatured alcohol

Place the alcohol into a container and dissolve the shellac fully. Brush the mixture on the bleached wood surface and allow it to dry before sanding the surface. This should eliminate the raised grain areas.

HARNESS WAX

You will need the following ingredients:

    90 Parts of oil of turpentine
    9   Parts of yellow wax
    1   Part of Prussian blue
    $1/2$ Part of Indigo
    5   Parts of Bone black

Place the wax and the oil in a double boiler and dissolve. In another container mix the other ingredients, making sure they are all well powdered, then add a small amount of the wax to this mixture and mix well. Add the powder mixture to the wax mixture and stir until well blended. Store in earthen boxes or the equivalent container.

MAKE A WOOD TABLE TOP ACID-PROOF
You will need the following ingredients:

Solution #1
- 4 *Parts of iron sulfate*
- 4 *Parts of copper sulfate*
- 8 *Parts potassium permanganate*
- 100 *Parts water*

Solution #2
- 15 *Parts of aniline hydrochlorate*
- 100 *Parts of cool tap water*

Place all the ingredients into an old pot and bring to a boil. Continue to boil while stirring well until the salts are fully dissolved, then remove from the heat and allow the solution to cool for a few minutes. Apply two coats of solution #1 with a brush while it is still hot. Apply a second coat of solution #1 as soon as the first coat dries. Keep solution #1 hot by covering the pot. Rub the surface well before applying two coats of solution #2 in the same manner. A black surface color will appear. It will take a few hours to see the results. Apply a coat of linseed oil after several hours.

TOOL & PAINT BRUSH CLEANER-UPPER
You will need the following ingredients:

- $1^1/2$ *Cup of baking soda (fresh)*
- $^1/2$ *Cup of white vinegar*
- 3 *Tablespoons of rubbing alcohol*
- 1 *Gallon of cool tap water*

Place all the ingredients into a bucket and mix well. Works great on tools and paint brushes. Store away from children.

SOFTEN HARD PAINT BRUSHES
You will need the following ingredients:

- $^1/2$ *Gallon of cool tap water*
- 1 *Cup of baking soda (fresh)*
- $^1/4$ *Cup of white vinegar*

Place the ingredients into a medium pot and mix well, then boil the hardened brushes until they become soft.

Chapter 13

In The
Garden

PLANT FOOD

DON'T LET THIS SLIP BY

Save your banana, peels, and eggshells to use as plant fertilizer. Banana peels are an excellent source of potassium and phosphorus, and eggshells contain a number of beneficial minerals, especially calcium. Crush the egg shells into a fine powder and slice the banana peels into very small pieces, then mix them together and place a small amount around the base of the plants or mix a small amount in with potting soil when you are transplanting.

BUGS NO MORE

APHIDS BEGONE

You will need the following ingredients:

1 *Small white onion*
2 *Medium cloves of garlic*
2 *Cup of cold tap water*
1 *Spray bottle*

Place the ingredients in a blender and mix on high for a few seconds until thoroughly blended. Strain the mixture through a piece of cheesecloth and pour the remaining liquid into a spray bottle. Set the spray bottle on fine mist and spray the solution on rose bushes. Both the tops and bottoms of the leaves must be sprayed.

   NOTE: a piece of aluminum foil placed around the base of rose bushes and tomato plants will keep the aphids from climbing the plants.

ARE MEALYBUGS ON YOUR PLANTS?

You will need the following ingredients:

> 1   Bottle rubbing alcohol
>   Cotton swabs

Wash the insect cluster on the plant with the alcohol on a cotton swab. Wash the area with an insecticidal soap and isolate the infected plant if possible.

ANT POISON FOR GARDENS

You will need the following ingredients:

> 2   Tablespoon of calcium sulfide
> 1   Quart of cool tap water
> 1   Egg white

Place all the ingredients into a container and mix well. Place small amounts in areas where you have an ant problem. Keep out of reach of children and pets.

ALKALI-FREE GENERAL INSECT ELIMINATOR

You will need the following ingredients:

> 1   Ounce of diglycol oleate
> 25 Ounces of pyrethum extract

Place the ingredients into a medium container and mix thoroughly, then spray as needed to eliminate most insects. If the solution becomes too thick, water may be added to dilute it.

HOUSEPLANT BUG KILLER

You will need the following ingredients:

> $1/2$ Cup of isopropyl alcohol (from drug store)
> $1/2$ Cup of insecticidal liquid hand soap
> 1   Cups of cool tap water

Place the ingredients in a small bucket and mix well, then place into a spray bottle and spray the bugs. Care should be taken not to spray too much on the plant leaves, especially ferns or leaves with hair-like projections. Never spray on food-bearing plants in or out of doors.

KILLING THE DREADED SPIDER MITE

You will need the following ingredients:

- *1/2 Cup buttermilk*
- *4   Cups of whole wheat flour*
- *5   Gallons of cold tap water*
- *1   Spray bottle*

Place the ingredients in a large bucket and mix thoroughly. Place a portion of the liquid in a spray bottle and spray the mites' living areas or anywhere the problem may exist. This formula will suffocate all species of mite.

ELECTROCUTE SLUGS

You will need the following ingredients:

- *Roll of copper wire*
- *Wire cutter*

Place a circle of copper wire around the base on the plant and the slug will electrocute itself. The minerals in the slugs body reacts with copper and causes enough current to kill them.

NATURAL INSECT REPELLENT

You will need the following ingredients:

- *3   Hot jalapeño peppers*
- *3   Cloves of fresh garlic*
- *3/4 Teaspoon of any liquid soap*
- *3   Cups of cold tap water*
- *1   Spray bottle*

Place the garlic and peppers in a blender and puree. Pour the puree into a spray bottle and add the liquid soap and water. Shake and allow to stand overnight. Strain the solution through a piece of cheesecloth and return the liquid to the spray bottle to be sprayed on tops and bottoms of leaves. Test the spray on a few leaves and allow it to sit for 2–3 hours before you spray all the plants. This solution can be used on all plants.

SPICY AND SMELLY BUG SPRAY

You will need the following ingredients:

- *1   Tablespoon of red pepper*
- *1   Small yellow onion*
- *10 Cloves of garlic (not 10 bulbs)*
- *1/2 Teaspoon of liquid mild hand soap (not detergent)*
- *1   Quart of warm tap water*

Place the garlic cloves and the onion in a blender and puree, then place in a container and add the red pepper and water. Mix well and steep for about 6 hours. Strain the mixture through a piece of cheesecloth, add the soap, and mix well. Spray on the tops and bottoms of the leaves. This will get rid of most bugs.

PROTECT TREES FROM BUGS
You will need the following ingredients:

    1 *Pound of canola oil*
1^1/$_2$ *Pounds of rosin*
    4 *Ounces of beeswax*

Place the ingredients into a double boiler and heat until all the ingredients are melted together and mixed. Remove from the heat and allow the solution to cool somewhat, then use a paintbrush to spread the solution around the tree in a 4-inch wide band from the bottom of the tree. Use care since some of these ingredients are flammable.

CATERPILLAR ELIMINATOR
You will need the following ingredients:

    8 *Ounces of pyrethrum*
  ^{1}/$_2$ *Pint of summer oil*
12^1/$_2$ *Gallons of cool tap water*

Place all the ingredients into a large basin and mix well. Place into a spray bottle and spray the leaves of your trees.

CONTROLLING WHITE BARK WORMS
You will need the following ingredients:

  2 *Ounces of granulated glue*
  1 *Pound of table salt*
  2 *Ounces of arsenate of lead powder (poison)*
  4 *Pounds of quicklime (poison)*
  2 *Ounces of nicotine sulfate (40%) (poison)*
  2 *Medium containers*
  1 *Large container*

Place 1 pint of cool tap water into one of the containers, then add the glue and dissolve fully. Place 2 quarts of cool tap water into the second container and dissolve the salt, then mix the two solutions together. Add the arsenate of lead and the nicotine sulfate and mix well. Place the quicklime into the large container and add sufficient cool tap water to prepare a creamy paste, then add this solution to the other solution and add additional water to prepare a heavy whitewash. Remove the soil from around the base of the tree and paint the solution on the bark from the base to about 18 inches above the ground. Replace the topsoil after the solution has dried sufficiently. Additional applications are sometime needed every 2 weeks, usually in May and June when the worms are active.

S.BEAN

GENERAL GARDEN FORMULAS

PEPPER-UPPER FOR HOUSE PLANTS

You will need the following ingredients:

> 1 *Tablespoon apple cider vinegar (5% acidity)*
> 1 *Gallon of cool tap water*

Place the ingredients into a medium bucket and mix well and add 2 teaspoons to your water whenever you water. This supplement will provide additional minerals for your houseplants.

ALL-AROUND PLANT PROTECTOR

You will need the following ingredients:

> 1 *Tablespoon of corn oil*
> 1 *Tablespoon of liquid hand soap*
> 1 1/2 *Tablespoons of baking soda (fresh)*
> 1 *Tablespoon of white vinegar*
> 1 *Gallon of cool tap water*

Place the vinegar, baking soda, and 1 cup of water in a medium bowl and mix well. Slowly add the white vinegar and mix. Pour the solution into a hand pump sprayer and add the rest of the water. Spray the tops and underneath sides of the leaves once per month for the best results. Will reduce the risk of disease and keep a number of pests away.

A GOOD HOME FOR BUGS

Many weeds seem to attract pests that may be harmful to your flowers and plants. Clover and lamb's quarter tend to be the favorite meal for rabbits. However, a few weeds will never hurt the garden. Weeds such as Queen Anne's lace are a favorite of many beneficial bugs. If you do need to kill them off, try using a natural chemical approach instead of the commercial weed killers that tend to foul the groundwater.

WEED KILLER
You will need the following ingredients:

       1   Quart of warm tap water
       1   Ounce of baby shampoo
       1   Ounce of white vinegar
     $1/2$ Shot of gin
       1   Spray bottle

Place all the ingredients in a small bucket and mix well. Spray the weeds with a stream, not a fine spray. The solution will adhere to the weed and dry them out. The gin helps to kill them and alleviate their suffering.

DANDELION KILLER
You will need the following ingredients:

       1   Pound of iron sulfate
       1   Gallon of cool tap water

Place the water in a small basin and dissolve the iron sulfate. Place the solution in a sprayer and spray on the area where the dandelion problem exists. This solution should cover an area of about 400 square feet. Don't be concerned if you notice that a slight burning of the grass, the grass will return in 2–3 days as good as new. A second application may be needed if the dandelions are especially stubborn.

FLOWER LIFE EXTENDER #1
You will need the following ingredients:

     $3/4$ Cup of granulated sugar
       4   Tablespoons of talc
       2   Tablespoons of yeast (fresh)
       1   Teaspoon of lime oil
       1   Quart of cool tap water

Place the sugar, talc, and yeast in a bowl and mix well, then add the lime and the water and blend. Add two tablespoons to about a pint of water that has been placed in a vase. Shake the mixture before using, since some settling may occur.

FLOWER LIFE EXTENDER #2

You will need the following ingredients:

3 *Tablespoons of granulated sugar*
2 *Tablespoons of white vinegar*
1 *Quart of warm tap water*

Place the ingredients in a small bowl and mix well, then pour the solution into the flower vase. The stems of the flowers should be in at least 3 inches of the solution.

MAKING NUTRIENTS MORE AVAILABLE

When your houseplants start looking a little sickly and pale, they are probably undernourished and need a booster. If you're using hard water to water them, the nutrients are more difficult for the plants to remove. A small amount of vinegar added to the water will make the minerals and nutrients more available and will produce a healthier, better-looking plant.

FERTILIZER FOR FLOWERING HOUSE PLANTS

You will need the following ingredients:

3 *Parts bonemeal*
3 *Parts cottonseed meal*
3 *Parts wood ashes*

Place all the ingredients into a large mixing bowl and blend thoroughly. All ingredients can be found at a nursery. Mix the fertilizer into the soil with a plastic fork. A six-inch pot will require about 1 teaspoon every 5–7 weeks to remain in super health.

ALL-AROUND GREAT FERTILIZER

You will need the following ingredients:

1 *Cup of pure apple juice*
1 *Cup of lemon scented liquid soap*
1 *Cup of household ammonia*
1 *Cup of liquid lawn fertilizer*
1 *Can of cola (not diet)*
1 *Can of cheap beer (do not drink)*

Place all the ingredients in a small bucket and mix well, then place the solution into a hose attached to a sprayer and go for it every 3 weeks, in the morning if possible.

FUNGAL DISEASE ELIMINATOR #1 (POISON)

You will need the following ingredients:

3 Quarts of cool tap water
$^1/_2$ Cup of crushed rhubarb leaves (poisonous)

Slice the leaves into small pieces and place in a pot of boiling water. Allow the leaves to steep for 8 hours. Strain the mixture through a piece of cheesecloth and place in a spray bottle. Spray on areas of the plant that have a fungal disease for a quick killer. Keep away from children and pets.

FUNGAL DISEASE ELIMINATOR #2 (POISON)

You will need the following ingredients:

1 Cup of dried horsetail
1 Quart of cool tap water

Place the water and dried horsetail in a medium saucepan and boil for 15 minutes, then allow the mixture to cool. Strain through a piece of cheesecloth and place into a spray bottle. Wear gloves and keep away from children and pets.

FIRST-AID FOR OAK TREES DAMAGED DURING PRUNING

You will need the following ingredients:

$1^3/_4$ Cups of zinc oxide powder (from drug store)
$3^1/_2$ Cups of pure mineral oil

Place the ingredients into a small bucket and mix well. Use a paintbrush to spread the mixture over the exposed area to seal it and protect it from possible diseases. Oak trees are very susceptible to diseases.

BLACK SPOTS ON YOUR ROSES?

You will need the following ingredients:

1 Large red onion
$^1/_2$ Cup of rubbing alcohol
15 Fresh tomato plant leaves

Place the ingredients into a small bowl and mix well. Allow to steep overnight, then remove any diseased leaves from the plant and rub the mixture on the plant stems and leaves with a small cotton swab. This should save the plant from getting any more black-spot fungus.

ELIMINATING BROWN AREAS ON YOUR LAWN #1

You will need the following ingredients:

> 1 *Tablespoon of a quality horticultural oil (from nursery)*
> 1 *Tablespoon of potassium bicarbonate (from nursery)*
> 1 *Gallon of cool tap water*

Place all ingredients in a bucket and mix thoroughly. Spray a small amount (do not saturate) on the affected area twice a week until the brown area has returned to green. This problem is usually caused by a fungus.

ELIMINATING BROWN AREAS ON YOUR LAWN #2

You will need the following ingredients:

> 2 *Ounces of mercurous chloride*
> 1 *Ounce of mercuric chloride*
> 2 *Pounds of clean sand*

Place the chlorides into a medium container and mix well, then mix with the sand and lightly sprinkle on affected area. This amount should be enough for about 800–1000 square feet. The lawn should be watered immediately afterwards.

GIVE PLANTS A BREATH OF FRESH AIR

You will need the following ingredients:

> 1 *Tablespoon of a non-detergent liquid soap*
> 1 *Tablespoon of liquid seaweed (from nursery)*
> 1 *Quart of warm tap water*

Place all ingredients in a spray bottle and shake to mix well. Spray on houseplants to cleanse them of indoor pollutants. This should be done once a month.

CREATE A THICK LUXURIOUS LAWN

You will need the following ingredients:

> 2 *Cups of seaweed extract (from nursery)*
> 2 *Cups of fish emulsion (from nursery)*
> 5 *Gallons of cool tap water*

Place all the ingredients in a large bucket and mix well. Use a hose with a sprayer to spray the lawn. This spraying is normally done in the spring and fall and should also help keep the weeds out of the lawn.

ORGANIC FERTILIZER

You will need the following ingredients:

> 3 *Pounds of cottonseed meal*
> 7^1/$_2$ *Pounds of granite dust*
> 1^1/$_2$ *Pounds of colloidal phosphate*

Place the ingredients into a very large bucket and mix well before using. This will replace most of the expensive chemical fertilizers.

SEED-STARTING FORMULA

You will need the following ingredients:

> 2 *Cups of sterilized sand (commercial sandbox sand is OK)*
> 2 *Cups of sterilized topsoil (or your own)*
> 2 *Cups of vermiculite (nursery supply store)*

Place all the ingredients into a bucket and mix well. Store is a sealed plastic bag until needed. Place seeds in this soil to give them a good start before transplanting.

GRAFTING WAX SHOOT PROTECTOR

You will need the following ingredients:

> 1 *Part zinc oxide (from drug store)*
> 5 *Parts paraffin wax*
> 3 *Parts diatomaceous earth (from nursery supply)*

Place the wax in a double boiler and slowly melt. Remove from the heat and mix in the diatomaceous earth and zinc oxide (wear mask and gloves). Re-heat the mixture to bring it to a form suitable for molding to the shoot that needs protection and support. Store the balance in a well-sealed container for future use.

BULB FERTILIZER

You will need the following ingredients:

> 2^1/$_2$ *Pounds of bloodmeal*
> 2^1/$_2$ *Pounds of pure bonemeal*
> 2^1/$_2$ *Pounds of clean wood ashes*
> ^{1}/$_2$ *Teaspoon of kelp*

Place all the ingredients in a large bucket and mix well. Spread a small amount over the area where the bulbs are planted every spring and fall. Store the mixture in a well-sealed container to keep the moisture out.

FERTILIZER FOR FRUIT TREES

You will need the following ingredients:

1 1/4 Teaspoon of fish emulsion (from a nursery)
5 Gallons of cool tap water

Place the water and fish emulsion in a large bucket and mix well. Fertilize three times the first year, once when the tree is first planted, then in the early spring, and again in the first part of the summer. Fertilize semi-annually until the tree has reached maturity. The concentration should be increased about 10% per year.

FERTILIZER FOR POTTED PLANTS #1

You will need the following ingredients:

1 Ounce of sodium phosphate
1 Ounce of sodium nitrate
1 Tablespoon of ammonium sulfate
2 Teaspoons of granulated sugar

Place all the ingredients into a medium container and mix well, then dissolve 1/2 teaspoon of the mixture into 1 quart of water to dilute. Potted plant fertilizers should only be used once per week. Excessive watering of potted plants will result in the decay of the roots, the browning of the leaves, and the death of the plant.

FERTILIZER FOR POTTED PLANTS #2

You will need the following ingredients:

2 1/2 Tablespoons of potassium nitrate
2 1/2 Ounces of table salt
2 1/2 Tablespoons of magnesium sulfate
2 Teaspoons of magnesia
1 Tablespoon of sodium phosphate

Place all the ingredients into a medium container and mix well, then dissolve 1 teaspoon of the mixture into 1 quart of water to dilute.

FERTILIZER FOR POTTED PLANTS #3

The following ingredients will be needed:

1 Teaspoon of ammonium chloride
4 Teaspoons of sodium phosphate
1 1/2 Teaspoons of sodium nitrate
5 Ounces of cool tap water

Place all the ingredients into a small container and mix well, then place 25 drops of the mixture into 1 quart of cool tap water to dilute before using.

FERTILIZER FOR DECORATIVE WINDOW BOX PLANTS

You will need the following ingredients:

> 3 Ounces of sodium nitrate
> 2 Ounces of dry sodium phosphate
> 2 Ounces of potassium sulfate

Place all the ingredients into a medium container and mix well. To fertilize the plants, place 1 tablespoon into 1 gallon of water to dilute and water the plants with about 1/2-pint every week (for a 12 inch planter box). Adjust the amount up or down depending on the size of the planter.

POTTING MIX FOR TRANSPLANTED SEEDLINGS

You will need the following ingredients:

> 1 Teaspoon of sharp sand
> 1 Teaspoon of loam
> 1 Teaspoon of leaf mold

Place all the ingredients into a small container and mix well. Mix the solution with the soil when transplanting.

POTTING MIX FOR PALMS AND GERANIUMS

You will need the following ingredients:

> 1 Teaspoon of sharp sand
> 2 Teaspoons of loam
> 1 Teaspoon of humus
> 1/2 Teaspoon of dried cow manure
> 1/4 Teaspoon of bone meal

Place all the ingredients into a medium container and mix well, then add use the mixture as you would any potting mix.

PONDS

ELIMINATING ALGAE FROM PONDS

You will need the following ingredients:

> 1 Gallon of sodium pentachlorophenate (from garden supply)
> 5 Gallons of cool tap water

Place the ingredients into a large bucket and mix well, then spray the solution on the surface of the pond. It will take about 1 gallon of the solution to cover a 1,000 square foot surface.

Chapter 14

Formulas
For Fishermen

FORMULAS FOR FISHERMEN

The following formulas will be effective when you place a small amount on your bait or lure. The ingredients can be found in a health food store, herbal shop, or pharmacy. Fishing supply houses in major cities may also carry the ingredients.

SUPER OIL-BASED FORMULA #1

You will need the following ingredients:

5   *Parts of oil of rhodium*
2   *Parts oil of cumin*
1   *Part tincture of musk*

Mix all the ingredients together in a small plastic bowl then pour into a sealed bottle.

SUPER OIL-BASED FORMULA #2

You will need the following ingredients:

2   *Ounces of oil of rhodium*
$1/2$ *Ounce of tincture of musk*
1   *Ounce of oil of cumin*
$1/2$ *Ounce juice of loveage root*
    Bread crumbs
    Cotton balls

Place all the liquid ingredients in a small bowl and mix well. Shred the cotton balls and mix the pieces with the bread crumbs, then pour the oil over the mixture and mix by hand, producing a paste. Try using small pieces of the cotton tied on to your hook as bait. Fish will fight to get to your hook.

SUPER OIL-BASED FORMULA #3

You will need the following ingredients:

1   *Pound ground aniseed*
$1/3$ *Pound ground allspice*
$1/8$ *Ounce of oil of cloves*

Place the aniseed and allspice in a medium bowl and mix them together. Sprinkle the oil of cloves over the mixture and mix thoroughly. Allow the mixture to ripen in a sealed jar for 3 days before using. Only 1 drop on the bait is needed to do the trick.

SUPER OIL-BASED FORMULA #4

You will need the following ingredients:

$^1/_2$ Cup of cod liver oil
5 Drops of red oil-soluble food coloring

Place the ingredients into a small bowl and mix thoroughly. Store in a small sealed jar. The bait should be dipped into the mixture for the best results.

SUPER OIL-BASED FORMULA #5

You will need the following ingredients:

1 Ounce gum benzoin
12 Ounces of virgin olive oil
30 Drops of oil of rhodium
3 Drops of patchouli
$1^1/_4$ Ounces of lard oil

Place the gum benzoin and olive oil in a double boiler and heat on low for 2 hours. Remove from the heat and allow it to stand for 1 week. Strain the mixture through a piece of cheesecloth, then add the rhodium and patchouli with a small medicine dropper. Mix the solution then add the lard oil and mix thoroughly. Only a drop or two is needed, preferably on a meat bait or worm.

SUPER OIL-BASED FORMULA #6

You will need the following ingredients:

$^1/_2$ Ounce of oil of rhodium
$^1/_8$ Ounce of oil of spearmint
$^1/_2$ Ounce oil of anise
1 Ounce of glycerin

Place all the ingredients in a small bowl and mix thoroughly. Store in a well-sealed jar. It only takes 1–2 drops on your bait to work.

SUPER OIL-BASED FORMULA #7

You will need the following ingredients:

1 Pint jar with lid
3–6 Ounces of dead worms (most any will do)
20 Drops of oil of rhodium

Put the worms in a jar with a loosely covered top (to allow air to enter) and place the jar far away from your house. A barn or garage will do fine. The worms will liquefy in about 10 days. Pour $^1/_2$ ounce of the liquid off (no need to measure too carefully) and add the rhodium to the liquid and mix. One drop of this is enough to drive fish wild.

SUPER OIL-BASED FORMULA #8

You will need the following ingredients:

   2   *Ounces of cod liver oil*
  20   *Drops of anise*

Place the ingredients in a small bowl and mix well. Store in a small well-sealed jar. Dip the bait into the jar for one of the best trout formulas ever.

SUPER OIL-BASED FORMULA #9

You will need the following ingredients:

  $^1/_2$ *Ounce of oil of rhodium*
  $^1/_2$ *Pint of virgin olive oil*

Place the ingredients in a small bowl and mix well. It will only take a drop or two on your bait to make the fish bite.

FISHERWOMEN'S INSECT REPELLENT #1

You will need the following ingredients:

   5   *Teaspoons of lavender flower water*
   1   *Drop of essential sandalwood oil*
   3   *Drops of citronella oil*
   3   *Drops of essential eucalyptus citiadora oil*

Place the lavender flower water in a small spray bottle, then add the essential oils and shake well to mix. Shake before using. Store in a cool, dry location and it should last for about 6 months.

FISHERMAN'S INSECT REPELLENT #2

You will need the following ingredients:

3 *Tablespoons of jewelweed (from health food store)*
1 *Quart apple cider vinegar*
1 *Teaspoon of eucalyptus oil*
1 *Teaspoon of pennyroyal oil*
1 *Teaspoon of orange oil or lemon oil*
1 *Teaspoon of citronella oil*
1 *Spray bottle*

Place the jewelweed in a jar and crush up as best you can, then pour the vinegar over it. Allow to steep for 3 days, then strain the mixture through a piece of cheesecloth and add the oils. Mix the repellent well and try a small dab on your arm to be sure that you are not allergic to it. Spray the repellent on clothing or any exposed areas of the body that you prefer not to be bitten.

Chapter 15

Cleaning
Around The Kitchen

POTS AND PANS

BRASS AND COPPER POTS FOR EVERYDAY USE

Most brass and copper pots and utensils have a lacquer coating that should be removed before using the item to hold or cook food. If the item is for decorative purposes only, then the lacquer coating should not be removed and the item should just be cleaned with lukewarm water with mild detergent. If the item is to be used with food, then the lacquer must be removed by placing the item into a bath of 1 cup of washing soda mixed with 2 gallons of boiling water. After a short time the lacquer will peel off easily.

BRASS AND COPPER CLEANER

The following ingredients are needed:

> $1/2$ Fresh lemon or 2 Tablespoons of lemon juice
> 1 Tablespoon of salt

Place the salt in a shallow dish and dip the exposed end of the lemon in the salt and use to scrub the stained area. Another method is to make a paste of lemon juice and salt and use a cloth dipped in the solution to clean the brass or copper surfaces. If the pot has a green spot, use a solution of ammonia and salt to remove the area that has turned green. Gloves should be worn when using ammonia and always try to avoid breathing the fumes and work in a well-ventilated area.

CAST IRON POTS

Mix the following ingredients together in a small bowl:

> 1 Teaspoon of ascorbic acid (vitamin C)
> 2 Cups of tap water

To remove rust from cast iron pots, briskly rub the area with a paste made from the ascorbic acid and water. If the rust spot persists, try allowing the mixture to remain on overnight.

ALUMINUM POT CLEANER

You will need the following ingredients:

> $1/2$ Cup white vinegar
> $1/4$ Cup soap flakes (or shaved bar of Ivory soap)
> $1/2$ Cup baking soda (fresh)
> $1/2$ Cup cream of tartar

Place the baking soda and the cream of tartar in a medium bowl and mix well, then add the vinegar and blend until a soft paste is formed. Add the soap flakes and mix thoroughly before placing in a well-sealed jar. This mixture should be applied with a steel wool pad, then rinsed with hot water.

WHAT IS IT AND IS IT SAFE TO USE?

Basically, teflon is a plastic material that has a high chemical and heat stability. Teflon is extremely difficult to destroy once it is produced. The coating has the ability to protect surfaces from friction and corrosion. Teflon is not really dangerous to humans unless it is heated above 4000°C. When this high temperature is maintained in a pan that is empty, fumes are released, causing teflon particles to become airborne and causing a poisoning known as "polymer fume fever." The fumes will easily kill birds and is very hard to diagnose. Teflon is very safe under normal cooking conditions. If a piece of teflon chips off and is swallowed it will not break down in the body but will pass through and be excreted.

TEFLON SURFACE CLEANER
You will need the following ingredients:

> 3 Tablespoons of baking soda
> 3 Lemon slices
> 1 Cup of hot tap water

Place the baking soda and the lemon slices on the stained area, then add the water to cover. Simmer the pot on low heat until the area appears clean.

SILVERSTONE POT CLEANER
You will need the following ingredients:

> 1/2 Cup of white vinegar
> 2 Tablespoons of baking soda (fresh)
> 1 Cup of cool tap water

Place all the ingredients into a container and mix well. Pour into the Silverstone pot and boil for 10–15 minutes; then rinse the pot in soapy water and rinse. Rub oil on the surface to re-season.

PORCELAIN CLEANER
You will need the following ingredients:

> 3 Tablespoons of cream of tartar
> 3 Tablespoons of alum

Place the ingredients into a container and shake well to mix. Sprinkle the powder onto a well-dampened surface and allow the powder to remain for 2–3 hours before cleaning with a sponge. Rinse the area well.

STAINLESS STEEL POT CLEANER

You will need the following ingredients:

> 1 *Tablespoon of household ammonia*
> 1 *Pint of cool tap water*

Place the ingredients into a container and mix well, then apply to the stainless steel pot.

ENAMELED POT OR SURFACE CLEANER

You will need the following ingredients:

> 3 *Tablespoons of sodium carbonate (from drug store)*
> 1 *Tablespoon of sodium metaphosphate (from drug store)*
> 2 *Tablespoons of Castile soap (powdered, from health food store)*
> 1 *Cup of pumice powder (very fine grain, from hardware store)*

Place all the ingredients into a container and blend well, then apply to the stained enameled surface with a damp sponge. Rinse with cool water.

TEAPOT LIME DEPOSIT CLEANER

You will need the following ingredients:

> $1^1/_2$ *Cups of apple cider vinegar*
> $1^1/_4$ *Cups of cool tap water*
> 3 *Tablespoons of table salt*

Place all the ingredients into the teapot and mix well, then boil the mixture for 15–20 minutes, then allow the mixture to remain for 10 hours before rinsing well with clear, cool tap water.

CLEANING SILVERWARE

DIRTY CUTLERY CURE

The following items are needed:

> 6 *Wide strips of aluminum foil*
> 1 *Quart of boiling water*
> 4 *Tablespoons of baking soda*

This formula should be used if you have a large amount of silverware to clean after a dinner party. Use a medium-sized plastic container and place the aluminum foil strips on the bottom of the container, then add all the silverware and cover with boiling water. Sprinkle the baking soda over the top of the mixture and allow the cutlery to soak for 10–15 minutes. If this is done after each use, the silverware should not tarnish as easily.

SILVER CLEANING CLOTH

The following items are needed:

Cotton cloth
Ammonia
Liquid silver polish
Cold water

In a small plastic bowl mix 2 parts ammonia (use gloves) with 1 part liquid silver polish and 10 parts cold water. Saturate the cloth and allow it to air dry overnight. More than one cloth may be made if so desired.

SILVER POLISH #1

You will need the following ingredients:

$1^1/2$ *Cups of warm tap water*
2   *Tablespoons of stearic acid (caution: flammable)*
$^1/2$ *Teaspoon of trisodim phosphate*
$^1/2$ *Teaspoon of washing soda*
1   *Cup of diatomaceous earth*

Place a double boiler with water on the stove and boil the water. Wear rubber gloves and a dust mask. The top of the double boiler will remain empty. Remove from heat and place the acid and water in the top of the double boiler and stir until the stearic acid has melted. Mix in the rest of the ingredients while continually stirring to produce a creamy paste. Polish silver.

SILVER POLISH #2

You will need the following ingredients:

1   *Pound of oleic acid*
1   *Pint of kerosene*
8   *Ounces of Tripoli powder*

Place all the ingredients into a container and add just enough water to prepare a paste.

SILVER POLISH #3

You will need the following ingredients:

8 *Parts of whiting*
2 *Parts of paraffin*
6 *Parts of paraffin oil*
1 *Part of oleic acid*

Place the paraffin and the paraffin oil in a double boiler and melt, then add the whiting and the oleic acid and blend. Remove from the heat and allow it to cool before placing in a well-sealed jar.

SILVER POLISH #4

You will need the following ingredients:

2 *Cups of cool tap water*
1/2 *Cup of whiting*
1/4 *Cup of soap flakes*
1 1/2 *Teaspoons of household ammonia*

Heat the water in a medium saucepan (not aluminum). Remove from the heat and dissolve the soap flakes. Add the whiting and beat vigorously until all the lumps are gone. Allow the mixture to cool before adding the ammonia; mix well. Shake well before each use.

GENERAL CLEANING

AIR FRESHENER

You will need the following ingredients:

2 *Cups of pure distiller water*
4 *Packages of Knox gelatin*
10 *Drops of rose essence fragrance*
2 *Tablespoons of table salt*
   Food coloring

Place one cup of distilled water in a medium saucepan and bring to a boil. Add the gelatin and blend until dissolved, then remove from the range and add the other cup of distilled water, the salt, and the rose fragrance. If you would like a colored freshener, add a few drops of food coloring. Place the mixture into small jars and allow it to remain at room temperature for about 12 hours. The result will be a very effective gel air freshener. The addition of the salt should eliminate the possibility of mold forming.

SCOURING POWDER #1

You will need the following ingredients:

> 1   Cup of baking soda
> 1/4   Cup of borax
> 1/4   Cup of washing soda

Place the ingredients in a sealed container and shake to mix well. Rinse well after using the powder.

SCOURING POWDER #2

You will need the following ingredients:

> 1   Cup of baking soda (fresh)
> 1   Cup of borax
> 1   Cup of table salt

Place all the ingredients into a glass jar and cover with a tight lid and shake to mix thoroughly. Use the same as any other cleanser.

SOFT-SCRUBBER CLEANSER

You will need the following ingredients:

> 1/4   Cup of baking soda
>   Liquid hand soap to make a paste

Place the baking soda into a small bowl and slowly add the liquid soap while stirring. You should end up with a creamy-textured soft cleanser.

NON-ABRASIVE CLEANSER

You will need the following ingredients:

> 1/4   Cup of chalk
>   Liquid hand soap to make a paste

Place the chalk into a small bowl and slowly add the liquid soap while stirring. You will end up with a creamy, non-abrasive cleanser that will not scratch surfaces.

REFRIGERATOR FRESHENER

You will need the following ingredients:

> 1   Teaspoon of baking soda
> 1   Teaspoon of lemon juice
> 2   Cups of very hot tap water
> 1   Spray bottle

Place the hot water into a spray bottle then add the ingredients and mix well. Spray a light mist inside the refrigerator the next time you clean it out. The spray can remain on the walls and shelves. Allow the mixture to dry for a few minutes. This spray freshener can be used anywhere you need a freshener.

LIQUID DISHWASHING SOAP

You will need the following ingredients:

> 3 Bars of soap (good use for those motel bars you have
>   been saving)
> 1 Grater
> 1 Container

Finely grate the bars of soap and place them in a small saucepan. Completely cover the fine gratings with water and simmer over low heat until they are all melted. Pour into the container and use the same as any liquid soap.

DISHWASHER SPOT REMOVER

You will need the following ingredients:

> 1 Cup of liquid chlorine bleach
> 1 Cup of white vinegar

After loading the dishwasher with only glass dishes or glasses (no silver, aluminum, or other metal) place the bleach into a small glass bowl and set it on the bottom shelf so that it will not spill. Run the washer cycle only, then turn off the dishwasher. Pour the vinegar into the bowl and run through the entire cycle.

DISHWASHER CLEANER

You will need the following ingredients:

> 2 Teaspoons of baking soda (fresh)
> 1 Teaspoon of cream of tartar
> 1 Teaspoon of borax

Place all the ingredients into a small cup and mix well, then add the mixture to the soap holder of the dishwasher when it is empty. Run the dishwasher on a hot water cycle or a pot cleaner cycle.

OVEN CLEANER #1

You will need the following ingredients:

> 2 Tablespoons of Castile soap (grated or liquid)
> 2 Tablespoons of borax

Place the soap and the borax into a spray bottle and fill with hot water, then shake well until all the soap and borax are in solution. Spray on oven stains and allow it to remain for about 20 minutes before rinsing with clear warm water. Some scrubbing may be needed for stubborn stains.

OVEN CLEANER #2

You will need the following ingredients:

4   Ounces of baking soda
$1/4$ Cup of washing soda
1   Teaspoon of table salt

Place all the ingredients into a small bowl and mix thoroughly, adding enough water to make a paste. Use a damp sponge to clean the area. For difficult spots, prepare some of the paste with more water to make it runny and allow it to sit on the spot for 1 hour before cleaning it off.

CLEANING THE OVEN OVERNIGHT

You will need the following ingredients:

$3/4$ Cup of household ammonia
1   Tablespoon of liquid hand soap
1   Quart of hot tap water

Pour the ammonia in a cup, close the oven door, and leave the cup in the oven overnight. The following morning remove the ammonia and clean the oven with the liquid soap and hot water. The ammonia fumes should turn the black stuck-on residues to dust.

FORMICA® COUNTER CLEANSER

You will need the following ingredients:

3   Tablespoons of white vinegar
$1/2$ Teaspoons liquid dish soap
$1/2$ Teaspoon of virgin olive oil
$1/2$ Cup of very warm tap water
1   Spray bottle

Place all the ingredients in a spray bottle and mix thoroughly. Spray the counter and wait a few seconds before wiping off with a damp sponge. Rinse the area well to remove all residue.

CLEANER FOR FOOD PROCESSORS

You will need the following ingredients:

$^1/_2$ *Cup of white vinegar*
$^1/_2$ *Teaspoon of liquid dish detergent*
$^1/_2$ *Cup of warm tap water*

Place the ingredients in a small bowl and mix. Blend in a food processor and run for 30 seconds. Remove the solution and rinse thoroughly.

HOUSEHOLD APPLIANCE, ANTISEPTIC CLEANER
(Harmful if ingested)

You will need the following ingredients:

2 *Cups of trisodium phosphate (TSP)*
1 *Cup of sodium bicarbonate*
1 *Cup sodium pyrophosphate*
2 *Drops of essential rose oil*

Place all the ingredients into a bucket and mix well (wear gloves and mask). Store the mixture in a glass container that can be well sealed. Dilute before using at about $^1/_2$ cup to each gallon of cool tap water.

PORCELAIN SINK STAIN REMOVER

You will need the following ingredients:

1 *Teaspoon of liquid detergent*
$^1/_2$ *Cup of liquid chlorine bleach*
$^1/_2$ *Cup of white vinegar*

Place a closure over the sink drain, then fill the sink with 2–3 inches of warm water. Place all the ingredients into the sink, mix well, and allow the mixture to remain for about 8–10 hours. Rinse with hot water.

KITCHEN ODOR REMOVER

You will need the following ingredients:

$^1/_4$ *Cup of chalk*
1 *Cup of Portland cement*
1 *Cup of vermiculite*
$^1/_4$ *Cup of silica gel*
    Cool tap water

Place all the ingredients except the water into a container and mix well, then slowly add the water and stir until the mixture turns into a creamy paste. Pour the mixture into molds and allow to air dry for 2–3 days, then place the molds into the oven at 350° F. for 2 hours. The cakes will last from 2–3 weeks and can be re-activated 3–4 times by placing them back in the oven at the 350° F. for 2 hours.

FLOOR CLEANING

GREASE CUTTER FOR SERIOUS CLEANING

You will need the following ingredients:

- $1/4$ Cup of white vinegar
- 1 Tablespoon of liquid dish soap
- $1/4$ Cup washing soda
- 2 Gallons of very warm tap water

Place all the ingredients into a bucket and mix well until sudsy. Mop the area with the solution. Not recommended for waxed floors—it may make the wax gunky.

Chapter 16

Adhesives

ADHESIVES

ADHESIVE FACTS:

Glue   One of the strongest adhesives.
Mucilage   Not as powerful as glue but will join lightweight articles.
Paste   Not as strong as mucilage or glue, but sufficient for
               light projects.
Cement   There are two types: an adhesive, and a mortar or filler.
Sealing wax Used to seal envelopes and paper packages

Most adhesives are composed of chemicals that tend to increase in volume when added to water or other organic solvents, then harden as the liquid evaporates. However, some adhesives have the tendency to melt when heated and then harden when cooled. The kind of adhesive chosen depends on the materials to be joined. Therefore, a variety of adhesives are necessary for different materials and projects. Choosing the right adhesive for your job is crucial to successful bonding and the permanence of the bond.

Many adhesive formulas contain poisonous chemicals including: sodium silicate, caustic soda, ammonium hydroxide, lime, potassium bichromate, ammonia, barium sulfate, white lead, chloral hydrate, carbolic acid, formaldehyde, and plaster of paris.

GLUES

GLASS TO GLASS GLUE

You will need the following ingredients:

1/2 Ounce unflavored gelatin
3 Tablespoons non-fat milk
2 Tablespoons of very cold water
5 Drops of oil of cloves
1 Small mixing bowl

Place the cold water in the small bowl and sprinkle the unflavored gelatin over the top of the water. Allow enough time for the gelatin to soften before using. Boil the non-fat milk (being careful not to burn it), pour the milk into the gelatin and stir the mixture until it is thoroughly blended. The glue should be used while it is still warm for the best results. Apply a thin layer with a brush to glue glass to glass. The glue will be waterproof. If you are going to store the glue, add 3 drops of lubricating oil and store in a well-sealed jar. Heat the mixture slightly before each use.

STANDARD GLASS GLUE

You will need the following ingredients:

5 Ounces of white gelatin
5 Ounces of acetic acid
6 Ounces of cool tap water

Place the gelatin and water in a medium bowl and allow the gelatin to soak for 12 hours, then place the mixture in a small saucepan and heat over low heat, allowing the gelatin to dissolve completely. Stir in the acetic acid and dilute to produce about a pint of glass glue. This glue will attach a paper or cardboard product to glass, or will work for glass to glass projects.

FABRIC AND LEATHER GLUE

You will need the following ingredients:

1 Packet of unflavored gelatin
3 Tablespoons of boiling water
1 Teaspoon of glycerin (from pharmacy)
1 Tablespoon of white vinegar

Place the gelatin into the boiling water and stir until the gelatin is completely dissolved. Add the white vinegar and glycerin and continue stirring until the solution is thoroughly mixed. Apply the glue to the fabric while it is still warm. The glue is waterproof and will work just as well gluing leather to leather. The glue can be stored in a well-sealed bottle but will gel. Just warm the glue slightly until it becomes soft enough to re-use. It should last for 3–4 months.

PAPER GLUE

You will need the following ingredients:

$1/2$ Cup of all-purpose flour
$1/2$ Cup of granulated sugar
$1^1/2$ Cups of hot tap water
$1/2$ Cup of cold tap water
$1/2$ Teaspoon of alum

Place the flour and sugar in a medium saucepan and mix well, then add the cold water and stir well (whisking works best) until the mixture is very smooth with no lumps. Add the hot water and heat on medium while continually stirring until the mixture comes to a boil and thickens. Remove from the heat, add the alum, and blend all ingredients well. Place into a heatproof container and allow it to cool before you use the paper glue.

GLUE FOR MAKING PAPER BOXES

You will need the following ingredients:

5   *Parts of chloral hydrate*
8   *Parts of white gelatin*
2   *Parts of gum arabic*
30 *Parts of boiling water*

Mix the chloral hydrate, gelatin, and gum arabic in a porcelain container and pour the boiling water slowly over the mixture. Allow it to stand for 24 hours. Stir the mixture vigorously at least 5–6 times during this period. If the mixture solidifies too much, place the container in a warm water bath for a few minutes. The glue will adhere to any surface.

OLD-FASHIONED LIBRARY GLUE

You will need the following ingredients:

2   *Tablespoons of yellow dextrin*
2   *Tablespoons of calcium chloride*
2   *Cups of cool tap water*

Place all the ingredients in a small saucepan and mix well, then slowly heat on low while continually mixing. Cook until it is the consistency of thin syrup—do not boil. Remove from the heat and allow the glue to cool, then place in a bottle with a good lid.

OLD-FASHIONED MOLASSES GLUE

You will need the following ingredients:

4   *Teaspoons of standard molasses*
1   *Teaspoon of quicklime (use with caution, do not inhale or get on skin)*
12 *Teaspoons of very warm tap water*

Place the water in a medium bowl and add the molasses, then stir until it is fully dissolved and add the quicklime. Place the mixture into a double boiler and heat to 167° F. while stirring frequently. Remove the mixture and allow the glue to cool and set for 3–4 days, then pour off the white liquid and use as glue.

GLUE FOR LEATHER SOLES

You will need the following ingredients:

6   *Parts of rosin*
4   *Parts of crepe rubber*
2   *Parts of varnish (good quality)*
3   *Parts of naptha*

Place the rosin, rubber, and varnish in a double boiler over low heat and stir until the ingredients are well blended, then remove the mixture from the heat and allow it to cool. When the mixture has cooled, add the naptha and stir well.

WATERPROOF GLUE #1

You will need the following ingredients:

8   Teaspoons of potassium bichromate
11 Teaspoons of gelatin glue
1   Teaspoon of alum

Place the gelatin glue into a medium bowl with just enough very hot water to allow the glue to dissolve, then add the potassium and mix well. Allow it to cool and use as waterproof glue.

WATERPROOF GLUE #2

You will need the following ingredients:

2   Packets of unflavored gelatin
2   Tablespoons of white vinegar
2   Teaspoons of glycerin
6   Tablespoons of cool tap water

Place the water into a small saucepan and bring to a boil, then remove from the heat and add the gelatin, stirring until it is fully dissolved. Stir in the vinegar and glycerin and continue to stir until it is well mixed. Allow the glue to cool for a few minutes before placing it into a well-sealed container. Waterproof glue is more effective when applied warm. If the glue gels, just warm it up and it will be usable. This mixture works best when used to glue paper to paper and leather to leather.

ACETIC ACID GLUE

You will need the following ingredients:

$^1/_2$ Pound of dextrin
2   Ounces of acetic acid
2   Ounces of gum arabic
1   Pint of boiling water
2   Ounces of ethyl alcohol

Place the dextrine in a medium bowl with the boiling water and dissolve. Strain the dextrine through a piece of cheesecloth, then add the acetic acid and mix well. Allow the mixture to cool to room temperature before adding the alcohol.

CELLULOID GLUE

You will need the following ingredients:

4 *Ounces of ethyl alcohol (or as strong as possible)*
2 *Ounces of shellac*
3 *Ounces of spirits of camphor*

Place the alcohol into a container and dissolve the shellac and spirits of camphor into it, then stir well. The glue should be stored in a warm location and in a well-sealed bottle. Use for adhering celluloid to wood or a metal surface.

MARINE GLUE

You will need the following ingredients:

1 *Part of para caoutchouc*
12 *Parts of benzol*
20 *Parts of powdered shellac*

Place the benzol into a pot and dissolve in the caoutchouc. Stir in the powdered shellac and place the mixture on low heat while continually stirring for a few minutes until the glue has an even consistency. Remove from the heat and allow the glue to cool somewhat before placing in a container.

FIREPROOF GLUE

You will need the following ingredients:

8 *Parts raw linseed oil*
1 *Part unsweetened gelatin*
2 *Parts quicklime*

Place the linseed oil in a pot and add the gelatin, then place the pot on low heat to melt the mixture while stirring. Remove the pot and allow the mixture to sit for 12 hours. When the mixture is blended into solution add the quicklime and stir well until the consistency is uniform. Spread the glue on a cookie pan and allow it to dry in a cool location.

MUCILAGE

To preserve mucilage, place a small piece of camphor in the storage bottle. The camphor will produce just enough vapor to kill any bacteria that might get into the bottle. This trick will preserve the adhesive quality of the mucilage.

MUCILAGE TO ADHERE PAPER TO GLASS

You will need the following ingredients:

8   Ounces of rye flour
1   Ounce of powdered acacia
2   Ounces of glycerine
40   Drops of oil of cloves

Place the acacia and rye flour in a mortar and pestle and grind into a very fine powder, then place the powder into a pot and add 8 ounces of cool tap water and mix well. Strain the mixture through a piece of cheesecloth, place the mixture back into the pot and add 1 pint of boiling water. Heat on low heat until the mixture obtains the desired thickness. Remove from the heat and allow it to cool until almost cold before adding the glycerin and oil of cloves, then mix well.

FLOUR MUCILAGE

You will need the following ingredients:

4   Ounces of whole wheat flour
1/2   Ounce of powdered acacia
1   Ounce of glycerin
20   Drops of oil of cloves
8   Ounces of cold water
1   Pint of boiling water

Place the cold water in a container and add the flour and powdered acacia. Mix into a smooth paste, then strain through a piece of cheesecloth. Dissolve the mixture into the boiling water, then heat the solution until it thickens. Remove from the heat and allow it to cool before adding the oil of cloves and glycerin. Mix well and store in a sealed container.

HONEY MUCILAGE

You will need the following ingredients:

4   Ounces of gum arabic
1 1/2   Ounces of pure honey
1   Pint of cool tap water

Place the water in a small pot and add the gum arabic, then boil the mixture while stirring continually until the gum is fully dissolved. Add the honey and mix until the mucilage is uniform in appearance.

S. DEAN

MUCILAGE FOR ENVELOPES

You will need the following ingredients:

- 1 *Teaspoon of gum arabic*
- 1 *Teaspoon of starch*
- 4 *Teaspoons of granulated sugar*

Place the gum arabic into a medium bowl and add enough water to dissolve it, then add the sugar and starch. Place the mixture into a small saucepan and heat until the starch dissolves. Add water to make the mucilage thin enough to easily apply with a small brush.

STICK MUCILAGE

You will need the following ingredients:

- 10 *Parts of powdered white glue*
- 2 *Parts of powdered gum arabic*
- 5 *Parts of granulated sugar*

Place the glue, gum, and sugar in a container and add sufficient cold tap water to prepare a smooth, thick mixture, then allow the mixture to stand for 12 hours. Add more cold water to make up for evaporation until the mixture has returned to a smooth, thick mixture. Place the glue in a greased cookie pan and when cold, slice into sticks. To use, just moisten the stick and apply it to the surface to be glued.

PASTE

FLOUR PASTE

You will need the following ingredients:

- 1 *Pound of rye flour*
- 3/4 *Ounces of rosin*
- 1 1/2 *Ounces of ethyl alcohol*
- 2 *Quarts of cool tap water*

Place flour and water into a medium saucepan and boil to incorporate the flour into the water. In a separate saucepan, dissolve the rosin in the ethyl alcohol over very low heat then add the flour mixture and stir well to mix.

DECORATORS' PASTE
You will need the following ingredients:

4 Parts of rye meal (powdered)
2 Parts of whiting (fine powder)
1 Part casein (powder)
1/2 Part of powdered alum

Place all the powders in a container and blend thoroughly, then add 1 pound of the powder to 1 pint of cold tap water and mix well.

WALLPAPER PASTE
You will need the following ingredients:

4 Pounds of rye flour
2 Quarts of cold water
1 1/2 Gallons of boiling water
2 Ounces of powdered rosin

Place the rye flour into the cold water and mix until it is the consistency of a smooth paste, then stir the paste into the boiling water and mix well. Add the powdered rosin to the mixture very slowly and continue to mix. Additional water may be added to thin the paste if necessary. Remove from the heat and allow it to cool to room temperature before using.

SUPER-HARDENING PAPIER MÂCHÉ PASTE
You will need the following ingredients:

1/2 Cup of whole wheat flour
1/2 Cup of warm tap water
1/4 Cup of powdered resin glue (from hardware store)
1 1/2 Cups of very hot tap water
3 Drops of essential cinnamon oil

Place the wheat flour and resin glue into a medium saucepan and, while stirring, add the 1/2 cup of warm tap water to form a paste. Add the hot water and blend all ingredients until there are no lumps, then place the saucepan over low heat and stir continually until the paste is clear and somewhat thick. Remove from the heat and allow the paste to cool for a minute, then add the essential cinnamon oil and blend well. Store the paste in a well-sealed jar. This paste will only last for 2–3 days.

PASTE FOR ADHERING CLOTH TO METAL

You will need the following ingredients:

   20 *Parts of starch*
   10 *Parts of granulated sugar*
    1 *Part of zinc chloride*
  100 *Parts of warm tap water*

Place all the ingredients into a pot and mix well, then place on low heat and warm until there are no lumps and the consistency is smooth. As soon as the liquid thickens, remove from the heat and allow the paste to cool.

BASIC FLOUR PASTE

You will need the following ingredients:

   2 *Pounds of wheat flour*
   1 *Quart of cold tap water*
   1 *Ounce of alum*
   4 *Ounces of very hot tap water*
  1/2 *Gallon of boiling water*

Place the cold water into a container and add the wheat flour. Mix very well until all lumps disappear. In another container, dissolve the alum in the 4 ounces of hot water and mix well. Add the alum mixture to the 1/2 gallon of boiling water and mix very well until it resembles an almost transparent paste. If it doesn't, boil the mixture until it has that look, then add the wheat flour mixture and mix well until you have made a fine quality paste for wallpaper or general use.

LABEL PASTE #1

You will need the following ingredients:

   1 *Ounce of tragacanth*
   4 *Ounces of acacia*
  14 *Grains of thymol*
   4 *Ounces of glycerin*
     Water

Dissolve the tragacanth and the acacia in 1 pint of water. In another container, add the glycerin to the thymol and mix. Mix both solutions together and add enough water to make 2 pints of paste. If allowed to stand, the mixture will separate but can be recombined by shaking before each use.

LABEL PASTE #2

You will need the following ingredients:

    3   Pounds of dextrine
    2   Ounces of borax
   20   Grams of glucose
    3   Pints + 2 ounces of warm tap water

Place the water in a double boiler and dissolve the glucose, then add the dextrine and borax and heat gently until they are all dissolved and the consistency is that of a smooth paste.

PAPER CRAFT AND WALLPAPER PASTE

You will need the following ingredients:

   1¹/2   Cups of all-purpose flour
    ¹/2   Cup of granulated sugar
     1   Tablespoon of alum
     2   Cups of boiling water
     1   Cup of cold tap water

Place the all-purpose flour and sugar into a bowl and mix well, then slowly add the cold tap water and blend well until there are no lumps. Place the mixture in a medium saucepan and heat on medium heat, then add the boiling water while stirring continuously. When the mixture starts to set, remove it from the heat and stir in the alum. Store in a well-sealed container. If the paste hardens, just add a small amount of warm tap water until the desired consistency is achieved.

LONG-LASTING PASTE

You will need the following ingredients:

    2   Ounces of alum
    2   Quarts of very hot tap water
  ¹/4   Ounce of powdered rosin
        All-purpose flour as needed

Place the hot water in a pot and dissolve the alum, then allow it to cool. Add just enough flour to prepare a paste, then stir in the powdered rosin. Boil the mixture on medium heat while stirring until it is very thick. Remove from heat and allow it to cool before using the paste. The paste may be thinned with warm water if it gets too thick.

PAPER TO METAL PASTE

You will need the following ingredients:

1 *Ounce of acetic acid*
2 *Ounces of dextrine*
5 *Ounces of cool tap water*
1 *Ounce of ethyl alcohol*

Place the water in a small saucepan on low heat, then dissolve the acetic acid and dextrine. Add the alcohol and blend thoroughly. Remove from the heat and allow it to cool before placing in a well-sealed container.

CEMENT

WATERPROOF CEMENT—STICK FORM

You will need the following ingredients:

1 *Ounce beeswax*
3 *Ounces resin*
5 *Ounces plaster of paris (talcum powder will work)*

Place the beeswax and resin in a double boiler and melt, then add the plaster of paris and mix until there are no lumps. Pour the mixture into a lightly greased flat pan with sides and slice into sticks before the cement hardens completely.

CHINA AND CROCKERY CEMENT #1

You will need the following ingredients:

1 *Tablespoon of beeswax*
4 *Tablespoons of rosin*

Place the ingredients into an iron pot and melt them together while stirring continually. Remove from heat and allow the cement to cool slightly before using. The cement works best when somewhat hot. Excellent for repairing china and crockery.

CHINA AND CROCKERY CEMENT #2

You will need the following ingredients:

3 *Tablespoons of gum arabic*
1 *Tablespoon of glycerin*
1/2 Teaspoon of cool tap water

Place all the ingredients into a container and mix well. Store in a well-sealed container. This cement will last about 1 year.

CHINA AND CROCKERY CEMENT #3

You will need the following ingredients:

3 *Tablespoons of gum arabic*
1/2 Teaspoon of cool tap water
Plaster of paris as needed

Combine the gum arabic and the water in a container, then add just enough plaster of paris to prepare a paste.

PIPE JOINT CEMENT #1

You will need the following ingredients:

5 *Ounces of fine yellow ocher*
2 *Ounces of ground litharge*
2 *Ounces of whiting*
1/4 Ounce of hemp (finely cut up)
Linseed oil

Place the ocher, litharge, whiting, and hemp in a container and mix well, then add just enough linseed oil to produce a stiff paste substance.

PIPE JOINT CEMENT #2

You will need the following ingredients:

3 *Parts of chalk (powdered)*
10 *Parts of graphite (powdered)*
4 *Parts of litharge (ground)*
3 *Parts of oil (boiled)*

Place the chalk and graphite into a container and mix well, then add the litharge. Add the mixture to the boiled oil to prepare a stiff paste. If stored in a cool location, the paste will remain in a somewhat plastic condition for some time.

CEMENT TO REPAIR MARBLE

You will need the following ingredients:

> 4 *Parts of gypsum*
> 1 *Part of finely powdered gum arabic*
> *Borax*
> *Cold water*

Place the gypsum and the gum arabic into a container and mix well. Mix the borax and cold water to form a mortar-like solution, then add the borax mixture to the gypsum mixture and blend well.

PAPER CEMENT

You will need the following ingredients:

> 2^1/$_2$ *Teaspoons of chloral hydrate*
> 4 *Teaspoons of white gelatin*
> 1 *Teaspoon of gum arabic*
> 15 *Teaspoons of boiling water*

Place the chloral hydrate, gelatin, and gum arabic into a porcelain container and add the boiling water, mix, and allow the mixture to stand for 10–12 hours. Stir 4 times during this period to avoid any serious setting. The cement will be ready to use after the 10–12 hour period. If the cement later becomes too hard, just place the container in a hot water bath for a few minutes to soften.

CEMENT TO ATTACH IRON TO MARBLE

You will need the following ingredients:

> 30 *Parts of plaster of paris*
> 10 *Parts iron filings*
> ^{1}/$_2$ *Part sal ammoniac*
> *White vinegar*

Place the first three ingredients into a container and mix well, then add sufficient vinegar to prepare a loose paste. Use the cement while it is fresh and discard leftovers. This cement must be made fresh for each use.

CEMENT TO ATTACH OBJECTS TO GLASS SURFACES

You will need the following ingredients:

1   Part rosin
2   Parts yellow wax

Place the ingredients into a double boiler and melt. Remove from heat and allow it to cool before storing in a well-sealed container.

CEMENT TO ATTACH COPPER TO GLASS

You will need the following ingredients:

1   Part caustic soda
3   Parts colophony
5   Parts of water
9   Parts of plaster of paris

Place the first three ingredients into a pot and bring to a boil, then add the plaster of paris and blend well. This is fast-hardening cement, if you need a slower-hardening cement, use slaked lime or zinc white in place of the plaster of paris.

CEMENT TO ATTACH BRASS TO GLASS

You will need the following ingredients:

1   Part of caustic soda (fine powder)
3   Parts of rosin (fine powder)
3   Parts of gypsum (fine powder)
5   Parts of water

Placer all the ingredients into a pot and bring to a boil, continually mixing. This is a fast-drying cement and needs to be used up in a short period of time.

CEMENTING GLASS TO IRON

You will need the following ingredients:

5   Ounces of rosin
1   Ounce of yellow wax
1   Ounce of Venetian red

Place the wax and rosin in a double boiler and melt. While continually stirring, slowly add the Venetian red, making sure it is well dried before using. Remove from the heat and allow to cool while continually stirring or the Venetian red will come out of suspension.

WATERPROOF CEMENT FOR GLASS AND METALS

You will need the following ingredients:

> 6 *Pounds of whiting*
> 3 *Pounds plaster of paris*
> 3 *Pounds of common sand*
> 3 *Pounds of litharge*
> 1 *Pound of rosin*
> *Copal varnish*

Place all the ingredients into a bucket and mix well, then add enough copal varnish to prepare a paste.

CEMENTING SUBSTANCES TO METALS

You will need the following ingredients:

> 4 *Ounces of sal ammoniac*
> 2 *Ounces of sulfur*
> 32 *Ounces of iron filings*

Place the ingredients into a container and mix well, then add just enough water to prepare a paste.

CRYSTAL CEMENT

You will need the following ingredients:

> 8 *Parts of caoutchoue*
> 100 *Parts of gum mastic*
> 600 *Parts of chloroform*

Place the chloroform in a container and add the other ingredients and dissolve well. This mixture must then be placed in a hermetically sealed container for 8 days before applying with a brush.

ALL-AROUND UNIVERSAL CEMENT

You will need the following ingredients:

> 100 *Parts gum arabic*
> 75 *Parts starch*
> 21 *Parts granulated sugar*
> 4 *Parts camphor*

Place the gum arabic in a small amount of water to dissolve. In another container, dissolve the starch in a small amount of water. Mix the two solutions together and stir well. Place into a pot and boil until the solution becomes the consistency of a paste. When applied, this cement will thicken and provide a super-strong bond.

LIQUID CEMENT FOR GLASS OR WOOD

You will need the following ingredients:

1 *Pound of shellac*
1 *Gallon of waterglass*
2 *Quarts of cool tap water*

Place the water into a large pot and add the waterglass while stirring, then place on low heat and slowly add the shellac while stirring until all the ingredients are fully blended. Remove from the heat and allow it to cool somewhat before placing the cement into a sealed container.

Chapter 17

Arts & Crafts

S. BEAN

MISCELLANEOUS

MAKE YOUR OWN WICKS THE OLD-FASHIONED WAY

Hundreds of years ago, candlewicks were made from the mullen. Mullen is a very hard-stemmed plant, which grows very straight. The plant is harvested when it is fully grown and the hard outer stem is removed to reveal a cord-like substance that can be twisted into a wick. After allowing it to dry for 3–4 weeks, this substance can be used as a wick in candles.

CANDLE WICKS

Mix the following ingredients together in a small bowl:

> 5 *Tablespoons of borax*
> 2 *Cups of warm tap water*
> 2 *Tablespoons of table salt*

Soak a quality string or twine in the solution until well saturated. Allow the wick to air-dry for at least 3 days to cure before rolling the wick up until needed. Cut off a portion of the wick to use as needed when making candles.

GREEN SEALING WAX

You will need the following ingredients:

> 4 *Ounces of Venetian turpentine (flammable)*
> 8 *Ounces of shellac*
> 2$^1/_2$ *Ounces of rosin*
> 1 *Ounce chrome yellow*
> $^1/_2$ *Ounce Prussian blue*
> 2 *Ounces of magnesia*

Place the rosin and turpentine in a pot and heat while continually stirring, then add the chrome yellow, Prussian blue, and magnesia. In another container, melt the shellac over low heat, then add in the first mixture with the turpentine. Stir until all the ingredients are well mixed and somewhat thick. Remove from heat and allow the mixture to cool. Use while still warm enough to pour.

INK THAT GLOWS IN THE DARK

You will need the following ingredients:

> 1 *Ounce of cinnamon oil*
> $^1/_4$ *Ounce of phosphorus (chemical supply house or pharmacy)*

Place the ingredients into a small bottle and close the lid. Place the bottle in a hot tap water bath (not on the stove) in a small pot on the counter.

Remove the bottle from the bath as soon as the ingredients have melted and blended together. This is not a formula for children to make. They should use the ink with adult supervision only. Store the bottle out of children's reach at all times.

PERMANENT BLACK DRAWING INK

You will need the following ingredients:

- *1/2* Cup of pure honey
- 1 Large egg yolk
- 1 Teaspoon of gum arabic (from pharmacy)
- *1/2* Teaspoon of lamp black (craft store or hold a plate over a lit candle)

Place the honey, egg yolk, and gum arabic in a small bowl and mix well. Add the lamp black and continue to mix until you have made a paste. Place the paste in a small well-sealed jar. When you are ready to use the ink, place a small amount of the paste in a small container and add just enough cold water to turn the paste into a fluid.

PERMANENT PRUSSIAN BLUE INK

You will need the following ingredients:

- *1/2* Cup boiling water
- 5 Teabags
- 1 Teaspoon of gum arabic (from pharmacy)

Place the teabags in a large bowl and pour the boiling water over them. Add the gum arabic and allow it to stand for 15 minutes. Extract the tannic acid in the tea by squeezing the teabags as hard as possible. The mixture should then be strained through a fine strainer. Allow the ink to cool before using it.

BLUE-BLACK WRITING INK

You will need the following ingredients:

- 1 Ounce of Naphthol Blue-Black
- *1/2* Ounce of powdered gum arabic
- *1/4* Ounce of carbolic acid (use with care)
- 1 Gallon of cool tap water

Place all the ingredients into a glass container and blend thoroughly. Place into a closed ink well.

RED WRITING INK

You will need the following ingredients:

1 *Ounce of eosine*
1 *Ounce of powdered gum arabic*
1/2 Ounce of carbolic acid (use with care)
1 *Gallon of cool tap water*

The directions are the same as for the blue-black writing ink.

INK THAT WRITES ON GLASS

You will need the following ingredients:

20 *Parts of shellac*
150 *Parts of ethyl alcohol*
35 *Parts of borax*
250 *Parts of cool tap water*
Water-soluble dye to color

Place the alcohol in a container and dissolve the shellac into it. In another container, dissolve the borax in the water, then pour the shellac solution very slowly into the borax solution. Dissolve the desired coloring into some water, add it to the solution, and blend well. This solution can be used to write on glass with a pen or thin brush.

TRANSFERRING PHOTOS TO FABRICS

You will need the following ingredients:

3 *Tablespoons of mild soap powder (not a harsh detergent)*
1/4 Cup of very hot tap water
3 *Tablespoon of turpentine*

Place the soap powder (finely grated Ivory soap will work) and hot water in a medium bowl and allow it to dissolve fully. Mix in the turpentine and allow it to cool. Use a standard watercolor brush to apply the solution on the face of the picture to be transferred. Wait 15 seconds then place a piece of white paper over the picture (attach with paper clips on all four sides) and rub the back of it with a teaspoon. It will take only a few seconds for the picture to transfer to the paper. If you wish to transfer to a fabric or T-shirt, just follow the same steps using the fabric instead of the paper. This special solution will store for 5–6 months in a well-sealed jar without refrigeration. Shake well before re-using.

TRANSFERRING IMAGES ON PAPER TO ANOTHER SURFACE

You will need the following ingredients:

 2 *Tablespoons of a non-detergent soap powder or finely grated Castile soap*
 1/4 *Cup of hot tap water*
 1 *Tablespoons of turpentine*

Place the soap into a medium bowl that contains the hot water and dissolve; then add the turpentine, mix well, and transfer the solution into a screw top jar. To use, just brush the solution over a picture in a magazine, comic book or newspaper and wait about 10 seconds. Place a sheet of clean white paper over it and rub with the back of a spoon. The picture will transfer to the paper and can then be transferred to a T-shirt, or other surface.

TRANSFERRING PHOTOS TO GLASS

You will need the following ingredients:

 1/4 *Ounce of glycerin*
 4 *Ounces of unflavored gelatin*
 3 *Ounces of ethyl alcohol*
 1 *Cup of cool tap water*

Place the water and gelatin in a saucepan and dissolve over low heat, then add the glycerin and mix. Place the alcohol in a container and very slowly pour the warm solution into the alcohol and mix well. Be sure that the glass that will accept the photo has been cleaned and dried thoroughly before wetting the glass with the mixture. Apply a thin layer of the mixture to the glass and evenly distribute on the area where the photo will go. Place the photo face down on the wet area and apply additional liquid over the photo. Remove any excess liquid and press slightly to remove any air bubbles. After the photo has dried it will become transparent. The photo that is used cannot include any writing or printed information on the back.

S. BEAN

PAPIER MÂCHÉ FORMULA #1

You will need the following ingredients:

^{1}/2 Cup of all-purpose flour
2 Cups of boiling water
3 Tablespoons of granulated sugar

Place the flour and cold tap water into a medium bowl and mix well. Add the mixture to the boiling water and bring to a boil. When the mixture returns to a boil, remove it from the heat and add the sugar, stirring continually. As the mixture cools it will thicken and be useable.

PAPIER MÂCHÉ FORMULA #2

You will need the following ingredients:

10 Ounces of paper pulp (wet)
5 Ounces of casein
2 Ounces of lime
20 Ounces of whiting

Place all the ingredients in a large bowl and mix well. This formula cannot be used in glue molds.

PAPIER MÂCHÉ FORMULA #3

You will need the following ingredients:

5^1/2 Ounces of rice flour
1 Cup of whiting
10 Ounces of paper pulp

Place all the ingredients into a double boiler and heat until it becomes a thick paste. Remove from heat and allow the mixture to cool before using. This will result in a very hard papier mâché when dry.

MARBLEIZING OBJECTS

You will need the following ingredients:

1 Pint of boiling water
5 Pints of cold tap water
8 Packets of unflavored gelatin (^{1}/4 oz. per packet)
1 Baking pan (low sides)
   Oil paints
   Turpentine

Place the gelatin into the boiling water in a medium saucepan. As soon as the gelatin melts completely, pour the mixture into the shallow baking pan and pour in the cold water (make sure the pan will hold 6 pints of water). Using separate bowls, place any color of oil paint and turpentine you wish to use, mixing the turpentine with the paint until it becomes thick and creamy. Drop a small dollop of the paint solution into the water in the shallow pan. If the colored dollop sinks to the bottom, the mixture is too thick, if the color spreads out into the entire pan, then it is too thin. The dollop of color must remain on the surface and not have a large area of spread. When this is achieved, drop small dollops of color on the surface of the water until you have enough. Swirl the color into a pattern and dip the object into the mixture. The object should pick up the colors. To clean the color out and replace it with a different color, just lightly touch the surface with a piece of newspaper and the color will attach to it.

PETROLEUM JELLY

You will need the following ingredients:

> 2 Ounces of beeswax (grated)
> 1 Cup of virgin olive oil

Place the ingredients into a double boiler and melt while stirring to blend well. Remove the solution from the heat and continue stirring until it cools. Store in a well-sealed glass container.

EASY-TO-MAKE PLASTIC

You will need the following ingredients:

> 11 Parts Epsom salts
> 36 Parts freshly calcined magnesite (chemical supply house)
> 2$^{1}/_{2}$ Parts lead acetate
> Cold tap water

Place the Epsom salts and the freshly calcined magnesite in a medium bucket and blend thoroughly. Add the lead acetate and mix thoroughly. Add water in small quantities just until the mixture holds together (do not saturate). When molding the plastic, place as much pressure as you can on the object for the best results.

SCENTED ROCKS

You will need the following ingredients:

> $^{1}/_{2}$ Cup of table salt
> $^{1}/_{2}$ Cup of all-purpose flour
> $^{2}/_{3}$ Cup of boiling water
> $^{1}/_{4}$ Teaspoon of essential oil (any)
> Food coloring

Place the salt and flour in a medium bowl and mix well. Add the boiling water and essential oil and mix. Form the mixture into small balls—these are your rocks—and allow them to dry overnight on a cookie sheet. Separate into different batches and add food coloring as desired.

THE HISTORY OF FINGERPRINTS

The first mention of the ridges, spirals, and loops in fingerprints was made in 1686 when Marcello Malpighi at the University of Bologna made the distinction—but no mention was made of their potential usefulness in identifying individuals. The first real information regarding the value of the fingerprint in identification was made in 1823 by John Evangelist Purinji at the University of Breslau when he published a thesis on nine different fingerprint patterns. Fingerprints were first used for identification in 1856 by Sir William Hershel in India to identify native contacts. Mark Twain wrote about fingerprints in 1883 and used them to identify a murderer in his book "Life on the Mississippi." Criminal identification using fingerprints actually began in England in 1901, in the United States by the New York Civil Service in 1902, and in 1903 by the New York Prison System.

FINGERPRINT DETECTION

You will need the following ingredients:

15   *Drops of tincture of iodine (poison)*
1   *Cotton ball*
1   *Small hollow glass tube*

Place the cotton ball in a small container and saturate with the iodine. Place the cotton ball in the glass tube and blow gently at the fingerprint. Do not inhale. The fingerprint will now be visible.

MOLDING WAX

You will need the following ingredients:

2   *Cups of beeswax*
4$^1/_2$ *Cups of Venice turpentine*
2   *Cups of pure lard*
1$^3/_4$ *Cups of powdered clay (talc may be used in place of the clay)*

Place the beeswax and turpentine in a double boiler and melt. Remove from the heat and add the lard. When all has melted, add the clay and mix thoroughly. The desired consistency of the molding wax can be adjusted by varying the amount of clay or talc added.

PROTECTIVE COATING FOR BOOK COVERS

You will need the following ingredients:

4   *Tablespoons of white shellac (flammable)*
4   *Tablespoons of denatured alcohol (flammable)*

Place the ingredients into a small container and mix well, then paint the cover, being careful not to get any of the mixture on the pages or they will be stuck together forever.

CLEANER FOR BLACKBOARDS

You will need the following ingredients:

1   Cups of white vinegar
$1/2$ Cup powdered hand detergent
$1/2$ Gallon of water

Place all the ingredients into a container and mix well. Wash the blackboard with a sponge and rinse with cold water.

PUTTY FOR SCULPTING

You will need the following ingredients:

3   Parts of boiled linseed oil
3   Parts of Fuller's earth
14   Parts of calcium carbonate (chalk)

Place all the ingredients into a large container and blend well.

COLORED BOTTLE WATER

You will need the following ingredients:

RED

$3^3/4$ Grams of potassium iodide (poison)
$3^3/4$ Grams of iodine (poison)
30   Grams of hydrochloric acid (use with extreme caution)
$2^1/4$ Quarts of distilled water

Slowly pour the acid into the water in a safe glass container and stir, then slowly add the other ingredients (avoid splashing) and mix well. The water will dilute the chemicals to a relatively safe level, but the bottle should be kept out of reach of children and pets.

BLUE

48   Grams of copper sulfate
6   Grams of sulfuric acid (use with extreme caution)
1   Pint of distilled water

Follow the directions for red colored water.

YELLOW

$1/2$ Ounce of potassium dichromate
$3^3/4$ Ounces of sodium bicarbonate
$2^1/4$ Quarts of distilled water

Place the ingredients into a bowl and mix well, then store in a well-sealed glass jar.

GREEN

> 6 *Grams of copper sulfate*
> 9 *Grams of hydrochloric acid*
> 1 *Quart of distilled water*

Follow the directions for red colored water.

CASTING WAX

You will need the following ingredients:

> 4 *Ounces of beeswax*
> 1 *Ounce of virgin olive oil*
> 4 *Ounces of starch (sifted)*

Place the beeswax and olive oil in a double boiler and melt, then slowly add the sifted starch until the mixture gets very thick, almost like bread dough. Remove from the heat and use as soon as it cools down, but is still easily workable. The wax will harden and will need to be warmed before each use. Force the metal object to be cast into the softened wax and tap the wax to remove. Plaster of paris can then be placed into the mold.

THERE ARE THOUSANDS OF USES FOR BEESWAX

The many uses for beeswax include: holding gemstones while they are being polished, candle-making, rubbing on irons, greasing doors and windows, waxing mustaches, using on leather straps, mixing with olive oil to make balm, using in dentistry, preserving sailboat masts, fly-tying, waterproofing tent seams, lining wooden water kegs, using in bone surgery, canning food, using as a flux for bullet casting, removing pin-feathers, keeping thread from tangling, waterproofing hunting boots, and many more.

BEESWAX CANDLES:

You will need the following ingredients:

> 1 *Pound of paraffin*
> 1 *Pound of beeswax*
> 1 *Ounce stearic acid*
> 3 *Drops of essential rose oil*

Place the paraffin and beeswax in a double boiler and melt to about 190° F., then add the stearic acid and the essential oil and mix well. Dip or mold the candles.

TRANSPARENT LACQUER

You will need the following ingredients:

2 *Parts gum mastic*
1 *Part camphor*
3 *Parts gum sandarac*
1 *Part gum elemi*
75 *Parts ethyl alcohol*

Place the alcohol in a pot, add the gums and heat on low, stirring well until the gums dissolve. Add the camphor and blend well. Remove from the heat and allow the lacquer to cool.

WATER VARNISH

You will need the following ingredients:

2 *Ounces of borax*
6 *Ounces of shellac*
1 *Pint of hot tap water*

Place the hot water in a container and dissolve the borax, then add the shellac and mix very well. Make sure your brush is very dry when applying the varnish. If the varnish becomes too thick you can heat it, then thin it out with hot boiled linseed oil and oil of turpentine. A small amount of alcohol will also thin out the varnish. Always allow one coat of varnish to fully dry before adding additional coats.

WHITE HARD VARNISH

You will need the following ingredients:

2^1/$_2$ *Pounds of gum sandarac*
8 *Ounces of gum mastic*
1 *Gallon of denatured alcohol*

Place all the ingredients in a sealed jar for 1 week and shake frequently until the varnish has fully liquefied. Strain the varnish and store in a well-sealed container. Follow the application directions above.

VIOLIN VARNISH

You will need the following ingredients:

2 *Parts of gum mastic*
1 *Part of gum dammar*
1 *Part of linseed oil*
20 *Parts of turpentine*

Place the turpentine in a container and dissolve the other ingredients into it. Lightly apply thin coats and allow each coat to fully dry before adding another coat. Store in a well-sealed container.

PAPER VARNISH

You will need the following ingredients:

> 1 *Pint of collodion*
> 1/2 *Ounce of castor oil*

Place all the ingredients into a container and mix well. Paint a thin coating of varnish on drawings, maps, or other paper products to form a protective coating. Lay the paper on a solid flat surface to stop any varnish from running. The paper will also become more pliable, which will prevent cracking.

FLOWER PRESERVATIVE

You will need the following ingredients:

> 1 *Pint of borax (powder)*
> 2 *Pints of cornmeal*

Place the borax and cornmeal into a shoe box and mix thoroughly. Place 3/4 of an inch of the mixture in the bottom of a container and place the flowers with their stems cut to about 1-inch long face down in the mixture. Make sure that the petals and leaves (if any) are spread out and lying flat. Space the flowers so that they do not touch one another, then place another 3/4 of an inch of the mixture on top of the flowers. Cover the box and allow the flowers to remain at room temperature for about 4 weeks.

THEATRICAL MAKE-UP

COLORED GREASEPAINT

You will need the following ingredients:

> 1 *Part coloring*
> 6 *Parts cocoa butter*
> *Oil of neroli (as needed)*

Place the cocoa butter in a double boiler and melt. Remove from the heat and add the coloring. Stir the mixture until it cools, then add perfume if you desire. The coloring needs to be finely powdered. Yellow greasepaint calls for the chemical ochre; brown is made from burnt umber; blue uses ultramarine; red uses carmine; and reddish brown requires burnt sienna.

WHITE GREASEPAINT
You will need the following ingredients:

  1 *Teaspoon zinc oxide*
  1 *Teaspoon cosmetic white*
  1 *Teaspoon white precipitated chalk*
     White Vaseline (as needed)

Place all the ingredients into a small bowl and mix well, then add the white Vaseline to make a paste.

VIVID RED GREASEPAINT
You will need the following ingredients:

  10 *Parts of zinc oxide*
  10 *Parts of bismuth subnitrate*
  10 *Parts aluminum oxychloride*
      Peppermint oil
      Camphor
      Eosine
      Almond oil

Place the zinc oxide, bismuth, and aluminum oxychloride in a container and mix well. Dissolve 2¼ grains of eosine in 15 drops of peppermint oil and 12 grains of camphor and add to every 4 ounces of the zinc oxide mixture. Mix well, then add just enough almond oil to prepare a usable paste.

BLACK GREASEPAINT
You will need the following ingredients:

  1 *Part of lampblack*
  1 *Part of expressed oil of almonds*
  1 *Part oil of coconut*
     Glycerin, as needed

Place the lampblack and oils into a container and add just enough glycerin to produce a stiff paste by beating the mixture.

CLOWN PAINT
You will need the following ingredients:

  1/8 *Cup of baby lotion (good quality)*
  1/2 *Teaspoon of liquid dish soap*
  1/4 *Teaspoon of tempera paint (powder)*

Place all the ingredients into a container and mix well. Any color of tempera paint may be used. Place a small amount on your skin to see if you allergic.

CLOWN NOSE PUTTY #1

You will need the following ingredients:

    1 Ounce of wheat flour
    2 Drams of powdered tragacanth
    Carmine as desired (red)

Place all the ingredients into a small bowl and mix well, then add a small amount of cool water to make a stiff paste. Place spirit gum on your nose before applying the nose putty. Store in a well-sealed jar.

CLOWN NOSE PUTTY #2

You will need the following ingredients:

    2 Ounces of white paraffin wax
    2 Ounces of bleached rosin
    1 Ounce of mutton tallow or suet
    Carmine as desired (red)

Place the wax, rosin, and tallow (or suet) in a double boiler and melt. Remove from the heat and add the carmine a small amount at a time while stirring continually until the desired shade of red is achieved. Paint the nose with spirit gum before applying the putty.

THEATRICAL STAGE BLOOD

You will need the following ingredients:

> 1 Cup of creamy peanut butter
> 1 Quart of liquid corn syrup
> 1/2 Cup of non-suds soap
> 1 Ounce of red food coloring
> 15 Drops of blue food coloring

Place the peanut butter and the corn syrup in a medium bowl and blend well. Add the soap and red food coloring and mix well, then add the blue food coloring a drop at a time until the desired color is obtained.

THEATRICAL ROUGE

You will need the following ingredients:

> 2 1/2 Ounces of zinc oxide
> 2 1/2 Ounces of bismuth subnitrate
> 2 1/2 Ounces of aluminum piumbate
> 15 Drops of eosine
> 30 Drops of essence bouquet
> 24 Grams of camphor
> 5 Drops of oil of peppermint
> Almond oil, as needed

Place the eosine in the essence bouquet and dissolve. Then mix with the camphor and oil of peppermint. Add the rest of the ingredients and blend into a paste using as much almond oil as needed.

Chapter 18

Dyes & Bleaches

S.BEAN

DYES

POPULAR IN GRANDMOTHER'S DAY

Dyeing fabrics at home was very common into the 1940's. The following formulas are for the more common dyes used on the fabrics of that day. Dyes will change the color of a fabric by saturating the fibers with a coloring agent. When dyeing, it is always best to use soft water since the presence of minerals may affect the final result. The container holding the dye must be spotless and the water temperature in most cases should be close to the boiling point.

Soak the garment in the dye solution for the specified amount of time to make the dye permanent. Silk, wool, and rayon can easily be dyed at a simmering temperature well below the boiling point. Silk and rayon are quick to accept dyes if they are associated with cotton fibers and if the dye solution is almost cold when starting out, then gradually heated. Tinting a piece of cloth is less permanent than dyeing. Tinting uses only warm water and the fabric is soaked in the dye for a shorter period of time. The following formulas will provide enough dye for about 1 pound of fabric.

COTTON DYES

You will need the following ingredients:

GREEN

5	Ounces of fustic
5	Ounces of blue vitriol
2^1/$_2$	Ounces of soft soap
2^1/$_2$	Teaspoons of extract of logwood
4	Gallons of very hot water

Place the hot water in a very large pot and mix in the extract of logwood, then mix in the fustic, blue vitriol, and soft soap, while bringing the solution to a boil. Remove from heat or turn the heat off and immerse the fabric for the length of time needed to achieve the desired color.

RED

^{1}/$_2$	Ounce of direct Congo red dye
2^1/$_2$	Ounces of table salt
4	Gallons of very hot water

Place the salt, Congo red dye, and water in a very large pot and heat until the temperature reaches 140° F. Add the fabric or garment and boil for 45 minutes. Remove the garment and rinse it in clear water.

BLUE

    2 *Ounces of blue vitriol*
    4 *Gallons of very hot water*

Place the water in a very large pot and add dissolve the blue vitriol. Soak the garment in the solution for 3 hours, then remove the garment and place it into a strong solution of lime and water to set the color.

BLACK

    1 *Ounce of direct black E dye*
  $4^3/4$ *Ounces of table salt*
    4 *Gallons of very hot water*

Place the water in a very large pot and dissolve the black dye and the salt, then heat to 140° F. and immerse the garment. Boil for 45 minutes before removing the garment and rinsing it in clear water.

WOOL DYES

You will need the following ingredients:

SCARLET

    5 *Teaspoons of cream of tartar*
  $2^1/2$ *Teaspoons of pulverized charcoal*
  $3^1/4$ *Ounces of tin chloride*
    2 *Gallons of very hot water*

Place the hot water in a large pot and dissolve the cream of tartar, charcoal, and tin chloride. Place the garment in the solution and stir for 15 minutes. Allow the garment to soak for another $1^1/2$ hours, stirring occasionally. Remove the garment and rinse in clear water.

BROWN

    4 *Ounces of camwood*
  10 *Ounces of fustic*
  $1/4$ *Ounce of blue vitriol*
    1 *Ounce of copperas*
    2 *Gallons of very hot water*

Place the hot water in a large pot and add the camwood. Boil for 20 minutes, then place the garment in for 30 minutes. Remove the garment, then add the fustic to the solution and mix well while boiling for 10 minutes. Remove from the heat and place the garment back in the water for 45 minutes, then remove and add the blue vitriol and copperas and mix. Place the garment back into the solution and soak for another 40 minutes.

PINK

    2 Ounces of alum
    7 Teaspoons of powdered cochineal
1³/4 Ounces of cream of tartar
    2 Gallons of very hot water

Place the hot water in a large pot and dissolve the alum, then place the garment into the solution and soak for 50 minutes. Remove the garment. Add the powdered cochineal and cream of tartar and mix well. Place the garment back into the solution and continue to soak until the desired shade is achieved. Remove the garment and rinse in clear water.

SILK DYES

You will need the following ingredients:

GREEN

¹/2 Ounce of direct green dye
2¹/2 Ounces of table salt
    4 Gallons of very hot water

Place the hot water in a very large pot and dissolve the green dye and the salt and mix well. Place the silk garment in the solution for 20–30 minutes, keeping the temperature between 180° F. and 200° F. Remove the garment and rinse in clear water, then hang up to dry.

RED

    3 Ounces of powdered cochineal
    2 Ounces of bruised nutgalls
³/4 Ounce of cream of tartar
    4 Gallons of very hot water

Place the water, cochineal, cream of tartar, and the nutgalls in a very large pot and boil for 10 minutes. Remove from the heat and allow the solution to cool. Place the garment in the solution and allow it to soak for 1 hour before removing and rinsing the garment very well in clear water. Hang up to dry thoroughly.

BLUE

¹/2 Ounce of direct blue 2B dye
2¹/2 Ounces of table salt
    4 Gallons of very hot water

Place the hot water, blue dye, and salt in a very large pot and mix well until dissolved. Place the silk garment in the solution for 20–30 minutes, keeping the temperature between 180° F. and 200° F. Remove the garment and rinse in clear water then hang up to dry.

LEATHER DYES

You will need the following ingredients:

BROWN

2   Ounces of deodorized kerosene
10   Ounces of benzol
$^1/_2$ Ounce of Pylam 123Y dye
$^1/_4$ Ounce of Sudan 5BA dye

Place all the ingredients into a container and blend well. Work the dye into the leather with a soft bristle brush. Make sure the dye is applied evenly, then allow the leather to air dry in a relatively dust-free area.

OAK BROWN

2   Ounces of raw umber
$^1/_4$ Ounces of lampblack
$8^1/_2$ Ounces of ox gall

Place all the ingredients in a container and mix well. Apply with a soft bristle brush and allow the leather to air dry in a dust-free area.

HARNESS DYE

You will need the following ingredients:

4   Ounces of glue
$1^1/_2$ Pints of white vinegar
2   Ounces of gum arabic
$^1/_2$ Pint of black ink
2   Drams of isinglass

Place the glue and the white vinegar into a saucepan and place over low heat, stirring until completely dissolved. Combine the gum arabic and the ink in another saucepan and heat on low heat. In a third saucepan place the isinglass in water to cover and heat to melt. Place the gum arabic solution into the glue solution and slowly heat, then add the isinglass solution and stir well. Allow the solution to cool. To use this dye, liquefy a small piece by heating it, then apply to the harness with a sponge and allow it to dry in a relatively dust-free area.

BLEACHES

ABOUT BLEACH

Bleach can be used to remove the color from dyed fabrics and garments as well as to whiten fabrics. Over time many garments will yellow and can be whitened with the use of bleach. However, a variety of methods can be used depending on the fabric to be bleached. Many of these chemicals should be handled with care since they are poisonous.

BLEACH FOR COTTONS AND LINENS

You will need the following ingredients:

> 1 Pound of chloride of lime
> 1 Pound of soda
> 1 Gallon of cool tap water
> 1 Gallon of boiling water

This formula should only be used on heavy fabrics since the lime will weaken the fibers of light linens or cotton garments.

Place the cool water in a medium basin and add the chloride of lime, stir, and cover the mixture loosely with a cloth. Allow the lime (poison) to remain in a safe location for 3 days to settle. Pour the clear liquid of lime off and save. Safely dispose of the remainder. Place the boiling water in a medium basin and place the soda in to dissolve, then place the garment in and allow it to soak for 12 hours, then boil for 30 minutes. Remove the garment and place it in the clear lime water for a few seconds to stabilize the bleach, then rinse in clear cool water.

BLEACH FOR SILK AND WOOL

You will need the following ingredients:

> 2 Ounces of oxalic acid
> 2 Ounces of table salt
> 1^1/$_2$ Gallons of cool tap water

Place the water, salt, and oxalic acid in a medium basin and mix well to dissolve. Soak the garment in the solution for 1 hour; then rinse with cool tap water until all the bleach has been removed. Hang the garment to air dry.

MAKING PAPER FIREPROOF

You will need the following ingredients:

    1   Ounce of ammonium sulfate
    3   Drams of boracic acid
    2   Drams of borax
 12^1/$_2$ Ounces of cool tap water

Place all the ingredients in a medium saucepan and stir to dissolve. Heat the solution to 122° F. Remove from the heat and dip the paper in the solution, remove it immediately, and allow it to dry.

MAKING PAPER WATERPROOF

You will need the following ingredients:

    12   Ounces of alum
    2   Ounces of Castile soap (grated)
    2   Quarts of tap water
  7^1/$_2$ Ounces of beeswax

Place the water in a medium saucepan and dissolve the alum and soap by bringing the water to a boil and mixing well. Remove the solution from the heat. Dip the paper into the solution then allow it to dry. Paper that was used to wrap items that were kept in a damp area used to be treated with this process.

HONEY, JUST LIGHT
IT ALREADY!

—I CAN'T!!

Chapter 19

Fun
Chemical
Experiments

S.BEAN

The following chemical experiments should be conducted by an adult only. They are not dangerous when the directions are followed, but some of the chemicals are poisonous. This should not deter you from having fun with these—just be sure to handle the chemicals with the same care you give to other common but dangerous household products.

MAKING A SULFUR PLASTIC

You will need the following ingredients:

20 *Grams of sulfur*
1 *Test tube*
1 *Bunsen burner*
1 *Metal test tube holder*
1 *Test tube rack*
1 *Pint of cold tap water*
1 *Small bowl or beaker*

Place the sulfur into the test tube and hold over the heat until it turns into a yellow liquid. Continue to heat and it will become a dark glob; when heated further it turns back into a liquid again. Remove the solution from the heat and carefully pour the liquid into the beaker with the cold water. The liquid will turn into a pliable and elastic substance.

THE VIOLET MYSTERY

You will need the following ingredients:

Pinch of crystal violet
Clear beaker or jar of water
Drop of oleic acid

Place the water in the beaker or jar and sprinkle the crystal violet in the water. The crystals will move rapidly and leave streaks of violet on the surface, covering the entire surface. Place the drop of oleic acid in the water and the layer of violet will sink to the bottom. The oleic acid will change the surface tension of the water and eliminate the buoyancy of the crystal violet.

MAKING A SOLID FROM TWO LIQUID SOLUTIONS

You will need the following ingredients:

Calcium carbonate
Potassium carbonate
Tap water
Two small beakers
One large beaker

Place water in one of the small beakers and add potassium carbonate until no more will dissolve. In the other small beaker, place calcium carbonate in a solution of water (make a strong solution), then mix the two in the large beaker. When mixed they will turn into a transparent solid mass.

MINI SPARKLER

You will need the following ingredients:

    10 Grams of zinc oxide
    10 Grams of flowers of sulfur
        Manganese dioxide
        Dammar varnish
     1 Porcelain crucible
     1 Bunsen burner

Place the zinc oxide and the sulfur in a small container and add the manganese dioxide a little at a time until the mixture darkens. Heat the mixture over a Bunsen burner in a covered porcelain crucible for 30 minutes. Remove from the heat. Apply a coat of dammer varnish to a card and sprinkle the mixture on the card before the varnish dries. Allow the varnish on the card to fully dry, then rub a hard object across the card and watch the multi-colored sparks fly. You can scrape the surface with your fingernail or any other hard object.

CHEMICAL ISLAND GARDEN #1

You will need the following ingredients:

     5 Pieces of porous coal
     6 Tablespoons of table salt
     6 Tablespoons of bluing
     6 Tablespoons of cool tap water
     1 Tablespoon of ammonia water
    10 Drops of green ink (fountain pen type)

Place the coal in a small dish with sides. Place the salt, bluing, water, and ammonia water in a small bowl and mix well. Pour this solution over the pieces of coal; then drop the green ink onto the coal and mix. You will notice a multi-colored growth start to appear in a few minutes and continue to grow. Rubbing Vaseline on the inside edges of the dish will keep the growth contained in the dish. Add a small amount of ammonia water from time to time to keep the reaction going.

CHEMICAL GARDEN #2

The following are directions and ingredients that will be needed:

Prepare a solution of sodium silicate dissolved in water to make about 1 cup of liquid. Pour this solution into a small fishbowl. The color of the crystals that will grow in this solution will depend on the chemicals you add to it.

Green: Add nickel nitrate crystals
Brown: Add ferric chloride crystals
Yellow: Add uranium nitrite crystals
Blue: Add cobaltous nitrate crystals

Only use one kind of crystal at a time for each solution your prepare. The green will produce particularly strange-looking plants.

HOW TO DETECT A COUNTERFEIT SILVER COIN

You will need the following ingredients:

24 *Grains of silver nitrate*
15 *Drops of nitric acid (handle with care)*
1 *Ounce of distilled water*

Place the distilled water in a glass beaker and add the silver nitrate and the acid, then stir well with a glass rod. Using thc glass rod, apply a drop to the silver coin. If a small black stain appears, the coin is not silver. Clean the coin with a solution of baking soda and water.

HOW TO DETECT A COUNTERFEIT GOLD COIN

The following are directions and ingredients that will be needed:

Dip a glass rod in nitric acid and apply the acid to the coin or jewelry. If it is not gold, a blue stain will appear—this is the formation of copper nitrate. The nitric acid should have no effect on true gold—even 14 karat gold. Clean the area off with a solution of baking soda and water to neutralize the acid.

SEEING BLUE STARS

You will need the following ingredients:

2   *Ounces of copper sulfide*
4   *Ounces of sulfur*
2   *Ounces of mercurous chloride*
8   *Ounces of potassium chlorate*
1   *Ounce of charcoal*

Place all the ingredients into a flat glass dish with sides and mix well. Small blue stars should appear as the chemicals unite with each other and form a new crystalline substance.

Chapter 20

Photographic Formulas

S. BEAN

ABOUT PHOTOGRAPHIC FORMULAS

This chapter will not provide directions for developing film. The formulas provided have been used for the last 50 years or longer and are still in use today by many photographers in their home photo labs. Many of these formulas use chemicals that need to be handled with care or are poisonous and need to be stored out of the reach of children and pets. A number of these formulas can be purchased ready-made from photographic suppliers, but many people still enjoy preparing their own solutions, which is why this chapter has been included in the formula book.

Basically, the negative or celluloid film is coated with a light-sensitive emulsion that is exposed to light. The negative is then placed in a chemical solution to bring out the image. The negative has a layer of gelatin, which contains crystals of specific silver salts. The developing solution reacts with the exposed crystals after they have been exposed to light and reduces them to metallic silver, leaving the unexposed crystals unchanged.

NEGATIVE DEVELOPERS

BUFFERED BORAX DEVELOPER
You will need the following ingredients:

    30 *Grains of metol*
    75 *Grains of hydroquinone*
  $3^{1}/_{2}$ *Ounces of sodium sulfite (anhydrous)*
    30 *Grains of borax*
  $^{1}/_{2}$ *Ounce of boric acid*
       Enough cool tap water to produce 32 ounces of developer

Place all the ingredients into a container and mix well in a tray developer. The developing time is about 21 minutes at 65° F.

GLYCIN DEVELOPER
You will need the following ingredients:

  $4^{1}/_{2}$ *Ounces of sodium sulfite (anhydrous)*
  $8^{1}/_{2}$ *Ounces of potassium carbonate*
  $1^{1}/_{2}$ *Ounces and 80 grains of glycin (agfa)*
       Enough cool tap water to produce 32 ounces of developer

Place all the ingredients into a container and mix well. For tank developing, dissolve 1 part of the solution in 15 parts of water. The developing time is about 23 minutes at 65° F. For tray developing, dissolve 1 part of the solution in 4 parts of water. The time for developing will be 5–10 minutes at 65° F.

MINIATURE FILM DEVELOPER

You will need the following ingredients:

24 *Ounces of water at 125° F.*
22 *Grains of metol (agfa)*
2¹/₂ *Ounces plus 80 grains of sodium sulfite (anhydrous)*
45 *Grains of hydroquinone (agfa)*
45 *Grains of borax*
7¹/₂ *Grains of potassium bromide*
   Enough cool tap water to produce 32 ounces of developer

Place all the ingredients into a container and mix well. The developing time is 10–15 minutes at 65° F.

RUBINOL DEVELOPER

You will need the following ingredients:

40 *Grains of rubinol*
800 *Grains of sodium sulfite (anhydrous)*
   Enough cool tap water to produce 16 ounces of developer

Place all the ingredients into a container and mix well. The developing time is18–20 minutes at 65° F.

RINSES

CHROME ALUM STOP-BATH

You will need the following ingredients:

1 *Ounce of potassium chrome alum*
30 *Ounces of cool tap water*

Place all the ingredients into a container and mix well. Agitate the film thoroughly in the solution and allow it to soak for 2 minutes. Stop-baths are used to remove a stain or spot left by the developer.

ACETIC ACID STOP-BATH

You will need the following ingredients:

25 *Cubic centimeters of 28% acetic acid*
16 *Ounces of cool tap water*

Place all the ingredients into a container and blend well. Agitate the film in the solution until any stain or spot has disappeared.

FIXING BATHS

BASIC HYPO BATH
You will need the following ingredients:

    8   *Ounces of hypo (sodium thiosulfate)*
   32 *Ounces of cool tap water*

Place the ingredients into a container and mix well. The time in the bath is about 20 minutes for most emulsions at a temperature of 65°–70° F. The fixing bath tends to act on the film's emulsion, which may contain some traces of silver salts. If these salts are not cleaned off, the film cannot be exposed to light without damage. The time in the fixing bath is about 2 minutes.

METABISULFITE FIXING BATH
You will need the following ingredients:

    1   *Pound of hypo (sodium thiosulfate)*
  $2^{1}/_{4}$ *Ounces of potassium metabisulfite*
        Enough cool tap water to produce 1 quart of the fixing bath

Place all the ingredients into a container and mix well. The total time for the film is 5–10 minutes at 65° F. This is a good formula when hardening of the emulsion is not needed.

REDUCERS

REDUCER FOR OVERDEVELOPED FILM
You will need the following ingredients:

    1 *Ounce of cool tap water*
   60 *Grains of ammonium persulfate*
   10 *Grains of sodium sulfite (anhydrous)*
   10 *Drops of sulfuric acid*
        Enough cool tap water to produce 3 ounces of solution

Place all the ingredients into a glass container with a good stopper and use 1 part of solution to 10 parts of cool tap water. The negative should remain in the reducer until the reduction is almost finished, then it should be placed in a fresh fixing bath for 5–10 minutes. Rinse the negative well with cool tap water and allow to dry.

BASIC FARMER'S REDUCER

The following ingredients will be needed to prepare 2 solutions:

Solution #1

4   *Ounces of cool tap water*
1/4   Ounce of potassium ferricyanide

Solution # 2

3   *Ounces of hypo (sodium thiosulfate)*
15   *Ounces of cool tap water*

Solution # 1: Place the water and potassium ferricyanide in a brown bottle and mix well.

Solution #2: Place the hypo and water into another bottle (doesn't have to be brown) and mix well.

Blend 1/2 ounce of Solution #1 and 2 ounces of Solution #2 with 16 ounces of cool tap water. Place the solution in a white tray and immerse the negative, watching carefully until the desired contrast is achieved. Remove the film immediately and rinse it in cool, water then hang the film up to dry. If any yellowing appears, place the negative in a new fixing bath for 2–3 minutes, then rinse again in cool water.

Reducers are used to decrease the contrast between light and shadow. Excessive contrast can be caused by overexposure or over-development of the film.

PRINT DEVELOPERS

Print developers are used after the negative has been processed to produce the print. A number of different types of paper are available for making prints depending on the type of processing and whether you will be enlarging or not. Any unexposed paper must be protected from the light or it will be ruined.

AMIDOL DEVELOPER

You will need the following ingredients:

8 *Ounces of water at 125° F.*
3/4 Ounce of sodium sulfite (desiccated)
46 *Grains of amidol*
10 *Grains of potassium bromide*
 Enough cool tap water to make 16 ounces of developer

Place all the ingredients into a container and blend well. The development time is $1^1/2$–2 minutes at 70° F. The amidol solution tends to produce purple tones.

PYRO DEVELOPER

You will need the following ingredients:

10 *Ounces of cool tap water*
22 *Grains of potassium metabisulfite*
1 *Ounce of sodium sulfite*
65 *Grains of pyro*
1 *Ounce of sodium carbonate*
65 *Grains of potassium bromide*
 Enough cool tap water to produce 24 ounces of developer

Place all the ingredients into a container and blend well. The development time is about $1^1/2$ minutes at 70° F. Pyro developer will produce warm tones.

METOL DEVELOPER

You will need the following ingredients:

5 *Ounces of cool tap water*
$12^1/2$ *Grains of metol*
55 *Grains of sodium sulfite*
$72^1/2$ *Grains of sodium carbonate*
21 *Grains of potassium bromide*
 Enough cool tap water to produce 14 ounces of developer

Place all the ingredients into a container and blend well. The development time is 1½ minutes at 68° F. If you notice that the solution is somewhat foggy, add more potassium bromide. Metol developer is used primarily for producing soft effects on bromide paper.

GLYCIN DEVELOPER
You will need the following ingredients:

20	Ounces of cool tap water
12	Grains of metol
2½	Ounces of sodium sulfite
115	Grains of hydroquinone
120	Grains of glycin
2½	Ounces of sodium carbonate
18	Grains of potassium bromide

Place all the ingredients into a container and mix well. Dissolve 1 part of solution in 4 parts of water and place in the developing dish. The developing time is 1½–3 minutes, depending on the depth of the tone desired. This developer will produce dark brown tones on chloro-bromide paper.

SHORT-STOP PRINT BATH

NEUTRALIZING STOP-BATH
You will need the following ingredients:

32	Ounces of cool tap water
1½	Ounces of acetic acid (28%)

Place all the ingredients into a container and mix well. Soak the print in the solution for 20–30 minutes, then remove and place in the fixing bath. The stop-bath stops the further development of the print.

FIXING BATH

ACID-HARDENING FIXER—AGFA 201
You will need the following ingredients:

Solution #1

16	Ounces of water at 125° F.
8	Ounces of hypo (sodium thiosulfate)

Solution #2

> 5 *Ounces of water at 125° F.*
> ¹/₂ *Ounce of agfa sodium sulfite (anhydrous)*
> 1¹/₂ *Ounces of agfa acetic acid (28%)*
> ¹/₂ *Ounce of agfa potassium alum*

Place the two solutions in separate containers and mix each of them well. Pour solution #2 into solution #1 and mix well. Add water to make 32 ounces of the solution. The fixing time is 15–20 minutes at 65°–70° F.

PREPARING WOODEN TRAYS

MAKING WOODEN TRAYS WATERPROOF

You will need the following ingredients:

> 10 *Ounces of methyl alcohol*
> 2 *Ounces of orange shellac*
> ¹/₂ *Ounce of rosin*
> ¹/₂ *Ounce of Venice turpentine*

Place all the ingredients into a double boiler and heat while stirring until they are all dissolved. Remove from the heat and allow the solution to cool before brushing on the wooden tray. Make sure that the tray is very clean before you start and apply at least 3 coats of solution, allowing each to dry thoroughly before adding the next coat.

CHEMICAL STAIN REMOVAL

REMOVING STAINS FROM YOUR HANDS AND TRAYS

You will need the following ingredients:

SILVER NITRATE STAINS

Solution #1

> 1 *Ounce of potassium ferricyanide*
> 1 *Ounce of potassium bromide*
> 32 *Ounces of cool tap water*

Solution #2

> 1 *Ounce of sodium bisulfite*
> 24 *Ounces of cool tap water*

Place the ingredients in separate containers and mix each well, then place your hands or the tray in solution #1 for a few seconds, then rinse in solution #2. Wash your hands or the tray thoroughly with clear, cool water.

GRAY OR BROWN STAINS
Solution #1
> 100 Grains of potassium permanganate
> 30   Ounces of cool tap water

Solution #2
> 3   Ounces of sodium bisulfite
> 30 Ounces of cool tap water

Place the two solutions into separate containers and mix each well, then place your hands in solution #1 for a few seconds and then into solution #2 for 2–3 minutes. Wash your hands well with clear water.

PYRO STAINS
Pyro stains can only be removed from your hands by immersing them into a solution of chlorinated lime and then rubbing the stained area with a citric acid crystal. If the stain does not disappear after the first procedure, try again and again until the stain is gone. Better yet, wear gloves—this is a tough one.

BASIC STAIN REMOVAL FOR TRAYS ONLY

Solution #1
> 30 Ounces of cool tap water
> 75 Grains of potassium permanganate
> 3   Drams of chemically pure sulfuric acid (use with caution)

Solution #2
> 30   Ounces of cool tap water
> $1/2$ Ounce of sodium bisulfite

Place the two solutions into separate containers and mix each well, then pour solution #1 into the tray and allow it to remain for 2–3 minutes, then rinse the tray with cool water. Pour solution #2 into the tray and allow it to remain for about a minute, then rinse in cool water.

Chapter 21

Plating
Metals

COPPER

ALUMINUM

GOLD

S. DEAN

ABOUT PLATING METALS

Plating metals at home can be done by using one of the following formulas. No electrical charges are needed and the plated metal can be polished and shined as desired. Always thoroughly clean the object you wish to plate in a solution of hot water with either borax or caustic soda. This will remove any dirt and grease particles that might interfere with the quality of the plating. If the metal to be plated has a small spot or two of rust, it can be removed with a solution made by dissolving 1 tablespoon of ammonium citrate in 1 quart of hot tap water. Rinse the object well and allow the metal to dry fully before plating it.

> **Remember:** many of the chemicals used below are poisonous or flammable and should be handled with care wearing the proper gloves and masks.

POWDERS FOR PLATING

You will need the following ingredients:

NICKEL PLATING

    20 *Parts of double nickel salts*
    1 *Part of magnesium powder*
    10 *Parts of chalk*

SILVER PLATING

    1 *Part of silver nitrate*
    1 *Part pure salt (do not use iodized)*
    14 *Parts of cream of tartar*

ZINC PLATING

    15 *Parts of zinc dust*
    5 *Ammonium sulfate*
    1 *Part of magnesium powder*
  $12^{1}/_{3}$ *Parts of chalk*

TIN PLATING

    5 *Parts of stannous chloride*
    5 *Parts of ammonium sulfate*
    1 *Part of magnesium powder*
  $23^{1}/_{3}$ *Parts of chalk*

Combine the ingredients for the metal you are going to plate in a container and mix well. Apply to the metal with a wet cloth.

BRONZING METALS

You will need the following ingredients:

TIN

- 1 *Part of green vitriol (copperas)*
- 1 *Part of sulfate*
- 20 *Parts of cool tap water*
- 4 *Parts of verdigris*
- 11 *Parts of distilled wine vinegar*

Place the water in a container and dissolve the green vitriol and the sulfate in the water and mix well. Place the tin object in the solution for a few seconds, remove, and allow to dry. Place the wine vinegar into another container and dissolve the verdigris into the vinegar and mix well. Place the tin object into the vinegar solution for a few seconds, remove, and rinse in clear water. Allow the tin object to dry fully before polishing it with English red.

ZINC

- 1 *Part of ammonium chloride*
- 1 *Part of potassium oxalate*
- 10 *Parts of white vinegar*

Place the vinegar into a container and dissolve the chloride and oxalate into the vinegar; then rub the zinc object with a clean cloth that has been dipped into the solution. Allow the metal to dry and then rinse with clear water and allow the object to dry.

IRON OR STEEL

Formula #1

- 1 *Part of ferric chloride*
- 1 *Part copper sulfate*
- 25 *Parts of cool tap water*
- 3/4 *Part of nitric acid (use with caution)*

Place the ingredients in a container and mix well. Make sure that the metal has been thoroughly cleaned with emery cloth and wiped off with a dry cloth, then place the metal in the solution for 1–2 minutes. Remove the metal and allow it to dry. Hold the object over the vapors from heated alcohol for about 30 seconds.

Formula #2

- $2^1/2$ *Ounces of copper sulfate*
- 2 *Ounces of nitric acid (use with caution)*
- 3 *Ounces of iron chloride*
- 6 *Ounces of antimony chloride (strong solution)*
- 5 *Ounces of cool tap water*

Place all the ingredients into a container and mix well, then sponge the solution onto the metal object and allow it to dry.

MAKING ANTIQUE BRONZE ON A COPPER SURFACE

You will need the following ingredients:

> 1 *Part of copper acetate*
> 1 *Part of potassium bitartrate*
> 1 *Part of pure salt (not iodized)*
> 3 *Parts of ammonium acetate*
> 3 *Parts of glacial acetic acid*

Place all the ingredients into a container and mix very well, then spread the solution on the copper. Allow the solution to remain on the copper for 10 hours, then rub the surface with a soft cloth that moistened with wax or oil.

SILVER PLATING FORMULAS

You will need the following ingredients:

FOR COPPER OR BRASS

> 2 *Ounces of silver nitrate*
> 6 *Quarts of cool tap water*
> 7 *Ounces of sodium cyanide*

Place 3 quarts of the water into a container and dissolve the silver nitrate into the water. In another container, place the other 3 quarts of water in and dissolve the sodium cyanide. Mix the two solutions together in a pot and heat the solution to 200° F. Immerse the metal and allow it to remain in the solution until it is evenly coated with silver. Remove the pot from the heat, remove the object, and rinse it in clear water. Allow the object to cool fully, then polish with a paste prepared from jeweler's rouge and water.

FOR IRON

> 1 *Part of chloride of antimony*
> 1/4 *Part of powdered arsenious acid*
> 2 *Parts of powdered hematite*
> 25 *Parts of alcohol (90%)*

Place the alcohol in a double boiler and dissolve the antimony, acid, and hematite into the alcohol, stirring gently for 30 minutes. Place a piece of cotton in the solution (wear rubber gloves) and gently press the wet cotton against the iron object forming a thin film of silver. Allow the object to dry and then polish with a dry, clean, soft cloth.

FOR BRONZE, COPPER, OR BRASS

> 1/2 *Part of silver nitrate*
> 50 *Parts of distilled water*
> 1 3/4 *Parts of potassium cyanide (98%)*

Wear gloves and mask. Place 25 parts of distilled water in a container and dissolve the silver nitrate in it, mixing well. In a second container, place the other 25 parts of distilled water and the potassium cyanide, mixing well to dissolve. Place both the solutions in an enameled pot and mix well, then heat to 176°–194° F. Immerse the object in the solution until it has an even coating of silver. Remove from the heat and allow to air dry, then polish with a dry, clean, soft cloth.

PASTE FOR SILVER PLATING ZINC, BRASS, OR COPPER #1
You will need the following ingredients:

¹/₂   *Part of nitrate of silver*
2¹/₂ *Parts of distilled water*
1¹/₄ *Parts of potassium cyanide*
  5   *Parts of whiting*
20 *Parts of potassium bitartrate*

Place the distilled water into a container and dissolve the nitrate of silver into the water. In another container, mix the potassium cyanide with enough additional distilled water to dissolve it fully. Mix the two solutions together, stirring well, then filter the solution. Use enough of the liquid added to the whiting and the potassium bitartrate to prepare a loose paste. Coat the metal using a brush and, when it has dried, wash off the paste with clear water. Dry the metal in sawdust.

PASTE FOR SILVER PLATING ZINC, BRASS, OR COPPER #2
You will need the following ingredients:

13 *Parts of carbonate of lime*
12 *Parts of sea salt (pure)*
 7   *Parts of cream of tartar*
 4   *Parts of nitrate of silver*

Place the cream of tartar and the nitrate of silver into a mortar and pestle and grind into a fine powder. Add the carbonate of lime and grind it into the powder. Add just enough water to prepare a paste, which should then be rubbed on the metal with a soft clean cloth. Rinse with clear water after the paste is completely dry. Store the paste in a well-sealed blue bottle in a cool, dry location.

BRASS PLATING SOLUTIONS FOR IRON OR STEEL
You will need the following ingredients:

2 *Quarts of cool tap water*
1 *Ounce of sulfate of copper*
1 *Ounce of protochloride of tin*

Place the water in a container and dissolve the copper and tin into the water, mixing well. Immerse the object into the solution until fully coated, then remove and allow it to dry. Rinse in clear water and polish with a clean dry cloth.

GOLD PLATING SOLUTIONS

You will need the following ingredients:

FOR BRASS

    1   *Part of caustic acid*
    1   *Part of lactose (milk sugar)*
  25 *Parts of cool tap water*
    1   *Part of blue vitriol*

Place the water in a pot and add the caustic soda and lactose. Boil for 15 minutes, mixing well. In another container place the blue vitriol in enough water to fully dissolve it and mix this solution into the lactose solution, stirring very well. Continue heating until the temperature of the solution is at 175° F. before immersing the brass object. When it appears to be plated (a few minutes at the most) remove it and allow it to dry before rinsing it with clear water and polishing it with a clean dry cloth.

FOR ZINC

    1   *Parts of gold chloride*
    1   *Part of distilled water*
    4   *Parts of potassium cyanide*
    4   *Parts of cool tap water*
  $1/4$ *Part of cream of tartar*
    5   *Parts of powdered chalk*

Place the distilled water and the gold chloride in a container and mix well to dissolve. In another container, place the potassium chloride and 4 parts of water and dissolve fully. Mix the two solutions together and stir well, then filter and add the powdered chalk and cream of tartar to prepare a paste. Use a brush to coat the zinc object with the paste and allow to fully dry before rinsing off with clear water.

COPPER PLATING SOLUTIONS

You will need the following ingredients:

FOR ZINC

    1   *Part of copper sulfate*
    1   *Part of spirits of sal ammoniac*
  $16^2/3$ *Parts of cool tap water*
        Hydrochloric acid (highly diluted)

Thoroughly clean the zinc object with a highly diluted solution of hydrochloric acid and rinse well with water. Place the water in a container and dissolve the copper sulfate and the spirits of sal ammoniac in the water and mix well. Immerse the object into the solution until it receives a coating; then remove it. Additional coating may be needed.

For Aluminum

 3 *Ounces of sulfate of copper*
 3 *Ounces of cream of tartar*
2^1/$_2$ *Ounces of soda*
 3 *Quarts of cool tap water*

Place the water into a container and dissolve the ingredients into it, mixing well. Immerse the aluminum object into the solution until it has been coated, then remove it and allow it to dry before rinsing well in clear water.

For Brass

^{3}/$_4$ *Part of tartar emetic*
^{3}/$_4$ *Part of powdered tartar*
25 *Parts of hot tap water*
2^1/$_2$ *Parts of hydrochloric acid (use with caution)*
2^1/$_2$ *Parts of powdered antimony*

Place the hot water in a porcelain or glass pot and dissolve the tartar emetic and the powdered tartar into the water, mixing well. Add the acid and the powdered antimony and mix well. Heat the solution to the boiling point and immerse the brass object. The object should turn gold and then a copper red color. After the copper coating has formed, remove the object immediately or it will change to purple. Rinse the object in clear water and allow it to dry.

CHEMICAL TESTS FOR PLATING

You will need the following ingredients:

Test For Tin Plating

To tell whether an object has been tin-plated, place a drop of hydrochloric acid or sulfuret of sodium on the object. Either chemical will remove tin plating. If you prefer not to excessively damage the object, immerse it in a solution of 6 parts of sea salt and 11 parts of cool tap water for 10 minutes. If the object has been plated it will acquire a slightly grayish cast.

Test for Silver Plating

To tell whether an object has been silver-plated, place some sulfuret of sodium on the object and it will turn black very quickly. If you wish to remove the silver plating, use nitric acid to dissolve it.

Test for Nickel Plating

To tell whether an object has been nickel-plated, first clean it thoroughly and apply a drop of hydrochloric acid to it. If the object has been plated the area will turn green. Sulfuret of sodium will not work on nickel.

Chapter 22

Making Polishes & Lubricants

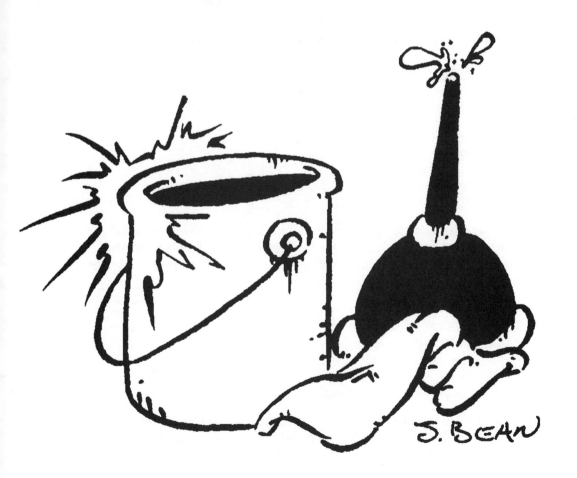

POLISHES

Polishes are used to provide a luster to many different types of surfaces. The most common ingredient in polishes is either a wax or oil. Wax will, in most instances, provide a more permanent finish but requires considerably more work to achieve the desired results. If water is used when preparing a polish, the formula must contain an emulsifying agent to keep the polish in suspension. This agent is usually soap or stearic acid. If an emulsifying agent is not added, the polish must be shaken (not stirred) to place all the ingredients back into suspension.

**The following ingredients used in polishes
and lubricants are poisons:**
acetic acid, caustic soda, sulfuric acid, aniline black,
Vienna lime, oxalic acid, barium stearate,
aniline dye, and sodium silicate.
These polish ingredients are flammable:
turpentine, kerosene, gasoline, alcohol, and oils.

METAL POLISHES

You will need the following ingredients:

BASIC PASTE POLISH #1
    9 *Parts of white petroleum jelly*
    3 *Parts of kieselguhr*
    1 *Refined paraffin wax*
    1 *Part refined whiting*
    1 *Part sodium hyposulfite*

Melt the paraffin wax and petroleum jelly in a double boiler, then add the other ingredients and blend thoroughly. Remove from the heat and stir until it turns into a paste. It may have to be returned to the heat if a paste is not produced.

BASIC PASTE POLISH #2
    8 *Ounces of kieselguhr*
    2 *Ounces of paraffin*
    6 *Ounces of lubricating oil*
    1 *Ounce of oleic acid*
   30 *Minims of oil of mirbane*

Place the paraffin and the lubricating oil in a double boiler and melt, then mix in the kieselguhr and add the other ingredients while continuing to stir until it becomes pasty.

LIQUID METAL POLISH #1
　　8　*Pounds of crude oleic acid*
　　2　*Pounds of mineral oil (unflavored)*
2^1/$_2$　*Pounds of kieselguhr*
　^{3}/$_4$　*Ounce of lemon oil*

Place all the ingredients into a container and blend well, then thin with water to make a liquid polish. The polish should be applied with one cloth and rubbed and polished with another.

LIQUID METAL POLISH #2
　　1　*Pound of Tripoli powder*
　　1　*Pound of whiting*
　　1　*Pound of prepared chalk*
　　1　*Pound of stearin*
　　1　*Gallon of leaded gasoline*
　　8　*Ounces of oleic acid*

Place the gasoline in a safe container. Dissolve the stearin into the gasoline, then stir in the oleic acid. Add the Tripoli powder, whiting, and the chalk. Mix well to keep lumps from forming.

BASIC POWDER METAL POLISH
　　1　*Part of magnesium carbonate*
　　1　*Part of chalk*
　　1　*Part of ferric oxide*

Place all the ingredients into a container and mix well.

SILVER COIN POLISH
　　1　*Part sulfuric acid (use with care)*
　　9　*Parts of cool tap water*

Wear gloves. Place the mixture in a glass bowl and mix well, then soak the coin in the mixture for 10 minutes. Rinse under running cold water, clean with Castile soap and a soft bristle brush, then rinse again. Dry the coin with a soft, cloth and polish with a piece of chamois.

ALUMINUM POLISH
　　1　*Part of virgin olive oil*
　　1　*Part of cheap rum*

Place the ingredients into a sealed container and shake to mix. Place the solution on a clean cloth and rub to polish. Buff with another clean, soft cloth.

COPPER POLISH

> 4   *Parts of finely powdered charcoal*
> 3   *Parts of spirit of wine*
> 2   *Parts of essence of turpentine*
> 3   *Parts of cool tap water*
> 1   *Part of oxalic acid*

Place the charcoal, spirit of wine, and essence of turpentine in a container and mix well. In another container, combine the water and oxalic acid, then mix with the first solution. Make sure the solution is well mixed and uniform—not streaky. Rub the solution onto the copper with a soft cloth.

TIN POLISH

> 1   *Part of Vienna lime*
> 1   *Part of chalk*
> 1   *Part of Tripoli*

Place the ingredients into a container and lightly dampen with alcohol. Apply to the tin with a brush and polish with a piece of chamois.

POLISHING CLOTH #1

You will need the following ingredients:

> 1   *Ounce of paraffin oil*
> 1   *Ounce of oil of cedar*
> 1   *Quart of gasoline*

Place the ingredients into a safe container and blend well. Keep away from a heat source since this formula is very flammable. Place a cloth in the mixture, remove, and allow to air dry. Baser metals such as iron or steel should be polished with a flannel cloth; other metals such as silver and gold should be polished with a soft cotton cloth.

POLISHING CLOTH #2

You will need the following ingredients:

> 3   *Ounces of gum benzoin*
> 1   *Quart of cottonseed oil*
> 3   *Quarts of liquid paraffin*

Heat the ingredients in a double boiler until the paraffin is melted and blend all ingredients are well-blended. Remove from the heat and dip the cloth into the solution, remove it right away, and allow it to dry. See instructions for Polishing Cloth #1 for which types of cloth to use on various types of metal. For baser metals sprinkle a small amount of fine emery powder on the cloth; for silver or gold metals use fine Tripoli powder.

OLD-TIME METAL STOVE POLISH

You will need the following ingredients:

4 Ounces of rosin
1 Gallon of turpentine
1 Pound of powdered graphite
1 Ounce of lampblack

Place all the ingredients into a container and blend well. A small amount of oil of cedar may be added for a pleasant aroma.

LEATHER SHOE POLISH

You will need the following ingredients:

BROWN SHOES

1 Part yellow wax
1 Part palm oil
3 Parts turpentine

Place the wax and the palm oil in a double boiler and melt, then add the turpentine and stir well. Remove from the heat and allow to fully cool before using.

BLACK SHOES

1 Pound of beeswax
1 Pound of ceresin
6 Ounces of carnauba wax
3 Pints of turpentine
6 Ounces of yellow soap shavings
   Oil-soluble black aniline dye (just enough to color)

Place the beeswax, ceresin, and carnauba wax into a saucepan and melt together over a low flame, then stir in the turpentine, soap shavings, and dye. If the mixture is too thick add a small amount of water. This solution can be used immediately after it is thoroughly mixed.

PATENT LEATHER POLISH
    1   *Part of wax*
    3   *Parts of virgin olive oil*
    1¹/₂ *Parts of oil of turpentine*

Melt the wax and olive oil in a saucepan over low heat then remove from the heat. When the mixture is just about cold, add the oil of turpentine and mix well.

WHITE SHOE DRESSING #1
    ¹/₂ *Pound of pipe clay*
    ¹/₄ *Pound of Spanish whiting*
    3   *Ounces of zinc white*
    2   *Ounces of precipitated chalk*
    1   *Dram of gum arabic*

Place all the ingredients into a container and add a small amount of water, just enough to produce a creamy consistency. Add a small amount of oil of cloves to prevent the gum from souring.

WHITE SHOE DRESSING #2
    3   *Ounces of cream of tartar*
    1   *Ounce of oxalic acid*
    1   *Ounce of alum*
    3   *Pints of whole milk*
    2   *Tablespoons of prepared chalk*
    2   *Tablespoons of magnesium carbonate*

Place all the ingredients into a container and blend well. Rub the solution on the shoes and allow them to dry before buffing with a clean cloth that has been dipped in a mixture of prepared chalk and magnesium carbonate.

HEEL POLISH
You will need the following ingredients:

     5 *Parts of carnauba wax*
     5 *Parts of Japanese wax*
     5 *Parts of paraffin*
    50 *Parts oil of turpentine*
     1 *Part lampblack*
     2 *Parts of wine black*

Place the wax and the paraffin in a double boiler and melt. Remove from the heat and allow the mixture to cool to lukewarm before adding the turpentine and mixing well. Add the lampblack and wine black and blend well, then pour into a metal can while it is still warm. Cover and store in a cool dry location until needed.

HARNESS POLISH

You will need the following ingredients:

> 1 *Part of natural yellow ceresin*
> 1 *Part of yellow beeswax*
> 1 *Part of Japan wax*
> 7$^1/_2$ *Parts of turpentine oil*

Place the waxes in a double boiler and when they begin to melt together, add the turpentine oil and mix well. Remove from heat and allow it to cool before using.

IVORY POLISH

You will need the following ingredients:

> 1 *Part of Armenian bole*
> 1 *Part of oleic acid*

Place the ingredients into a container and prepare a paste. Rub the polish on the ivory with a clean linen cloth (or toothbrush depending on the item) and wash the ivory with Marseilles soap, then dry and polish with a chamois skin, then a piece of silk.

LUBRICANTS

Lubricants lengthen the useful life of a piece of machinery by reducing the friction between moving metal parts. This is accomplished by applying a substance to form a smooth film. Some lubricants such as grease and oil will also help to prevent rust. Lubricants are more sensitive to temperature changes than other products, which means most lubricants need to be made specifically for that metal. Lubricants for leather are usually made to soften the leather and make it more flexible and resistant to excessive wear.

VALVE LUBRICANT

You will need the following ingredients:

5 *Parts of barium stearate*
4 *Parts of mineral oil*
1 *Part of talc*

Place the barium stearate and the mineral oil in a pot and heat to 250° F. while continually stirring, then add the talc and continue to stir until the solution is uniform in texture. Remove from the heat and allow the lubricant to cool. This lubricant is capable of withstanding high temperatures.

POWDERED LUBRICANT

You will need the following ingredients:

1 *Parts of zinc stearate*
1 *Part of talc*

Powder the ingredients using a mortar and pestle. The resulting lubricant may be used on electrical devices, such as washing machines. The lubricant will not stain cloth.

SEWING MACHINE LUBRICANT #1

You will need the following ingredients:

9 *Ounces of pale oil of almonds*
3 *Ounces of rectified benzoline*
1 *Ounce of foreign oil of lavender*

Place all the ingredients into a container and mix well.

SEWING MACHINE LUBRICANT #2

You will need the following ingredients:

1 *Part of petrolatum*
7 *Parts of paraffin oil*

Place the ingredients into a container and mix well.

FIREARM LUBRICANT

You will need the following ingredients:

3 *Parts of white petrolatum*
1 *Part of acid-free bone oil*

Place the ingredients in a pot and mix while on low heat. Stir until well-blended and remove from heat. Allow the lubricant to cool before using.

LUBRICATING PENCIL

You will need the following ingredients:

4 *Ounces of beeswax*
1 *Ounce of diglycol stearate*
5 *Ounces of graphite powder*

Place all the ingredients into a double boiler and heat until they
are mixed well. Remove it from the heat and allow it to
cool somewhat before pouring it into a greased, flat-
bottomed pan. After it has cooled and solidified,
cut into pencil-sized
pieces to lubricate
door hinges. This
lubricant will not
attract dust and will not stain.

LEATHER LUBRICANT #1

You will need the following ingredients:

8 *Ounces of Russian tallow*
3 *Ounces of beeswax*
2 *Ounces of black pitch*
1¹/₂ *Pounds of castor oil*
4 *Ounces of soft paraffin*
¹/₄ *Ounce of oil of citronella*

Heat the tallow, beeswax, black pitch, castor oil, and soft paraffin together
in a double boiler until well blended. Remove the mixture from the heat
and allow it to cool before adding the citronella; mix well.

LEATHER LUBRICANT #2

You will need the following ingredients:

10 *Ounces of Neat's foot oil*
2 *Ounces of oil of turpentine*
4 *Ounces of petrolatum*
¹/₂ *Ounce of lampblack*

Place the petrolatum in a saucepan and place on low heat until melted.
Place the Neat's foot oil, oil of turpentine, and lampblack into a container
and mix well, then add to the melted petrolatum and blend well. Remove
from the heat and allow the lubricant to cool before using. This is highly
recommended for black harnesses.

PENETRATING OIL
You will need the following ingredients:

> 2 *Parts of kerosene*
> 7 *Parts of light mineral oil*
> 1 *Part of secondary butyl alcohol*

Place the mineral oil into a container and dissolve the other ingredients into it. This oil will remove rusted screws, bolts, etc.

1930's AXLE GREASE
You will need the following ingredients:

> 19^1/$_2$ *Parts of tallow (acid-free)*
> 14 *Parts of palm oil*
> 5^1/$_2$ *Parts of sal soda*
> 3 *Parts of cool tap water*

Place the water into a container and dissolve the sal soda. In a pot, melt the tallow, then stir in the palm oil. Remove the tallow mixture from the heat and add the mixture to the sal soda and water. Make sure all ingredients are thoroughly blended. If you prefer grease that is not as solid, add more palm oil. This grease was commonly used on heavy vehicle axles.

GRAPHITE GREASE
You will need the following ingredients:

> 7 *Parts of ceresin*
> 7 *Parts of tallow*
> 3 *Parts of graphite*

Place the ceresin and the tallow in a double boiler or pot and heat to a temperature of 176° F. Add the graphite and mix well until the grease is uniform in appearance.

Chapter 23

Beverages &
Food Formulas

The following beverages were popularized during the 1940's and 1950's. When you're in a nostalgic mood, try making one of these old favorite formulas.

BEVERAGES FROM FRUIT JUICES

PARTY PUNCH
You will need the following ingredients:

> 1 *Cup of orange juice*
> 1 *Cup of pineapple juice*
> 1 *Cup of grapefruit juice*
> 1/2 *Cup of lemon juice*
> 1 *Quart of carbonated water*
> *Granulated sugar (as desired)*

Place all the juices into a punch bowl and blend well. Add sugar (as desired) and a small block of ice that has been made by freezing water in an empty milk carton. Decorate with slices of orange and float cherries in the punch. Makes enough for 8–12 servings.

LOGANBERRY DELIGHT
You will need the following ingredients:

> 4 *Lemons (juice only)*
> 2 *Cups of strong tea*
> 2 *Cups of loganberry juice*
> *Ice cubes or crushed ice*
> *Ginger ale*

Place the tea into a container and add the juice of 4 lemons and the loganberry juice. Fill a tall glass 1/2 full of crushed ice (or ice cubes) and add 1/4 of a glass of the mixture, then fill the glass with ginger ale and stir well.

GRAPE JUICE BONANZA
You will need the following ingredients:

> 2 *Cups of purple grape juice (or red)*
> 1 *Cup of orange juice*
> 1 *Tablespoon of lemon juice*
> 2 *Whole cloves*
> 1 *Slice of lemon peel*
> *Maraschino cherries (as desired)*

Place the first 5 ingredients into a cocktail shaker with ice and shake well. Strain into glasses and add one maraschino cherry to each glass.

STRAWBERRY COCKTAIL
You will need the following ingredients:

>   1 *Quart of fresh strawberries*
>   1 *Lemon*
>   1 *Orange*
>   1 *Pound of granulated sugar*
>   3 *Pints of cool tap water*

Place the strawberries into a sieve and press well, then combine the strawberry juice with the juice of the lemon and orange and add the water. Mix well and allow to stand for 2 hours. Pour the mixture over the sugar and stir until it is all dissolved. Serve the drink in small cocktail glasses.

WINTERTIME COCKTAIL
You will need the following ingredients:

>   1^1/2 *Cups of ruby red grapefruit juice (any will do)*
>   1^1/4 *Cups of red raspberry juice*
>   2 *Oranges (or equivalent juice)*
>   2 *Lemons (or equivalent juice)*

Place the juice from the orange and lemon in a bowl, mix and add the grapefruit and raspberry juices, then blend well and serve over ice or chill before serving.

CRANBERRY CORDIAL
You will need the following ingredients:

>   4 *Cups of fresh cranberries*
>   4 *Cups of boiling water*
>   4 *Whole cloves*
>   1 *Slice of lemon peel*
> ^{3}/4 *Cup of granulated sugar*

Place the cranberries, cloves, and lemon peel in a pot with the boiling water and cook over low heat for 15 minutes, crushing the cranberries with the back of a spoon. Add the sugar and continue cooking for another 5 minutes. Remove from the heat and strain through a fine sieve or piece of cheesecloth. Allow the mixture to cool, then place it in the refrigerator. When you are ready to serve, place the mixture in a cocktail shaker with ice, shake, and serve.

LEMON POWDER BEVERAGE

You will need the following ingredients:

$3^1/4$ Ounces of sodium bicarbonate
3 Ounces of tartaric acid
$6^1/4$ Ounces of granulated sugar
Lemon oil (as desired)

Place the sodium bicarbonate, acid, and sugar into a bowl and mix well. Add a small amount of lemon oil to taste and shake the mixture with ice in a cocktail shaker. Serve in cocktail glasses with a stuffed green olive if desired. Provides 12 servings.

RASPBERRY POWDER DELIGHT

You will need the following ingredients:

1 Pound of granulated sugar
1 Ounce of bicarbonate of soda
1 Ounce of tartaric acid
2 Drams of essence of raspberry

Place the sugar and the essence of raspberry in a medium bowl and mix thoroughly, then add the other ingredients and blend well. Store the powder in an airtight plastic bag or well-sealed jar. Humidity and moisture will affect the quality of the powder. Place about $1/2$ teaspoon of the powder (or to taste) into a glass, and add water and ice to prepare a sparkling beverage.

VEGETABLE JUICE BEVERAGES

Juice drinks were popular long before the present juicing trend. These were some of the more popular veggie drinks.

LOST INTEREST IN SEX?

In ancient Greece, carrot juice was used to induce the desire for sex in both sexes. Carrots were considered a cure for psychological impotency. If you really want to increase their potency, add a little parsley and a few caraway seeds.

CARROT JUICE DRINK

You will need the following ingredients:

2   *Ounces of carrot juice*
2   *Ounces of celery juice*
1/4   *Teaspoon of table salt*

Place all the ingredients into a glass and mix well.

THE LUV VEGGIE

If you are interested in astrology, you may be aware that rhubarb is considered the "love food" and one that has protective qualities. Rhubarb originated in China and is commonly used as a medicinal vegetable. The leaves are poisonous and should never be consumed.

RHUBARB COCKTAIL

You will need the following ingredients:

2   *Ounces of rhubarb stalk juice (never use the leaves)*
1   *Teaspoon of pure honey*

Place the ingredients into a cup and blend well. This was also used as a summer purge.

TOMATO JUICE BEVERAGE

You will need the following ingredients:

1   *Pint of tomato juice*
1/2   *Teaspoon of table salt*
1   *Tablespoon of lemon juice*
1   *Teaspoon of minced onion*
1   *Teaspoon of minced celery*
1   *Slice of lemon peel*

Place all the ingredients in a sealed jar and refrigerate until cold. Place the mixture in a cocktail shaker with ice; mix and strain into glasses.

THE DEATH PENALTY FOR STEALING CABBAGE

Cabbage was such an important vegetable to the Greeks that they passed a special law that gave the death penalty to anyone caught stealing a head of cabbage. Consuming 10 cups of cabbage a day was thought to ward off insanity and even cure it. Cabbage was also thought to eliminate nightmares if consumed just before bedtime.

SAUERKRAUT JUICE COCKTAIL

You will need the following ingredients:

1 *Quart of sauerkraut juice*
2 *Teaspoons of lemon juice*
$1/4$ *Teaspoon of paprika*
$1/4$ *Teaspoon of table salt*

Place the sauerkraut and the lemon juice into a bowl and mix well, then add the paprika and salt. Place the mixture into the refrigerator and chill well before serving.

MILK BEVERAGES

MAKING OLD-FASHIONED CHOCOLATE SYRUP FOR MILK

You will need the following ingredients:

2 *Squares of unsweetened chocolate*
2 *Cups of granulated sugar*
$1^1/2$ *Cups of whole milk (low-fat is okay)*
2 *Tablespoons of unsalted butter (not margarine)*
2 *Drops of real vanilla extract*

Place the unsweetened chocolate (broken into small pieces), sugar, butter, and milk into a double boiler. Allow the mixture to heat (without stirring) until it looks like thick syrup. Remove from the heat and add the vanilla, then mix and store in a well-sealed glass jar. If the syrup is allowed to heat too much, you will end up with a great fudge recipe.

OLD-FASHIONED CHOCOLATE MALTED MILK

You will need the following ingredients:

4 *Tablespoons of chocolate syrup*
$1/2$ *Pint of milk (any)*
2 *Tablespoons of vanilla or chocolate ice cream*
1 *Teaspoon of malt*

Place the chocolate syrup in a tall glass, then add the other ingredients and blend well. An electric blender works great.

S. BEAN

OLD-FASHIONED VANILLA MALTED MILK

You will need the following ingredients:

4   *Tablespoons of vanilla syrup*
$^1/_2$ *Pint of milk (any)*
2   *Tablespoons of vanilla ice cream*
1   *Teaspoon of malt*

The directions are the same as for the chocolate malt.

CHOCOLATE CREAM SODA #1

You will need the following ingredients:

4   *Tablespoons of chopped ice*
4   *Tablespoons of chocolate syrup*
6   *Tablespoons of whipped cream*
$^1/_2$ *Cup of carbonated water*

Place all the ingredients into a large glass and blend well.

CHOCOLATE CREAM SODA #2

You will need the following ingredients:

2   *Tablespoons of chocolate syrup*
2   *Tablespoons of real cream or whole milk*
3   *Tablespoons of chocolate or vanilla ice cream*
    Carbonated water to fill glass

This may be mixed in a blender. Substitutions may be made to reduce the fat and cholesterol.

VANILLA CREAM SODA

You will need the following ingredients:

1   *Tablespoon of corn syrup*
2   *Drops of vanilla extract*
2   *Tablespoons of real cream of whole milk*
3   *Tablespoons of vanilla ice cream*
    Carbonated water to fill glass

Place the corn syrup, vanilla extract, and cream (or milk) into a glass and blend well. Add the ice cream and fill the glass with the carbonated water and mix well or use a blender.

STRAWBERRY CREAM SODA

You will need the following ingredients:

    1 *Tablespoon of strawberry jam (not low sugar)*
    2 *Tablespoons of real cream or whole milk*
    3 *Tablespoons of strawberry ice cream*
       Carbonated water to fill glass

Place the strawberry jam, cream (or milk), and ice cream in a glass, then fill the glass with carbonated water and mix or blend well.

RASPBERRY CREAM SODA

You will need the following ingredients:

    1 *Tablespoon of raspberry jam*
    2 *Tablespoons of real cream or whole milk*
    3 *Tablespoons of vanilla ice cream or raspberry sherbet*
       Carbonated water to fill glass

This soda comes out better if real cream is used with either raspberry ice or sherbet. If you wish to use milk, then ice cream should be used.

MAKING MILK MALT

You will need the following ingredients:

    1 *Ounce of powdered malt*
    2 *Ounces of powdered oatmeal*
    4 *Ounces of milk sugar*
    1 *Pound of roasted all-purpose flour*

Place all the ingredients in a jar, cover with a tight lid, and shake well to blend. Shake before each use. Add one teaspoon to each cup of milk.

SLEEPYTIME BEVERAGES

A BEDTIME BEVERAGE #1

You will need the following ingredients:

    1 *Glass of hot tap water*
  1$^1/_2$ *Tablespoons of pure honey*
       Juice of $^1/_2$ lemon

Place the lemon and honey into the hot water and blend well.

BEDTIME BEVERAGE #2

You will need the following ingredients:

1 *Warm milk*
1 *Tablespoon of pure honey*

Place the honey in the warm milk and fully dissolve before drinking.

MISCELLANEOUS BEVERAGES

SARSAPARILLA SYRUP

You will need the following ingredients:

20 *Ounces of simple syrup*
$1/2$ *Teaspoon of sarsaparilla flavoring or extract*
Caramel to color

Thoroughly mix together the flavoring, the caramel, and the simple syrup. Place 3 tablespoons of the syrup in a glass and add enough carbonated water to fill the glass, then blend well.

SPRUCE BEER

You will need the following ingredients:

$1/2$ *Ounce of essence of spruce*
1 *Pound of granulated sugar*
1 *Gallon of boiling water*
2 *Ounces of yeast (fresh)*

Place the boiling water in a container and add the sugar and essence of spruce and mix well. Allow the mixture to cool a little, then add the yeast and allow the beverage to remain still for 12–14 hours before bottling it.

GINGER BEER #1

You will need the following ingredients:

1 *Pound of brown sugar*
1 *Gallon of boiling water*
$1/2$ *Ounce of cream of tartar*
1 *Ounce of bruised ginger*
$1/4$ *Pint of yeast (fresh)*

Place the boiling water in a container and add the ginger, mix and add the sugar and cream of tartar, then blend well. Strain the mixture after it has become lukewarm, then add the yeast and allow it to remain still for 12–14 hours before pouring the ginger beer into bottles.

GINGER BEER #2

You will need the following ingredients:

15 Ounces of bruised ginger
20 Ounces of granulated sugar
1 Lemon, sliced very thinly
1 Ounce of pure honey

Boil the ginger in 3 pints of water for 30 minutes. Add the lemon slices and the sugar to the hot solution. Stir in the honey and 1 gallon of water. Strain the solution and allow the liquid to stand for 4 days before bottling.

1920's GINGER BEER RECIPE #3

You will need the following ingredients:

1^1/$_2$ Pounds of ginger (bruised)
20 Pounds of sugar
1 Dozen lemons (bruised & sliced)
1 Pound of honey
20 Gallons of water

Soak the ginger in 3 gallons of water in a large tub for ^{1}/$_2$ hour. Then add the sugar, lemons, honey, and 17 gallons of water and mix well. Strain the mixture well, then wait 3–4 days before bottling.

A VERY OLD BREW

Beer is a generic name for any beverage that is produced by the process of fermentation of extracts of a cereal grain, usually barley. The history of beer can be traced back nine-thousand years to the coarse milling of a prehistoric grain, called "emmer." The Babylonians produced over 20 varieties of beer and the Egyptians and Greeks were avid beer drinkers. The Germans started producing the brew in about 800 BC.

HOP BEER

You will need the following ingredients:

3 Ounces of hops
5 Quarts of cool tap water
2 Ounces of bruised ginger
2 Pounds of granulated sugar
^{1}/$_2$ Pint of yeast (fresh)

Boil the hops in 2^1/$_2$ quarts of tap water for 3 hours. Strain the mixture and add the bruised ginger and the

S. BEAN

other 2^1/$_2$ quarts of water. Boil for a few more minutes and then strain the mixture again and stir in the sugar. After the mixture has cooled a little, add the yeast and allow the beer to stand for 24 hours before placing in bottles.

MAKING BEER AT HOME
You will need the following ingredients:

> 4 *Gallons of bottled spring water*
> 5 *Gallon crock*
> 1 *Quart of red top malt*
> 2 *Cakes of fresh yeast*
> 5 *Pounds of granulated sugar*

Place 2 gallons of water in the crock and heat. While it is heating, stir in the malt and sugar. When they are fully dissolved, allow the mixture to cool and add 2 more gallons of water, then add the yeast. Mix and keep the crock in a warm location for about 4 days or until all the foam settles. The beer may now be bottled and cooled to your taste.

FIRST SODA POP IN THE UNITED STATES

The first soda was sold in the United States in the mid-1800's and was invented by James Vernor, who named the drink Vernor's Ginger Ale. The extract used to produce the drink was aged for 4 years in oak casks. Ginger ale was the most popular soda pop until the 1920's. Ginger ale became associated with alcohol during prohibition when it was the most popular mixer of the day. Vernor's Ginger Ale is still being sold today through select distributors.

GINGER ALE
You will need the following ingredients:

> 3 *Ounces of cream of tartar*
> 1 *Ounce of bruised ginger*
> 24 *Ounces of granulated sugar*
> 2 *Drams of citric acid*
> 1 *Ounce of yeast (fresh)*
> 1^1/$_2$ *Gallons of boiling water*

Place the first four ingredients into the boiling water and dissolve fully. When the water starts to cool, strain the mixture and add the yeast. Allow the ginger ale to rest overnight before bottling.

ROOT BEER, 1650'S STYLE

In the 1600's the colonists made a root beer out of sassafras root, water, sugar, and a small amount of ale or bread yeast placed in warm water. However, recent laboratory studies now show that rats can develop cancer from consuming safrole, the active ingredient in sassafras. The FDA has now banned sassafras from being sold other than as a raw food product by health food stores.

ROOT BEER EXTRACT

You will need the following ingredients:

    1³/4 Cups of raisins (chopped, not too fine)
    3 Cups of boiling water
    2 Gallons of cool tap water
    1¹/2 Ounces of dried sassafras root bark
    15 Cups of granulated sugar

Place the raisins in a pan and pour the boiling water over them, cover and allow the raisins to steep for about 45 minutes. In another large pot, place the 2 gallons of water and the sassafras bark over medium heat. While the water is heating, slowly add the sugar while continually stirring and simmer for about 40 minutes. Remove from the heat and set aside. Strain the raisin solution through a piece of cheesecloth, reserving the liquid, and place the raisin liquid into the bark mixture and let it sit uncovered for about 30 minutes. Pour the extract into 1 quart canning jars and proceed with normal canning instructions.Can with normal bands and lids.

MAKING ROOT BEER WITH EXTRACT

You will need the following ingredients:

    3 Quarts of cool tap water
    1 Quart jar of root beer extract
    ¹/8 Teaspoon of ale yeast

Place the extract into a pot (warm slightly to remove from container) with the water and heat on low. The mixture should only become luke-warm, never hot. Mix gently and add the yeast, then place the root beer into bottles and allow them to remain in a dark location. Check the root beer after about 2 days to be sure that the carbonation is forming well and again after 3 days. When the carbonation looks right, refrigerate the beverage.

OLD-FASHIONED CHERRY-VANILLA SODA

You will need the following ingredients:

- 1   Cup of cool tap water
- 4   Tablespoons of brown sugar
- 4   Inches of fresh vanilla bean
- 1   Gallon of cherry juice at room-temperature (a blend is okay if cherry juice is listed first on the label and it's 100% juice)
- 1/8   Teaspoon of ale yeast
- 1/4   Cup of lukewarm tap water

Place the cool water, sugar, vanilla bean, and 2 cups of the cherry juice into a small pot and heat on medium to just below boiling, then simmer for 15 minutes while stirring until all the sugar dissolves. Remove from the heat and allow the mixture to stand for 20 minutes, then pour the rest of the cherry juice into a large jug and add the contents of the pot. Place the lukewarm water into a cup and add the yeast, shake gently to mix or place a lid on and turn over 2–3 times. Allow the yeast to remain still for 5–6 minutes before adding the yeast mixture to the jug. Place a cap on the jug and turn it upside down 3–4 times to mix. Bottle the soda and allow it to remain in a dark location for 2 days before checking on the carbonation level. When the carbonation seems to be right, refrigerate the soda.

FOOD-RELATED FORMULAS

THE MYSTERY OF BAKING POWDER REVEALED

Baking powder is a mixture of chemicals that has the ability to leaven bread. The main chemicals are calcium acid phosphate, sodium aluminum sulfate or cream of tartar, and sodium bicarbonate. This mixture of acids and bases produces a chemical reaction when water is added producing carbon dioxide gas. When this occurs, the gas creates minute air pockets or will enter already existing ones in the dough or batter.

When you place the mixture in a hot oven or on a hot plate, the dough rises, since the heat causes the release of carbon dioxide from the baking powder as well as expanding the trapped carbon dioxide gas, thus creating steam. The pressure of the steam swells the dough or batter and it expands and rises. Always combine the wet and dry ingredients separately. A wet measuring spoon should never be placed into baking powder. Use 1 teaspoon of baking powder for each 1 cup of flour for the best results. If you are mixing a batter for fried foods, reduce the amount to half and you will have a lighter batter.

BAKING POWDER FORMULA #1

You will need the following ingredients:

- *1/2 Teaspoon of cream of tartar*
- *1/4 Teaspoon of baking soda (fresh)*
- *1/4 Teaspoon of cornstarch*

Place the ingredients into a small bowl and mix. This will make 1 teaspoon of baking powder. The baking powder must be used immediately to be effective. The cornstarch will prevent moisture from the air getting into the powder, giving you enough time to use the powder.

BAKING POWDER FORMULA #2

You will need the following ingredients:

- *2 Tablespoons of potassium bitartrate*
- *1 Tablespoon of sodium bicarbonate*
- *1 Tablespoon of cornstarch*

Place all the ingredients into a small bowl and blend well. This formula needs to be used immediately since it will not keep well.

CHEF'S FAVORITE ALL-AROUND BREADING

You will need the following ingredients:

- *2 Cups of whole wheat pastry flour*
- *1/2 Tablespoon of paprika*
- *1 Tablespoon of dry mustard*
- *3/4 Teaspoon of finely ground celery seed*
- *1 Teaspoon of ground black pepper*
- *1 Teaspoon of dried basil*
- *1 Teaspoon of dried marjoram*
- *1 Teaspoon of dried thyme*

Place all the ingredients into a medium bowl and mix thoroughly, then store in the refrigerator until needed. Before using, remove from the refrigerator and let it sit for 20 minutes to bring it to room temperature.

MAYONNAISE BY ANY OTHER NAME

Mayonnaise must contain at least 65% oil by weight to be called "mayonnaise." If it has any less it must be called "salad dressing." Most fat-free mayonnaise contains more sodium than "real" mayonnaise. A tablespoon of "real" mayonnaise contains only 5–10mg of cholesterol, since very little egg yolk is actually used and most mayonnaise has a soy base.

STANDARD MAYONNAISE

You will need the following ingredients:

1 *Large egg*
1/2 *Teaspoon of table salt*
1 *Teaspoon of mustard (optional)*
1/4 *Teaspoon of ground white pepper*
11/2 *Teaspoons of white wine vinegar*
1 *Cup of corn oil*
11/2 *Teaspoons of lemon juice*

Place the egg, salt, mustard, pepper, and vinegar in a blender and blend for 6 seconds, then place the mixture in a food processor and process for 15 seconds while adding the oil in a small, slow stream. As soon as all the oil has been added, stop the processor and add the lemon juice to taste. If the mayonnaise is too thick, add a small amount of water; if it is too thin, process for a little longer.

COFFEE SUBSTITUTE FROM WHEAT

You will need the following ingredients:

6 *Cups of 100% wheat*
1 *Cup of whole milk (low-fat is okay)*
1/2 *Cup of molasses*
1/2 *Teaspoon of table salt*

Grind the wheat in a coffee grinder, then place it in a large bowl. Add the milk, molasses, and salt and mix until it has the consistency of a paste. Spread the paste on a cookie sheet and bake it at 350° F. until brown (do not burn). As soon as the mixture is brown, reduce the heat to its lowest point and allow the wheat paste to dry until crisp. Break up the crispy mass and grind it all up in a coffee grinder, then store in a sealed container in a cool, dry location until used.

ALUM BAKING POWDER

You will need the following ingredients:

15 *Parts of ammonium alum anhydrous*
18 *Parts of sodium bicarbonate*
67 *Parts of cornstarch*

Place all the ingredients into a bowl and blend well.

CHEWING GUM

You will need the following ingredients:

4 *Parts of balsam of tolu*
1 *Part of benzoin*
1 *Part of white wax*
1 *Part of paraffin*
1 *Part of powdered sugar (10X)*

Place all the ingredients into a pot and blend well over low heat; then remove and allow the mixture to cool. Roll into small individual chewing gum sticks.

1920 FORMULA FOR CHOW CHOW

You will need the following ingredients:

10–20 *New pickles*
3 *Ounces of curry powder*
5 *Ounces of mustard powder*
8 *Grams of cayenne pepper*
3 *Ounces of ginger*
9 *Grams of black pepper*
2 *Ounces of turmeric*
5 *Grams of coriander*
5 *Grams of allspice*
8 *Grams of celery seed*
2 *Gallons of apple cider vinegar*
2 *Grams of mace*
2 *Grams of savory*
2 *Grams of thyme*

Place all the dry ingredients into a very large pot and mix well, then add the vinegar. Mix and allow to steep on low heat for 3 hours, mixing occasionally. The pickles should be par-boiled with salt, then drained well. Pour the vinegar mixture over the pickles while they are still warm and store in small, well-sealed jars in a cool, dry location.

HERE LITTLE FISHY

Anchovies are usually only about 4–6 inches long and are commonly used on pizza, Caesar salad, or sold in cans. They have a very high sodium (salt) content but can be somewhat de-salted by soaking in ice water for about 15 minutes. After soaking, place them in the refrigerator for 45 minutes before using. Because of their high salt content anchovies will last about 1 year in a can and still be fresh. If you open the can but do not finish it, just cover the anchovies with olive oil and refrigerate and they should last for about 2 months.

ANCHOVY PASTE

You will need the following ingredients:

7   Pounds of anchovies
9   Pints of cool tap water
1   Pound of table salt
1   Pound of all-purpose flour
1/4   Ounce of capsicum
1   Grated lemon peel
4   Ounces of mushroom ketchup

This recipe is designed for commercial purposes. For home use, reduce as needed. Place all ingredients into a large bowl and blend well into a smooth paste. Add the water slowly so as not to make the paste too watery.

Appendix

Appendix A
Common Names Of Chemicals

The following list will provide you with the chemical name of some of the more common chemicals used in the book. This may help you locate them.

Common Name	Chemical Name
Alum	Potassium aluminum sulfate
Aqua fortis	Nitric acid
Baking soda	Sodium bicarbonate
Blue vitriol	Copper sulfate
Borax	Sodium tetraborate
Brimstone	Sulfur
Butter of antimony	Antimony trichloride
Carbolic acid	Phenol
Caustic potash	Potassium hydroxide
Chalk	Calcium carbonate
Chloride of lime	Calcium hypochlorite
Cinnabar	Mercury sulfide
Copperas	Ferrous sulfate
Cream of tartar	Potassium bitartrate
Epsom salts	Magnesium sulfate
Fluorspar	Calcium fluoride
Grain alcohol	Ethyl alcohol or ethanol
Green vitriol	Ferrous sulfate
Gypsum	Calcium sulfate
Hypo	Sodium thiosulfite
Kaolin	Aluminum silicate
Litharge	Lead monoxide
Lye	Sodium hydroxide or Potassium hydroxide
Magnesia	Magnesium oxide
Methylated spirits	Methyl alcohol or methanol
Minium	Red oxide of lead

Muriatic acid	Hydrochloric acid
Oil of vitriol	Sulfuric acid
Pearlash	Potassium carbonate
Plaster of paris	Calcium sulfate
Plumbago	Graphite
Prussian blue	Ferric-ferrocyanide
Pyro	Pyrogallic acid
Quicklime	Calcium oxide
Red lead	Red oxide of lead
Rochelle salt	Potassium tartrate
Sal ammoniac	Ammonium chloride
Sal soda	Crystalline sodium carbonate
Sal volatile	Ammonium sesquicarbonate
Salt	Sodium chloride
Saltpeter	Potassium nitrate or Sodium nitrate
Slaked lime	Calcium hydroxide
Soda ash	Sodium carbonate
Spar	Barite
Spirits of salt	Hydrochloric acid
Sugar of lead	Lead acetate
Tartar emetic	Antimony tartrate and Potassium tartrate
Verdigris	Copper acetate
Washing soda	Sodium carbonate
Waterglass	Sodium silicate
White copperas	Zinc sulfate
White lead	Basic lead carbonate
White vitriol	Zinc sulfate
Whiting	Calcium carbonate
Wood alcohol	Methyl alcohol or methanol
Zinc white	Zinc oxide

Appendix B	
Sources Of Ingredients	
The products needed to make the formulas will be found at the following locations:	
Acetone	Drugstore/Chemical supply house
Alcohol	Drugstore/Hardware store
Alum (aluminum sulfate)	Drugstore/Supermarket
Aluminum oxide (alumia)	Chemical supply house
Aluminum powder	Paint store
Aluminum stearate	Chemical supply house
Ammonia	Supermarket/Chemical supply house
Ammonium carbonate	Substitute: double-acting baking powder
Ammonium hydroxide (ammonia water)	Chemical supply house/Supermarket
Ammonium nitrate (saltpeter)	Chemical supply house/ Pharmacy
Ammonium oleate (ammonia soap)	Supermarket
Ammonium sulfate	Garden supply house
Amyl acetate (banana oil)	Drugstore
Antimony sulfide	Plumbing supply store
Barium sulfide (black ash)	Chemical supply house
Beeswax	Hobby shop/Hardware store
Borax	Supermarket/Drugstore
Buckwheat hulls	Health food store
Calcium carbonate (chalk)	Chemical supply house
Calcium chloride	Chemical supply house
Calcium oxide (lime)	Chemical supply house
Camphor	Drugstore/Chemical supply house

Carbonic acid (seltzer)	Supermarket/Chemical supply house
Carbon tetrachloride (cleaning fluid)	Dry cleaner/Chemical supply house
Carnauba wax	Chemical supply house
Castile soap	Drugstore
Castor oil	Drugstore/Supermarket
Ceresin wax	Paint store/Hardware store
Chalk	Paint store/Hardware store
Charcoal	Chemical supply house
Chlorinated lime	Hardware store
Citric acid (vitamin C)	Health food store/Drugstore
Clay	Health food store
Coconut oil	Health food store
Copper sulfate (bluestone)	Chemical supply house
Diatomaceous earth	Garden or swimming pools supply
Dyes	Hobby shop
Essential oils	Health food store
French chalk	Sewing center
Fuller's earth	Drugstore/Hardware store
Glucose (corn syrup)	Supermarket
Glycerin	Drugstore
Graphite	Drugstore
Gum arabic (acacia)	Drugstore/Chemical supply house
Hydrated lime	Garden supply house/Hardware store
Hydrochloric acid (muriatic acid)	Chemical supply house/Pool supply
Hydrogen peroxide	Supermarket/Drugstore
Iodine	Drugstore

Ipecac	Drugstore
Isopropyl alcohol (rubbing alcohol)	Drugstore
Jewelers' rouge	Chemical supply house/ Jewelry store
Kerosene	Paint store/Chemical supply house
Lacquer	Paint store/Hardware store
Lanolin	Drugstore
Lard	Supermarket
Lemon oil	Drugstore
Linseed oil	Hardware store/Paint store
Lye	Supermarket/Garden store
Magnesium carbonate	Chemical supply house
Magnesium hydroxide	Drugstore (milk of magnesia)
Magnesium sulfate (Epsom salt)	Supermarket/Drugstore
Mineral oil	Drugstore
Mineral spirits	Paint store
Montan wax	Chemical supply house
Naphtha soap	Supermarket/Hardware store
Neat's foot oil	Hardware store
Oil of Mirbane	Drugstores
Oleic acid	Chemical supply house
Orris root	Health food stores
Oxalic acid	Chemical supply house
Paraffin	Supermarket/Hobby shop
Peppermint oil	Health food store/Drugstore
Pigments	Paint store
Phenol (carbolic acid)	Drugstore/Chemical supply house
Plaster of paris (calcium sulfate)	Hardware store
Portland cement	Building supply/Hardware store

Potash	Chemical supply house
Potassium alum	Drugstore/Chemical supply house
Potassium carbonate (cream of tartar)	Supermarket
Potassium chlorate	Drugstores
Potassium chloride (potash)	Drugstore/Chemical supply house
Potassium hydroxide (caustic potash)	Chemical supply house
Potassium sorbate	Health food store
Pumice	Hardware store/Paint store
Shellac	Hardware store/Paint store
Silica gel	Hardware store/Hobby shop
Soap flakes	Supermarket
Sodium bicarbonate (baking soda)	Supermarket
Sodium borate (borax)	Supermarket
Sodium carbonate (washing soda)	Supermarket
Sodium citrate	Drugstore/Chemical supply house
Sodium hydroxide (caustic soda)	Supermarket/Photographic supply
Sodium hypochlorite	Chemical supply house
Sodium oxide (sand)	Hardware store
Sodium perborate	Drugstore
Sodium silicate (waterglass)	Drugstore/Chemical supply house
Sodium sulfate (Glauber's salt)	Drugstore
Sodium thiosulfate	Photographic supply
Stearic acid	Chemical supply house
Strontium chloride	Aquarium supply/Pet store
Sucrose (cane sugar)	Supermarket

Sulfuric acid (oil of vitriol)	Chemical supply house/ Supermarket
Talc (magnesium silicate)	Hardware store/Chemical supply house
Tincture of benzoin	Drugstore
Tinctures	Health food stores
Tripoli (brown buffing compound)	Lapidary supply house
Trisodium phosphate	Hardware store/Builders supply
Turpentine	Paint store/Hardware store
Vinegar (acetic acid)	Supermarket (3-5% solution)
Washing soda	Supermarket
Waterglass (sodium silicate)	Drugstore/Chemical supply house
Whiting	Paint store/Hardware store
Witch hazel	Drugstore
Zinc sulfate (white vitriol)	Chemical supply house
If chemicals cannot be located try looking the chemical up in the O.P.D. Chemical Buyers Directory	

Appendix C	
Tables Of Weights And Measures	
Apothecary Weights	5 Grams = 7^1/$_2$ Grains 20 Grains = 1 Scruple 3 Scruples = 1 Dram 8 Drams = 1 Ounce 12 Ounces = 1 Pound
Apothecary Fluid Measures	60 Minims = 1 Fluid Dram 8 Drams = 1 Fluid Ounce
Standard Weights	437^1/$_2$ Grains = 1 Ounce 16 Drams = 1 Ounce 16 Ounces = 1 Pound 7000 Grains = 1 Pound
Standard Liquid Measures	4 Gills = 1 Pint 2 Pints = 1 Quart 4 Quarts = 1 Gallon 31^1/$_2$ Gallons = 1 Barrel 2 Barrels = 1 Hogshead
Small Amount Information	^{1}/$_4$ Teaspoon = ^{1}/$_4$ Dram = 15 Drops 1 Teaspoon = 1 Dram = 60 Drops 8 Teaspoons = 1 Ounce 4 Teaspoons = 1 Tablespoon 2 Tablespoons = 1 Ounce
Metric Conversions	^{1}/$_4$ oz. = 7g. ^{1}/$_4$ oz. = 15g. 1 oz. = 30g. 2 oz. = 55g. 1 lb. = 455g.

English Weights & Measures	1 Pound = 16 Ounces =
	   256 Drachms = 7,000 Grains
	   (Troy) = 453.60 Grams
	1 Gallon = 8 Pints = 128 Ounces =
	   1,024 Drachms = 61,440 Minims

Miscellaneous	1 Drachm = 4 Grams 8 Drachms = 1 Ounce 1 Drachm = ^{1}/$_8$ Ounce = 15 Drops

Glossary

Glossary

Acacia.   A gum obtained from trees belonging to the mimosa family. Normally found in Africa and Australia.

Accelerator.   A substance that has the ability to speed up a reaction.

Acetic Acid.   A biting, colorless liquid that tends to congeal in cool temperatures and smells like vinegar. Vinegar can be substituted for acetic acid in a number of formulas.

Acetone.   Colorless, inflammable liquid that has an odor similar to ether. May be sold as dimethyl ketone.

Agar-Agar.   Gelatin-like substance that is derived from certain varieties of seaweed.

Alcohol, Ethyl.   Colorless liquid, usually made from the fermentation of grains, that is easily mixed with water or caustic soda and is flammable. Absolute ethyl alcohol is produced by removing water through distillation.

Alcohol, Denatured.   Ethyl alcohol that has been changed by the addition of other chemicals, making it unusable for human consumption and alcoholic beverages.

Alum.   A natural mineral crystalline substance that is often used for pickling and as a fixative for dyes. Can be a natural astringent.

Amidol.   White or gray powder used for photographic developing solutions.

Ammonia, Household.   A commercial chemical used in many manufacturing processes. The fumes may be irritating and may react with other household chemicals, such as hydrogen peroxide, etc. Care is recommended when mixing or using this product.

Ammonium Chloride.   White, soluble crystalline powder. Also known as sal ammoniac.

Ammonium Sulfate..   A fertilizer prepared by neutralizing ammonia water with sulfuric acid and then evaporating the liquid.

Amyl Acetate.   Oily, flammable, colorless liquid also known as banana oil since it smells like bananas.

Aniline.   Colorless, oily liquid derived from benzene and used in the manufacture of dyes. Highly poisonous.

Arnica, Tincture of.   An alcoholic solution derived from the flowers of the herb *Arnica montana*.

Arsenate of Lead.   Highly poisonous, white crystals usually used in insecticides.

Aspirin.   A mild acid used in many cleaning formulas

Baking Soda.   Bicarbonate of soda. An effective cleaning agent and deodorizer.

Balsam Peru.   Aromatic, sticky resin that varies from black to brown. Obtained from a tree grown in San Salvador.

Barium Sulfate.   Poisonous, white substance that is used in photographic chemicals and in the production of imitation opals. Also called "Mountain Snow."

Beeswax.   Made from the wax that honeybees secrete when they construct their comb. Available in either white or yellow. The natural color is yellow, which is bleached to produce the white beeswax.

Benzene.   Colorless liquid usually produced by the fractional distillation of coal tar. Benzene is flammable and should not be inhaled.

Benzol.   A liquid similar to benzene.

Bergamot Oil.   Golden oil that mixes easily with alcohol and is produced from the fruit of the *Citrus bergamia*.

Blue Vitriol.   Poisonous substance sold as blue crystals. Sometimes called copper sulfate.

Bluing.   Blue compound, usually sold in liquid form, containing ultramarine blue, soluble Prussian blue, or coal tar blue. Primarily used to whiten fabrics.

Borax.   Borax is usually mined in desert areas and makes an excellent water softener and is a common ingredient in many household cleaning products. It also has abrasive qualities when prepared as a paste.

Boric Acid.   Colorless powder that is easily mixed with water or alcohol and is produced by adding hydrochloric or sulfuric acid to a borax solution, then crystallizing it.

Calcium Carbonate.   White power also known as chalk that is easily mixed with water or acid and usually obtained from limestone.

Calcium Chloride.   White, porous, granular substance that is produced by the dehydration of white hexahydrate of calcium using a heat source.

Calendula.   An herb from the marigold family that has been used historically to treat nausea. Was also used externally as a first-aid remedy and as a cleanser and a cream. Also used effectively as an ointment to treat inflamed areas of the skin.

Carbolic Acid.   A poisonous, colorless, caustic crystal, also known as phenol. Produced from the distillation of coal tar and sometimes sold as an oily liquid.

Carmine.   A vivid crimson pigment produced from cochineal.

Carnauba Wax.   A natural wax made from the leaves of the Brazilian palm tree. It is the hardest natural wax known to man.

Casein.   A white milk protein substance derived by separating it from milk by means of a curdling process using rennet or acid.

Castile Soap.   A very mild soap manufactured with olive oil and used to produce a foaming base for a number of products. Commonly available in drug stores or health food markets.

Caustic Soda.   Also called sodium hydroxide and sold in white chips, which can easily be mixed with water or alcohol. Produced by the electrolysis of a salt solution. When mixed with water, caustic soda will heat up and may burn exposed skin areas. Should always be stored in an airtight container.

Ceresine Wax.   Also called mineral wax and available in yellow or white. The wax mixes easily with alcohol and is produced by purifying ozocerite with sulfuric acid, then filtering the solution through a charcoal filter.

Chamomile.   Herb that can be purchased in liquid form. Chamomile will repel a number of beetles and insects, especially when Tabasco is added to it.

Chloral Hydrate.   A white, crystalline narcotic that used to be known as "knock-out-drops."

Cholesterin.   Odorless and tasteless crystalline alcohol that is usually obtained from nerve tissue, egg yolk, or bile.

Citra Solv.   A citrus concentrate, available at most markets or health food stores.

Citric Acid.   Derived from citrus fruits and used as a pH modifier and regulator in many facial-care products. Citric acid is a safe product for many uses.

Citronella Oil.   Obtained from citronella grass. Used to keep flying insects away and to increase the effectiveness of ant formulas.

Clay.   A natural substance composed mainly from aluminium, silicon and oxygen. It has excellent absorbing qualities and is used extensively in facial masks. Also used in shampoos as a thickener.

Cochineal.   A dye used to produce crimson and other shades of red. Produced from the dried bodies of female insects of the *Dactylopius coccus* species.

Collodion.   A viscous liquid produced by dissolving pyroxylin in acetone or alcohol and ether.

Copperas.   Poisonous green salt that may be called green vitriol or sulfate of iron (ferrous sulfate). Copperas turns brown when exposed to the air.

Cream of Tartar.   White crystalline substance with a somewhat gritty texture and acidic taste. It is produced from purifying crude tartar obtained from the fermentation of grape juice.

Dammar.   A resin obtained from certain trees grown in Australia, New Zealand, and the East Indies.

Dextrine.   A white, odorless, gummy powder that is produced from the decomposition of starch using acids, heat, or enzymes.

Diatomaceous Earth.   Derived from dead sea creatures called diatoms. These remains contain high levels of minerals and are nearly 88% silica. Sold in either brick or powder form.

Dragon's Blood.   A dark red resinous substance obtained from a number of tropical trees, including the Malaysian palm.

Drier.   A substance that is dissolved in a varnish or paint to speed up the drying process.

Essential Oils.   Oils derived from a plant's fragrance and used as a base for perfumes. Usually extracted by steam distillation or by soaking the plant in alcohol or oil.

Ethyl Alcohol.   Common alcohol found in alcoholic beverages, such as liquor, beer, and wine. When recipes call for ethyl alcohol, just use any inexpensive vodka.

Eucalyptus Oil.   Colorless oil with a pungent aroma that easily mixes with water and alcohol. Eucalyptus oil should never be ingested since it is somewhat toxic.

Formaldehyde.   A solution made by the oxidation of synthetic methanol and used to preserve organic tissue. This is very toxic and should not come in contact with your skin.

Fuller's Earth Clay.   Natural clay used in a number of cleaning formulas because of its ability to draw out stains from porous surfaces. Found in health food stores.

Fusel Oil.   A heavy, flammable, oily fluid that has a disagreeable aroma. It consists of amyl alcohol and is found in liquors that have not been adequately distilled.

Gelatin.   Produced by boiling animal by-products with water. Capable of absorbing many times its weight in liquid.

Glycerin.   Produced from glycerol, which is a natural-occurring fat found in vegetables and animals. Easy to find at drug stores or health food markets.

Gum arabic.   A transparent, colorless, water-soluble gum obtained from certain plants of the mimosa family.

Gum Elemi.   A pleasant-smelling resin obtained from certain tropical trees.

Hydrochloric Acid.   A poisonous, colorless liquid that is corrosive in concentrated form. Also known as muriatic acid. It is actually a solution of hydrogen chloride gas that has been mixed with water. It is not flammable but will produce strong irritating fumes.

Hydrogen Peroxide.   Colorless dilute aqueous solution that is very toxic if taken internally without diluting it with water.

Hypo.   The chemical name is sodium thiosulfate, which is a salt used in photographic chemical solutions. Sold by photographic supply stores in the form of a clear crystal or white powder

Isinglass.   An almost pure form of gelatin produced from the air bladders of codfish, carp, and other fish. Sometimes thin sheets of mica used in curtains for old stagecoaches were called isinglass curtains.

Isopropyl Alcohol.   Also known as rubbing alcohol and included in a number of cleaning formulas. It is available from most pharmacies.

Jeweler's Rouge.   Also called *colocothar*. A reddish-brown iron oxide that is produced from heating ferrous sulfate and keeping the oxide as a residue.

Kaolin.   Also called *Cornish clay* or aluminum silicate. It is soft white clay that is usually sold as a powder.

Kieselguhr.   A porous, loose form of the earthy mineral known as *diatomite*. It is normally used in formulas as an abrasive.

Lampblack.   A fine black soot produced by condensing a substance that contains carbon, such as coal, pitch, or oil.

Linseed Oil.   The oil is best if purchased from a health food store instead of a hardware store. The hardware store product contains petroleum-based material and may be somewhat volatile. The food grade linseed oil is a natural, safe product.

Litharge.   Usually sold as a powder and produced by allowing lead oxide to melt.

Lye.   A very caustic chemical that will easily dissolve in water. The crystals will cause a skin burn and care should be taken when handling them. Lye is very toxic if swallowed and immediate medical attention is required. If lye is spilled on skin, flush the area with vinegar, then cold water as soon as possible. Always work with lye in a well-ventilated area and wear protective gear.

Metol.   Used as a photographic developing agent and sold as a white crystalline powder.

Montan Wax.   Hard white wax produced through the extraction of lignite from coal.

Neat's Foot Oil.   Yellow oil that can be mixed with alcohol or kerosene. Produced by boiling the shinbones and feet (no hoofs) of cattle. The oil is separated from the fat.

Neroli, Oil of.   Yellowish oil produced from the distillation of orange flowers.

Nitric Acid.   Also known as aqua fortis. A corrosive and very poisonous liquid that is usually colorless and produced by the action of sulfuric acid on nitrates.

Nutgalls.   May also just be called "galls." They are actually round swellings made by insects such as the gall midge and the gallfly found on certain varieties of oak trees. They are about the size of a hazelnut and are either blue or green.

Jungle Rain.   Produced from citrus oils and peppermint soap.

Oleic Acid.   Produced from animal tallow or certain vegetables oils and easily mixed with alcohol or organic solvents. The color ranges from yellow to reddish orange.

Olein.   Also called *glyceryl oleate*—a colorless, liquid fat at room temperature. It is found in most animal and vegetable fats.

Orris Root.   The rootstock of a European iris plant.

Oxalic Acid.   Colorless crystalline substance that is poisonous and has no aroma.

Paraffin Wax.   Sold in white blocks and soluble in warm alcohol, turpentine and olive oil. Produced through the distillation of crude petroleum oil. Paraffin wax is flammable.

Patchouli Oil.   Oily perfume extracted from the leaves and branches of a plant called *Pogostemon patchouli*, which grows in Asia.

Pearlash.   May also be sold as potassium carbonate or purified potash. It is a white salt that will produce a strong alkaline solution when dissolved in water. Pearlash is mainly produced from potassium chloride and wood ashes but can be made from sugar beets and wood scourings.

Petrolatum.   Also sold as Vaseline. White or yellowish petroleum jelly. When in its pure form it is odorless and tasteless.

Pine Oil.   Oil produced by steam distillation of pine and usually sold as an oily, light amber liquid.

Pitch.   Dark-colored sticky residue produced from the distillation of coal, tar, petroleum, and similar substances. Naturally occurs as asphalt.

Plaster of paris.   Also known as calcium sulfate. Plaster of paris forms a paste when mixed with water. Usually sold as a white, powdery substance.

Precipitated Chalk.   Purified form of white calcium carbonate.

Pumice Powder.   Abrasive powder produced from a porous rock.

Pyrethrum.   A substance prepared from crushed pyrethrum chrysanthemum flowers.

Resin.   A transparent or translucent substance that varies from yellow to brown and is easily melted or softened by heat. Resins are derived from certain trees, plants, coal, lignite, and asphalt beds.

Sal Soda.   Also known as sodium carbonate, washing soda, or soda ash. It is a white, strongly-alkaline salt composed of transparent crystals.

Sandarac.   An aromatic resin derived from fragrant wood of the sandarac tree, which grows in Africa.

Shellac.   Natural resin secreted by the insect *Laccifer lacca* and deposited on certain trees in India. It is easily mixed with alcohol.

Silicon Dioxide (sand).   White crystalline powder that is only soluble in hydrofluoric acid. May be produced from waterglass.

Soap Flakes.   A very difficult product to locate these days. You can make your own by grating a bar of soap.

Stearic Acid.   Also known as stearine. A white, fatty, crystalline substance obtained from hard fats such as tallow.

Stearin.   White crystalline solid found in many types of fats.

Sulfuric Acid.   Also known as oil of vitriol. A poisonous corrosive acid.

Talc or **Talcum.**   A soft mineral that is somewhat greasy to the touch. Usually sold as a powder.

Tallow.   The solid rendered fat of cattle or sheep. It is usually white or yellow depending on the level of purity.

Tannic Acid.   Yellow crystals which should be mixed well with water, benzene, and alcohol. Tannic Acid is extracted from certain nutgalls or tree bark using water and alcohol. Can be toxic if ingested or inhaled.

Tartaric Acid.   White crystalline powder that can easily be mixed with water or alcohol. Produced from maleic anhydride and hydrogen peroxide. Exercise caution when using.

Tea Tree Oil.   Essential oil derived from the tea tree. An effective ant repellent.

Thymol.   White, somewhat aromatic crystal with antiseptic qualities. Derived from the fragrant oil of a plant known as thyme.

Tragacanth.   A gum that swells up when placed in water and is obtained from the *Astralagus gummifer* herb mainly grown in Europe.

Tripoli.   A relatively soft, crumbly mineral that is produced by the decomposition of siliceous limestone and usually sold in powdered form. Tripoli is not the same as tripolite (diatomaceous earth).

Trisodium Phosphate (TSP).   Sold as a colorless crystal or white powder. Mixes well with water and alcohol. Produced by precipitating calcium carbonate (chalk) from a solution of dicalcium phosphate and soda ash.

Turpentine or **Oil of Turpentine.**   Clear, colorless, oily liquid that is produced by the steam distillation of turpentine gum from certain pine trees. *Caution:* very toxic if ingested.

Vinegar.   Produced by the fermentation of fruits and grains. Normally brown but can be further distilled to a white color. Balsamic vinegar is made from grapes.

Washing Soda.   Also called sodium carbonate, soda ash, or sal soda. Excellent cleaner for greasy, petroleum product messes. Found in most laundry sections of the supermarket.

Whiting.   A white powdery mixture of ground chalk (or other source of calcium carbonate). Used as a filler in paints, whitewash, and even putty. Liquid whiting is also known as liquid bluing. Used to clarify water and as a bleach.

Witch Hazel.   Clear astringent liquid that mixes well with water and alcohol.

Index